The Modern Concept of Nature

The Modern Concept of Nature

Essays on Theoretical Biology
and Evolution by H. J. Muller

Edited by Elof Axel Carlson

State University of New York Press   1973

The Modern Concept of Nature
First Edition
Published by State University of
New York Press
99 Washington Avenue,
Albany, New York 12210
© 1973 State University of New York
Printed in the United States of America
Library of Congress Cataloging
in Publication Data
Muller, Hermann Joseph, 1890-1967.
The modern concept of nature.
1. Genetics. 2. Evolution. 3. Muller,
Hermann Joseph, 1890-1967. I. Carlson, Elof Axel, ed.
II. Title. [DNLM: 1. Evolution—Essays. 2. Genetics, Human—
History—Essays. QH431   M958m   1973]
QH430.M84 1973   575   74-170884
ISBN 0-87395-096-8
ISBN 0-87395-196-4 (microfiche)

Contents

Preface

From his early childhood, H. J. Muller was committed to an evolutionary world view. His undergraduate exposure to E. B. Wilson's courses on the chromosome theory provided the basis for associating heredity with evolution. As early as 1910, when he was 20 years old, he began to speculate about mutations in the genes as the essential mechanism of Darwinian variation. Muller was both a scientist and a social reformer. He believed in rationalism and applied, where he could, the findings of his experiments and the implications of his theories to human concerns. He became a chief spokesman for protecting the world's population from exposure to radiation hazards. He advocated differential reproduction, by voluntary germinal choice, as a solution to the ever-increasing load of mutations which arises each generation in man.

These essays emphasize the scientific contributions which Muller made to the studies of mutation and the gene, especially to their bearing on the Darwinian theory of evolution. He was a staunch materialist and accepted the role of chance mutation as the basis for the newly arising variations on which natural selection acts. He carefully assessed the properties of genes and mutation, devising elaborate genetic stocks to test these features. Eventually he used radiation to induce mutations and chromosome breaks and exploited these for a thorough foundation of facts and principles of radiation genetics.

The development of molecular biology has not led to the rejection of the theoretical properties of the gene advocated by Muller. Rather, there remains a continuity in gene theory and a widely accepted underlying world-view of molecular biology that the gene, as genetic nucleic acid, provides a basis for understanding cell function and for tracing evolution from the origin of life itself.

A companion volume of Muller's major essays on science and humanity, *Man's Future Birthright*, was also published by State University of New York Press.

ELOF AXEL CARLSON

Muller's Evolutionary World-View

The modern concept of nature is derived from the unity of the physical and life sciences. It incorporates the atomic composition of the universe and the cellular composition of life. The laws of physics and chemistry have been sufficient, so far, for the analysis of living matter. The molecular structure of proteins and nucleic acids, while difficult to work out for any given molecule, is nevertheless comprehensible to the biologist with only a modest background in biochemistry. The advances in molecular biology may even be conveyed to the layman who lacks a formal scientific background.

The structure of matter, living and inanimate, is only part of the modern concept of nature. From Darwin's insights we have assimilated time as an essential part of our quest to construct and reconstruct our view of the universe. Cosmology, stellar evolution, the formation of the planets, and the origin of earth's benevolent blanket of air are seen by us through a hindsight liberated from the creation mythologies imposed on our forebears.

The unification of evolutionary, biological, chemical, and physical interpretations of the universe is a twentieth-century endeavor. It was Muller's privilege to live through the formative years of that emerging world-view and to have contributed to it, especially through his insights into mutation and the gene.

Although the rediscovery of Mendel's paper in 1900 is the usual birthdate attributed to genetics, the science was not named until William Bateson chose that term in 1906. Furthermore, the conception of heredity as a product of fundamental physiological units within cells may be attributed to Charles Darwin (in his *Animals* and *Plants under Domestication*, 1868), to Herbert Spencer (in his *Principles of Biology*, 1866), and in retrospect, to Gregor Mendel ("Experiments in Plant Hybridization" in *Verhandlungen des naturforschenden Vereines in Brunn*, Vol. 4 [1865]). The relation of Darwinism to Mendelism was by no means clear during the rediscovery period. Bateson saw in Mendelism a basis for discontinuous rather than gradual evolution of species. In this view he had good company. Hugo de Vries, one of Mendel's rediscovers, thought Darwinism was outmoded and he proposed instead that new species arose suddenly by dramatic changes, or *mutations* as he called them, in the progeny. The newly arising species in the primroses he studied would often fail to breed with their parental types. Championing Darwinism were the British biometricians, especially W. F. R. Weldon and Karl Pearson. They repudiated Mendelism as a spurious oversimplification of Sir Francis Galton's statistical analysis of inheritance, which was based on studies of populations rather than individuals.

This acrimonious controversy was not resolved for some time. Entering the lists in support of Hugo de Vries was Thomas Hunt Morgan at Columbia University. He attacked Mendelism and the chromosome theory; he saw no credence in the pitifully slow changes proposed by Darwin for speciation. But in 1910 he found his first mutations in the fruit fly, *Drosophila*. During the next three years he was assisted by three energetic and brilliant students— A. H. Sturtevant, C. B. Bridges, and H. J. Muller. Through their daily meetings, research, debates, and intense analysis of each newly arising mutation, this *Drosophila* Group worked out the principles of classical genetics. The Group was not especially harmonious, but the excitement of the new facts and ideas predominated over personality differences. Throughout these formative years Morgan, the skeptic, needed continual prodding to accept the Darwinian basis of evolution.

Muller's ideas of coincidence and interference in crossing-over resolved the inaccuracies of chromosome maps which Sturtevant had worked out. Muller devised the means to dissect the chromosomes genetically, localizing the numerous minor genes whose combined effects intensified or diminished a character's expression. Later he clarified the relation between genes and characters.

It was clear to him that variable, quantitative traits in man and other organisms had their basis in the same multigenic and environmental interplay that he had analyzed originally for wing shape in the fruit fly.

Muller's major interest in genetics shifted to the gene and to the nature of mutation. Throughout the 1920s at Columbia and at the University of Texas, Muller pursued these twin themes. The individual gene had the unique property of replicating itself and its variations. The variations in the individual genes were the mutations upon which natural selection could act. Most mutations were deleterious; they were usually recessive; they were infrequent; they arose singly and indeterminately; and most mutations had mild effects on a character. From these properties Muller drew three conclusions: (1) the variations for Darwinism were mutations in the individual genes and new species arose gradually from the natural selection of these minor variations; (2) the gene was the basis of life, producing all other cellular components and thereby affecting all physiological and morphological features of the organism; and (3) the origin of life could be dated with the appearance of the first replicating molecules, probably virus-like molecules, which he called "naked genes."

These three tenets became the basis of Muller's neo-Darwinian interpretation of life. The implications from this theory of the gene provided the direction of his research for the near- and long-range future. Muller attempted to measure mutation frequency, devising special genetic stocks for the detection of one of the most commonly occurring type of mutations—lethal mutations which kill unless protected by a normal allele or gene for that function.

The frequency of mutation occurring spontaneously was variable but rare enough to make a deliberate effort to induce mutations. Muller chose X rays because of their known biological effects and because the individual paths of ionization were indeterminate and highly localized to a minute portion of the cell volume. In 1926 Muller began radiation exposures of his flies and by 1927 he published his findings as "The Artificial Transmutation of the Gene" (*Science* 66, no. 1699: 84–87).

After the founding of radiation genetics, Muller used radiation as a tool for studying gene structure. He rejected the oversimplified application of target theory to determine gene size but hoped the alteration of the gene by X rays would spur physicists to bring their special outlook to a study of life. He also ruled out, experimentally, the origin of spontaneous mutations in *Drosophila* from radiation sources, internally or externally. By combining X ray studies of genetically altered arrangements in the sequence of genes and by applying microscopy to a study of these chromosome changes, Muller enlarged his view of the evolutionary process. He looked upon duplication of genetic material as the raw material for gene evolution, the duplicated genes diverging into new functions through independent mutations over large numbers of generations.

Muller's concept of nature incorporated his theoretical treatment of mutation and the gene. The evolution of the galaxies, the solar system, the earth's atmosphere, and life itself were part of an immensely vast and immensely ancient universe. Too often, however, biology was left out of the "exact" sciences; too often biologists failed to see that life was part of the same universe explored by physicists and chemists. Muller wanted a new biology with physics and chemistry playing a leading role in the study of genic material. He saw such a possibility fifty years ago with bacteriophage; he hoped radiation mutagenesis would stimulate this new approach; and he urged physicists to adopt enough biology—neo-Darwinian biology—to study the gene as genetic material having the unusual crystalline property of replicating its imperfections.

Muller's urgings were less influential, however, than his philosophical treatment of the gene, which was accepted by the earliest founders of molecular biology. Max Delbrück, through the influence of N. W. Timoféeff-Ressovsky, in Berlin, adopted this outlook. Timoféeff had been stimulated by Muller's radiation experiments and benefitted, in 1933, from his association when Muller arrived on a Guggenheim Fellowship for research in his laboratory. Erwin Schrödinger, whose influential book, *What is Life?* (New York: MacMillan, 1944) recruited physicists and chemists to biology, obtained his major ideas on the gene from the review papers of Timoféeff-Ressovsky, K. G. Zimmer, and Delbrück.

The recognition of nucleic acids as the chemical basis of heredity ushered in the molecular biology of today. Muller lived to see the molecular basis of the special property of gene replication in the "double helix model" of DNA, and it gave him satisfaction that J. D. Watson attributed his interest in the gene to Muller's advanced course, "Mutation and the Gene," which Watson took as a graduate student at Indiana University.

In another area, radiation genetics, Muller also worked out and emphasized the genetic basis of radiation sickness, cell death, and embryonic malformation characteristic of exposure to higher doses of radiation. He calculated the mutation frequency per roentgen of radiation received by germinal material and applied his analysis to human somatic and germinal damage. Muller's views were frequently ignored or scorned by physicists and biologists who did not accept the genetic basis of radiation damage or who believed that recuperation from such excess exposure to radiation somehow applied to the mutational damage also. Muller's most far reaching interpretation of the damage from induced and spontaneous mutations, however, was his concept of the load of mutations which accumulated in man. Increases in this genetic load, he believed, were a direct result of cultural evolution which nullified the rigorous checks of natural selection on survival. Thus the long-range consequence of indifference to the genetic load would lead to greater human suffering and genetic deterioration.

It is no surprise that there is a common theme in the widespread concern over the radiation danger, in the problem of our load of mutations, in the present concern over chemical mutagens and pollutants, in the developments of molecular biology from the synthesis of functional viral nucleic acids to the deciphering of the genetic code, and in the neo-Darwinian interpretation of evolution. They all reflect a partial dependence on the theoretical insights developed by Muller through his studies of mutation and the gene.

ELOF AXEL CARLSON

The Modern Concept of Nature

Mutation

I N the first two decades of the twentieth century the term *"mutation" was used in conflicting ways. Hugo de Vries conceived mutations to be the basis of evolution by a discontinuous process. New species, as he observed in his studies of the evening primrose, Oenothera, arose suddenly, without intermediate form. Muller summarized the known facts about mutations in Drosophila from his own experiments and those of the Drosophila Group. His theory of mutation, summarized in fourteen points, is incompatible with de Vries's mutation theory; rather, it provides the basis for Darwinian variation. The passage of nearly a half-century has not altered some facts often ignored today: most mutations are harmful; they are usually hidden or recessive; they do not arise in a directed response to the environment; and they are usually as stable as the original normal gene.*

Beneath the imposing building called "heredity" there has been a dingy basement called "mutation." Lately the searchlight of genetic analysis has thrown a flood of illumination into many of the dark recesses there, revealing some of them as ordinary rooms in no wise different from those upstairs that merely need to have their blinds flung back, while others are seen to be subterranean passageways of quite a different type. In other words, the term mutation originally included a number of distinct phenomena, which, from a genetic point of view, have nothing in common with one another. They were classed together merely because they all involved the sudden appearance of a new genetic type. Some have been found to be special cases of Mendelian recombination, some to be due to abnormalities in the distribution of entire chromosomes, and others to consist in changes in the individual genes or hereditary units. It seems incumbent upon us, however, in the interests of scientific clarity, to agree to confine our use of the term mutation to one coherent class of events. The usage most serviceable for our modern purpose would be to limit the meaning of the term to the cases of the third type, that is, to real changes in the gene. This would also be most in conformity with the spirit of the original usage, for even in the earlier days mutations were conceived of as fundamental changes in the hereditary constitution, and there were never intentionally included among them cases merely involving redistribution of hereditary units—when these cases were recognizable as such. In accordance with these considerations, our new definition would be "mutation is alteration of the gene." And "alteration," as here used, is of course understood to mean a change of a transmissible, or at least of a propagable, sort.

In this trimming down the scope of our category of mutation we do not deprive it of the material of most fundamental evolutionary significance. For all changes due to the redistribution of individual genes or of groups of genes, into new combinations, proportions, or quantities, are obviously made possible only by the prior changes that make these genes differ from each other in the first place. It should in addition be noted that changes due merely to differences in the gross proportions of entire groups of genes must be relatively incapable of that delicate adjustment which is required for evolutionary adaptation. And as to the question, frequently raised, whether all evolution is ultimately due to mutation, this is necessarily answered in the affirmative by our definitions of the gene and of mutation, which designate the gene as any unit of heredity, and mutation as any transmissible change occurring in the gene. The question of the basic mechanism of evolution thus becomes transferred to the problem of the character, frequency, and mode of occurrence of mutation, taken in this precise, yet comprehensive sense. And since eugenics is a special branch of evolutionary science it must be equally concerned with this problem.

In choosing the body of data wherewith to attack these questions of mutation, in their new form, it must unfortunately be
recognized that the results with the evening primrose, *Oenothera*,
although they formed the backbone of the earlier mutation theory,
can no longer be regarded as having a direct bearing on the modern problem, since they cannot be shown to be due directly to
changes in the genes. Certain of them, such as *gigas*, *lata*, *scintil-
lans*, etc., have been proved by S. J. Geerts, F. E. Lutz, R. R. Gates,
and others, to be due to abnormalities in the apportionment of
the chromosomes. Very valuable information on the genetics of
cases of this sort is now being obtained, especially in the work of
A. F. Blakeslee, J. Belling, and M. E. Farnham on much clearer cases
of similar character in the Jimson Weed, and, finally, in work of
Bridges on the fruit fly *Drosophila*. Most of the other so-called
mutations in the evening primrose appear to be due to the normal
hereditary processes of segregation and crossing-over, working on
a genetic constitution of a special type. Evidence for this was obtained in my analysis of the analogous case existing in the fly
Drosophila, as follows. It had previously been shown by de Vries,
and further elaborated by O. Renner, that germ cells or individuals
of *Oenothera* bearing certain genes always died, in such a way that
all the surviving individuals were heterozygous (hybrid) in regard
to these genes. I later showed, through work on *Drosophila*, that
when such a condition (there called "balanced lethal factors")
exists, the situation tends to become still further complicated
through the presence of other heterozygous genes, which are
linked to those which cause death. When one or a group of these
nonlethal genes crosses-over (separates) from the lethals, as they
occasionally do, they may become homozygous, producing a visible effect. Thus new types of individuals appear which may be
ascribed to "mutation," whereas they are really due to crossing-
over. The work of Frost on stocks has shown that a precisely
analogous situation exists in that form also, and G. H. Shull is obtaining evidence for the same conclusion in the evening primrose
itself. In any event, it must be granted that so long as this interpretation cannot be definitely refuted, these variations cannot be used
as examples on which to base our theory of gene change. In place,

then, of the elaborate system of conclusions which has derived its support chiefly from the results in the evening primrose, it will be necessary for our present theory of gene change to erect an independent structure, built upon an entirely new basis.

The data upon which the new theory must be built consists of two main sorts, which may be called direct and indirect. (1) In the cases giving the direct evidence, the occurrence of the gene change can be proved, and it is possible to exclude definitely all alternative explanations, such as contamination of the material, emergence of previously "latent" factors, nondisjunction, etc. So far, the only considerable body of such evidence is that gotten in the *Drosophila* work, where mutations have (in this sense) been actually observed in at least 100 loci. Considered collectively, however, there exist in other organisms enough scattered data to afford ample corroborative evidence for the generality of occurrence of mutations like those observed in the *Drosophila* work. In addition several specially mutable genes have been found in a number of plants (as well as in *Drosophila*) that are giving highly valuable information along their particular lines. And a number of selection experiments that have been performed on nonsegregating lines of various organisms have also given us direct evidence, if not of the frequency, then at least of the infrequency, of mutations. (2) As for the indirect data, these may be gotten by examination of Mendelian factor-differences of all kinds, on the assumption that they must have arisen through mutation. Although this assumption can be shown to be fully justified, these cases cannot provide information concerning the manner of origin of the mutants, nor can they furnish a reliable index of the frequency of mutations, since the mutant genes may have been subjected to an unknown amount of selective elimination or selective propagation before the observations were taken. As for the still more indirect data, derived from studies of phylogenetic series and comparisons between different species, genera, etc., these occasionally give suggestive results, but where crosses cannot be made or where the differences cannot be traced down to the individual genes, such facts can seldom lead to trustworthy genetic conclusions.

On these various data, duly weighted, we may found our new

mutation theory. We know nothing, as yet, about the mechanism of mutation, or about the nature of the gene—aside from the fact that nearly all genes hitherto studied behave like material particles existing in the chromosomes. Nevertheless there is always evidence for a number of empirical principles regarding the changes of the genes, some of which may conveniently be listed here in the form of fourteen statements. I shall have opportunity merely to present these principles, without attempting any adequate explanations of how they have been derived from the data.

1. The first and probably most important principle is that most genes—both mutant and "normal"—are exceedingly stable. Some idea of the degree of this stability may be obtained from some quantitative studies of mutation which E. Altenburg and I have made in the fruit fly *Drosophila*. It may be calculated from these experiments that a large proportion of the genes in *Drosophila* must have a stability that—at a minimum value—is comparable with that of radium atoms. Radium atoms, it may be recalled, have a so-called "mean life" of about 2,000 years.

2. Certain genes are, however, vastly more mutable than others. For example, a gene causing variegation in corn, studied by R. A. Emerson, and another in the four-o'clock, studied by D. C. E. Maryatt, ordinarily have a mean life of only a few years; and that causing bar eye in *Drosophila* has a mean life of only about 65 years, as is shown by the results of C. Zeleny. (In expressing these results we are here using the physicists' index of stability, which seems most appropriate for the present purpose also.)

3. External agents do not ordinarily increase the mutability sufficiently (if at all) to cause an obvious "production" of mutation.

4. The changes are not exclusively of the character of losses; this is shown by the well-established occurrence of reverse mutations, in bar-eyed and white-eyed *Drosophila*, in Blakeslee's dwarf *Portulaca*, Emerson's variegated corn, and probably in a number of other recorded instances. It is known that mutations having an effect similar to that of losses do occur, however, and they may be relatively frequent.

5. The change in a given gene is not in all cases in the same direction, and it does not even, in all cases, involve the same characters. The latter point is illustrated by a series of mutations which I am investigating in *Drosophila,* which all involve one gene, but which produce, as the case may be, either a shortened wing, an eruption on the thorax, a lethal effect, or any combination of these three.

6. The direction of mutation in a given gene is, however, preferential, occurring oftener in some directions than in others. This is well illustrated in the studies on variegated corn and four-o'clocks, and on the bar eye and white eye and other series in *Drosophila.*

7. The mutability and preferential direction may themselves become changed through mutation, as illustrated by some of the same cases.

8. The mutations do not ordinarily occur in two or more different genes at once. In only two instances in *Drosophila* have mutations been found in two different, separated [1] genes in the same line of cells of one individual. But a recurrent case, apparently of this kind, has recently been described in oats, by H. Nilsson-Ehle.

9. Not only does the mutation usually involve but one kind of gene—it usually involves but one gene of that kind in the cell. That is, the allelomorphs mutate independently of one another, just as totally different genes do. There is evidence for this derived from corn, *Portulaca,* and *Drosophila.*

10. Mutations are not limited in their time of occurrence to any particular period of the life history. This has been proved in the above mentioned studies on mutable plants, in *Drosophila,* and in other cases.

11. Genes normal to the species tend to have more dominance than the mutant genes arising from them. This is very markedly the case in *Drosophila,* where even the relatively few mutant genes that have been called dominant are very incompletely so, and might more justly be called recessive. In other organ-

---

1. Contiguous genes may be affected in the rare cases known as "deficiencies," found by Bridges and Mohr.

isms, the same condition of things is strongly suggested, although the direct data on occurrence of mutations is as yet too meagre to allow of certainty.

12. Most mutations are deleterious in their effects. This applies not only to the organism as a whole but also to the development of any particular part: the delicate mechanisms for producing characters are more likely to be upset than strengthened, so that mutations should more often result in apparant losses or retrogressions than in "progressive" changes. This is both an a priori expectation and a phenomenon generally observed.

13. Mutations with slight effects are probably more frequent than those with more marked effects. This must not be understood as referring to the different mutations of each given gene, but it applies in a comparison of the mutations occurring in different genes. Thus, there are more than a dozen mutations, in different loci, which reduce the size of the wing in *Drosophila* so slightly as to leave it more than half its original length, whereas only four reduce it to less than half-length. Mutant genes with effects so slight as to be visible only by the aid of specific co-genes seem to arise still more frequently. It is resonable to conclude that the mutations with slighter effects would more often take part in evolution, because they should usually be less deleterious, and this conclusion is borne out by observations on the multiplicity with which such factor-differences with relatively slight effects are found in species crosses.

14. The range of those mutations which are of appropriate magnitude to be visible is probably very small, in comparison with the entire "spectrum" of mutations, so that there are many more lethals than visible mutations, and probably subliminal than visible.

The above empirical and semiempirical principles must be regarded as a mere preliminary scaffolding, for the erection of a later, more substantial, theory of mutation. Time does not permit me here to discuss which directions of research, and what methods, seem the most promising for future results. Suffice it to say that it is especially important to obtain accurate data concerning the effect of various conditions upon the rate of mutation. This seems one of the logical routes by which to work toward the artificial production of mutation and consequent more perfect control of evolution. At the same time such results should also give a further insight into the structures of the gene. The way is now open, for the first time, to such studies on mutation rate, first through the finding, by Emerson, E. Baur, Maryatt, Zeleny, and Blakeslee, of a number of specially mutable factors in different organisms, and second, through certain special genetic methods which I have elaborated in *Drosophila,* for the detection of lethal and other mutations there.

It has now become recognized that advances in theoretical or "pure" science eventually carry in their train changes in practice of the most far-reaching nature—changes which are usually far more radical than those caused by progress in the applied science directly concerned. It may therefore be asked at this point by eugenists: "Are there any applications of the knowledge which has already been gained about mutation in general, to eugenics and to the principles which should govern us in guiding human reproduction?" I think that one such application is already clearly indicated.

In order to understand the nature of this application it will be necessary first to consider the proposition—emphasized by East and Jones in their book, *Inbreeding and Crossbreeding*—that the only way for a genetically sound stock to be formed is by its going through a course of inbreeding, with elimination, by natural or artificial selection, of the undesirable individuals that appear in the course of this inbreeding. The truth of this proposition depends upon the fact that many recessive genes of undesirable character are apt to exist in a population. Since the frequency with which these genes are able to produce their characteristic effects, i.e., to "come to light," depends on the closeness of the inbreeding, it is evident that inbreeding will be necessary in order to recognize the genes adequately, and hence to eliminate them.

Our present theory of mutation, however, carries us further than the proposition just considered. It shows that these undesirable genes have arisen by mutation; in fact, as stated in point 12, the *great majority* of mutations are deleterious, probable even to the degree of being lethal, and it is also known, as noted in point 11, that many—probably the great majority—are recessive. In other words, our mutation theory shows that probably the majority of the mutations that are occurring are giving rise to genes of just the type specified in the above discussion. This immediately shows us that not only are inbreeding and selection desirable for raising the genetic level of a population, but they are absolutely necessary merely in order to maintain it at its present standard. For the same process of mutation which was responsible for the origination of these undesirable genes in the past must be producing them now and will continue to produce them in the future. Therefore, without selection, or without the inbreeding that makes effective selection possible, these lethals and other undesirable genes will inevitably accumulate, until the germ plasm becomes so riddled through with defect that pure lines cannot be obtained, and progress through selection of desirable recessive traits can never more be effected, since each of them will have become tied up with a lethal. To avoid such a complete and permanent collapse of the evolutionary process, it is accordingly necessary for man or nature to resort to a periodically repeated, although not continuous, series of inbreedings and selections in the case of any biparental organism.

This conclusion is more than a mere speculation, or even a deduction from our principles. The reality of this process of mutational deterioration has been directly proved, in the case of *Drosophila,* through experiments that I have conducted on lines in which the processes that usually accompany inbreeding and selection were prevented: in these lines there was found an accumulation of lethal genes so rapid that it would have taken but a few decades to have brought about the presence of a lethal gene in practically every chromosome of every fly. Although the same general thesis undoubtedly applies also to mankind we do not yet know the speed of the process here. Its speed depends upon the actual frequency of mutations, which it will be very important— and extremely difficult—to determine in the case of mankind. Meanwhile, no matter what this rate may be, the process remains a real one, which must eventually be reckoned with, and either grappled in time, and conquered, or else yielded to.

I have dwelt at length upon this particular application to eugenics of some of the mutation studies. I believe, however, that this is but one example of such applications, and that from an increasing knowledge of our theoretical science there will inevitably flow an increasingly adequate technique for coping with our refractory human material. Meanwhile, the crying need is for more of the theoretical knowledge—and for the support of pure science —in its investigation of the processes lying at the root of the germ plasm.

Variation Due to Change
in the Individual Gene

T HE unusual view adopted by Muller in this essay was the centrality of the gene in biological theory. Few in his audience were prepared to accept such a novelty. This full display of Muller's imaginative treatment of the gene was regarded by some as fanciful or a hoax. It is here that Muller introduces the key feature of gene construction: its ability to reproduce its mutations. It is here that a single replacement of a conjunction by a preposition converts nineteenth-century Darwinism to twentieth-century neo-Darwinism: "Thus it is not inheritance and variation which bring about evolution, but the inheritance of variation, and this in turn is due to the general principle of gene construction which causes the persistence of autocatalysis despite the alteration in structure of the gene itself."

The Relation between the Genes and
the Characters of the Organism

The present paper[1] will be concerned with problems, and the possible means of attacking them, rather than with the details of cases and data. The opening up of these new problems is due to the fundamental contribution which genetics has made to cell

1. Contribution No. 156, University of Texas. In Symposium on "The Origin of Variations" at the thirty-ninth annual meeting of the American Society of Naturalists, Toronto, Can., 29 December 1921.

physiology within the last decade. This contribution, which has so far scarcely been assimilated by the general physiologists themselves, consists in the demonstration that, besides the ordinary proteins, carbohydrates, lipoids, and extractives, of their several types, there are present within the cell *thousands* of distinct substances—the "genes"; these genes exist as ultramicroscopic particles; their influences nevertheless permeate the entire cell, and they play a fundamental role in determining the nature of all cell substances, cell structures, and cell activities. Through these cell effects, in turn, the genes affect the entire organism.

It is not mere guesswork to say that the genes are ultramicroscopic bodies. For the work on *Drosophila* has not only proved that the genes are in the chromosomes, in definite positions, but it has shown that there must be hundreds of such genes within each of the larger chromosomes, although the length of these chromosomes is not over a few microns. If, then, we divide the size of the chromosome by the minimum number of its genes, we find that the latter are particles too small to give a visible image.

The chemical composition of the genes and the formula of their reactions remain as yet quite unknown. We do know, for example, that in certain cases a given pair of genes will determine the existence of a particular enzyme (concerned in pigment production), that another pair of genes will determine whether or not a certain agglutinin shall exist in the blood, a third pair will determine whether homogentisic acid is secreted into the urine (alkaptonuria), and so forth. But it would be absurd, in the third case, to conclude that on this account the gene itself consists of homogentisic acid, or any related substance, and it would be similarly absurd, therefore, to regard cases of the former kind as giving any evidence that the gene *is* an enzyme, or an agglutinin-like body. The reactions whereby the genes produce their ultimate effects are too complex for such inferences. Each of these effects, which we call a "character" of the organism, is the product of a highly complex, intricate, and delicately balanced system of reactions, caused by the interaction of countless genes, and every organic structure and activity is therefore liable to become increased, diminished, abolished, or altered in some other way, when the balance of the reaction system is disturbed by an alteration in the nature or the relative quantities of any of the component genes of the system. To return now to these genes themselves.

The Problem of Gene Mutability

The most distinctive characteristic of each of these ultramicro-scopic particles—that characteristic whereby we identify it as a gene—is its property of self-propagation: the fact that, within the complicated environment of the cell protoplasm, it reacts in such a way as to convert some of the common surrounding material into an end-product identical in kind with the original gene itself. This action fulfills the chemist's definition of "autocatalysis"; it is what the physiologist would call "growth"; and when it passes through more than one generation it becomes "heredity." It may be observed that this reaction is in each instance a rather highly localized one, since the new material is laid down by the side of the original gene.

The fact that the genes have this autocatalytic power is in itself sufficiently striking, for they are undoubtedly complex substances, and it is difficult to understand by what strange coincidence of chemistry a gene can happen to have just that very special series of physiochemical effects upon its surroundings which produces—of all possible end-products—just this particular one, which is identical with its own complex structure. But the most remarkable feature of the situation is not this oft-noted autocatalytic action in itself: It is the fact that, when the structure of the gene becomes changed, through some "chance variation," the catalytic property of the gene may[2] become correspondingly changed, in such a way as to leave it still *autocatalytic*. In other words, the change in gene structure—accidental though it was—has somehow resulted in a change of exactly *appropriate* nature in the catalytic reactions, so that the new reactions are now accurately adapted to produce more material just like that in the new changed gene itself. It is

2. It is of course conceivable, and even unavoidable, that *some* types of changes do destroy the gene's autocatalytic power, and thus result in its eventual loss.

this paradoxical phenomenon which is implied in the expression, "variation due to change in the individual gene," or, as it is often called, "mutation."

What sort of structure must the gene possess to permit it to mutate in this way? Since, through change after change in the gene, this same phenomenon persists, it is evident that it must depend upon some general feature of gene construction, common to all genes, which gives each one a *general* autocatalytic power—a "carte blanche"—to build material of whatever specific sort it itself happens to be composed of. This general principle of gene structure might, on the one hand, mean nothing more than the possession by each gene of some very simple character, such as a particular radicle or "side-chain", alike in them all, which enables each gene to enter into combination with certain highly organized materials in the outer protoplasm, in such a way as to result in the formation, "by" the protoplasm, of more material like this gene which is in combination with it. In that case the gene itself would only initiate and guide the direction of the reaction. On the other hand, the extreme alternative to such a conception has been generally assumed, perhaps gratuitously, in nearly all previous theories concerning hereditary units; this postulates that the chief feature of the autocatalytic mechanism resides in the structure of the genes themselves, and that the outer protoplasm does little more than provide the building material. In either case, the question as to what the general principle of gene construction is that permits this phenomenon of mutable autocatalysis, is the most fundamental question of genetics.

The subject of gene variation is an important one, however, not only on account of the apparent problem that is thus inherent in it, but also because this same peculiar phenomenon that it involves lies at the root of organic evolution, and hence of all the vital phenomena which have resulted from evolution. It is commonly said that evolution rests upon two foundations—inheritance and variation; but there is a subtle and important error here. Inheritance by itself leads to no change, and variation leads to no permanent change, unless the variations themselves are heritable. Thus it is not inheritance *and* variation which bring about evolution, but the inheritance *of* variation, and this in turn is due to the general principle of gene construction which causes the persistence of autocatalysis despite the alteration in structure of the gene itself. Given, now, any material or collection of materials having this one unusual characteristic, and evolution would automatically follow, for this material would, after a time, through the accumulation, competition, and selective spreading of the self-propagated variations, come to differ from ordinary inorganic matter in innumerable respects, in addition to the original difference in its mode of catalysis. There would thus result a wide gap between this matter and other matter, which would keep growing wider, with the increasing complexity, diversity and so-called "adaptation" of the selected mutable material.

A Possible Attack through Chromosome Behavior

In thus recognizing the nature and the importance of the problem involved in gene mutability have we now entered into a cul de sac, or is there some way of proceeding further so as to get at the physical basis of this peculiar property of the gene? The problems of growth, variation, and related processes seemed difficult enough to attack even when we thought of them as inherent in the organism as a whole or the cell as a whole—how now can we get at them when they have been driven back, to some extent at least, within the limits of an invisible particle? A gene can not effectively be ground in a mortar, or distilled in a retort, and although the physicochemical investigation of other biological substances may conceivably help us, by analogy, to understand its structure, there seems at present no method of approach along this line.

There is, however, another possible method of approach available: that is, to study the behavior of the chromosomes, as influenced by their contained genes, in their various physical reactions of segregation, crossing-over, division, synapsis, etc. This may at first sight seem very remote from the problem of getting at the structural principle that allows mutability in the gene, but I am inclined to think that such studies of synaptic attraction between chromosomes may be especially enlightening in this connection, because the most remarkable thing we know about genes—besides their mutable autocatalytic power—is the highly specific attraction which like genes (or local products formed by them) show for each other. As in the case of the autocatalytic forces, so here the attractive forces of the gene are somehow exactly adjusted so as to react in relation to more material of the same complicated kind. Moreover, when the gene mutates, the forces become readjusted, so that they may now attract material of the new kind; this shows that the attractive or synaptic property of the gene, as well as its catalytic property, is not primarily dependent on its specific structure but on some general principle of its makeup, which causes whatever specific structure it has to be autoattractive (and autocatalytic).

This autoattraction is evidently a strong force, exerting an appreciable effect against the nonspecific mutual repulsions of the chromosomes, over measurable microscopic distances much larger than in the case of the ordinary forces of so-called cohesion, adhesion, and adsorption known to physical science. In this sense, then, the physicist has no parallel for this force. There seems, however, to be no way of escaping the conclusion that in the last analysis it must be of the same nature as these other forces which cause inorganic substances to have specific attractions for each other, according to their chemical composition. These inorganic forces, according to the newer physics, depend upon the arrangement and mode of motion of the electrons constituting the molecules, which set up electromagnetic fields of force of specific patterns. To find the principle peculiar to the construction of the force-field pattern of genes would accordingly be requisite for solving the problem of their tremendous autoattraction.

Now, according to Troland (1917), the growth of crystals from a solution is due to an attraction between the solid crystal and the molecules in solution caused by the similarity of their force field patterns, somewhat as similarly shaped magnets might attract each other—north to south poles—and L. T. Troland maintains that essentially the same mechanism must operate in the autocatalysis of the hereditary particles. If he is right, each different portion of the gene structure must—like a crystal—attract to itself from the protoplasm materials of a similar kind, thus molding next to the original gene another structure with similar parts, identically arranged, which then become bound together to form another gene, a replica of the first. This does not solve the question of what the general principle of gene construction is, which permits it to retain, like a crystal, these properties of autoattraction,[3] but if the main point is correct, that the autocatalysis is an expression of specific attractions between portions of the gene and similar protoplasmic building blocks (dependent on their force-field patterns), it is evident that the very same forces which cause the genes to grow should also cause like genes to attract each other, but much more strongly, since here all the individual attractive forces of the different parts of the gene are summated. If the two phenomena are thus really dependent on a common principle in the makeup of the gene, progress made in the study of one of them should help in the solution of the other.

Great opportunities are now open for the study of the nature of the synaptic attraction, especially through the discovery of various races having abnormal numbers of chromosomes. Here we have already the finding by Belling, that where three like chromosomes are present, the close union of any two tends to exclude their close union with the third. This is very suggestive, because the same thing is found in the cases of specific attractions between inorganic particles that are due to their force field patterns. And through Bridges' finding of triploid *Drosophila,* the attraction phenomena can now be brought down to a definitely genic basis, by the introduction of specific genes—especially those known to influence chromosome behavior—into one of the chromosomes of a triad. The amount of influence of this gene on attraction may then be tested quantitatively, by genetic determination of the frequencies of the various possible types of segregation. By extending

3. It can hardly be true, as Troland intimates, that all similar fields attract each other more than they do dissimilar fields, otherwise all substances would be autocatalytic, and, in fact, no substances would be soluble. Moreover, if the parts of a molecule are in any kind of "solid," three dimensional formation, it would seem that those in the middle would scarcely have opportunity to exert the molding effect above mentioned. It therefore appears that a special manner of construction must be necessary, in order that a complicated structure like a gene may exert such an effect.

such studies to include the effect of various conditions of the environment, such as temperature, electrostatic stresses, etc., in the presence of the different genetic situations, a considerable field is opened up.

This suggested connection between chromosome behavior and gene structure is as yet, however, only a possibility. It must not be forgotten that at present we cannot be sure that the synaptic attraction is exerted by the genes themselves rather than by local products of them, and it is also problematical whether the chief part of the mechanism of autocatalysis resides within the genes rather than in the "protoplasm." Meanwhile, the method is worth following up, simply because it is one of our few conceivable modes of approach to an all-important problem.

It may also be recalled in this connection that besides the genes in the chromosomes there is at least one similarly autocatalytic material in the chloroplastids, which likewise may become permanently changed, or else lost, as has been shown by various studies on chlorophyll inheritance. Whether this plastid substance is similar to the genes in the chromosomes we cannot say, but of course it cannot be seen to show synaptic attraction and could not be studied by the method suggested above.[4]

The Attack through Studies of Mutation

There is, however, another method of attack, in a sense more direct, and not open to the above criticisms. That is the method of investigating the individual gene, and the structure that permits it to change, through a study of the changes themselves that occur in it, as observed by the test of breeding and development. It was through the investigation of the *changes* in the chromosomes, caused by crossing-over, that the structure of the chromosomes was analyzed into their constituent genes in line formation; it was through study of molecular changes that molecules were analyzed

4. It may be that there are still other elements in the cell which have the nature of genes, but as no critical evidence has ever been adduced for their existence, it would be highly hazardous to postulate them.

into atoms tied together in definite ways, and it has been finally the rather recent finding of changes in atoms and investigation of the resulting pieces that has led us to the present analysis of atomic structure into positive and negative electrons having characteristic arrangements. Similarly, to understand the properties and possibilities of the individual gene, we must study the mutations as directly as possible and bring the results to bear upon our problem.

The Quality and Quantity of the Change

In spite of the fact that the drawing of inferences concerning the gene is very much hindered in this method on account of the remoteness of the gene-cause from its character-effect, one salient point stands out already. It is that the change is not always a mere loss of material, because clear-cut reverse mutations have been obtained in corn, *Drosophila, Portulaca,* and probably elsewhere. If the original mutation was a loss, the reverse must be a gain. Secondly, the mutations in many cases seem not to be quantitative at all, since the different allelomorphs formed by mutations of one original gene often fail to form a single linear series. One case, in fact, is known in which the allelomorphs even affect totally different characters: this is the case of the truncate series, in which I have found that different mutant genes at the same locus may cause either a shortening of the wing, an eruption of the thorax, a lethal effect, or any combination of two or three of these characters. In such a case we may be dealing either with changes of different types occurring in the same material or with changes (possibly quantitative changes, similar in type) occuring in different component parts of one gene. Owing to the universal applicability of the latter interpretation, even where allelomorphs do not form a linear series, it can not be categorically denied, in any individual case, that the changes may be merely quantitative changes of some *part* of the gene. If all changes were thus quantitative, even in this limited sense of a loss or gain of part of the gene, our problem of why the changed gene still seems to be autocatalytic would in the main disappear, but such a situation is excluded a priori since in that case the thousands of genes now existing could never have evolved.

Although a given gene may thus change in various ways, it is important to note that there is a strong tendency for any given gene to have its changes of a particular kind and to mutate in one direction rather than in another. And although mutation certainly does not always consist of loss, it often gives effects that might be termed losses. In the case of the mutant genes for bent and eyeless in the fourth chromosome of *Drosophila,* it has even been proved, by Bridges, that the effects are of exactly the same kind, although of lesser intensity, than those produced by the entire loss of the chromosome in which they lie, for flies having bent or eyeless in one chromosome and lacking the homologous chromosome are even more bent, or more eyeless, than those having a homologous chromosome that also contains the gene in question. The fact that mutations are usually recessive might be taken as pointing in the same direction, since it has been found in several cases that the loss of genes—as evidenced by the absence of an entire chromosome of one pair—tends to be much more nearly recessive than dominant in its effect.

The effect of mutations in causing a loss in the characters of the organism should, however, be sharply distinguished from the question of whether the gene has undergone any loss. It is generally true that mutations are much more apt to cause an apparent loss in character than a gain, but the obvious explanation for that is, not because the gene tends to lose something, but because most characters require for proper development a nicely adjusted train of processes, and so any change in the genes—no matter whether loss, gain, substitution, or rearrangement—is more likely to throw the developmental mechanism out of gear and give a "weaker" result than to intensify it. For this reason, too, the most frequent kind of mutation of all is the lethal, which leads to the loss of the entire organism, but we do not conclude from this that all the genes had been lost at the time of the mutation. The explanation for this tendency for most changes to be degenerative, and also for the fact that certain other kinds of changes—like that from red to pink eye in *Drosophila*—are more frequent than others—such as

red to brown or green eye—lies rather in developmental mechanics than in genetics. It is because the developmental processes
are more unstable in one direction than another, and easier to
push "downhill" than up, and so any mutations that occur—no
matter what the gene change is like—are more apt to have these
effects than the other effects. If now selection is removed in regard to any particular character, these character changes which
occur more readily must accumulate, giving apparent orthogenesis,
disappearance of unused organs, of unused physiological capabilities, and so forth. As we shall see later, however, the changes are
not so frequent or numerous that they could ordinarily push evolution in such a direction against selection and against the immediate interests of the organism.

In regard to the magnitude of the somatic effect produced by
the gene variation, the *Drosophila* results show smaller character
changes occurring oftener than large ones. The reason for this is
again probably to be found in developmental mechanics, because
there are usually more genes slightly affecting given character than
there are those playing an essential role in its formation. The evidence proves that there are still more genes whose change does
not affect the given character at all—no matter what this character
may be, unless it is life itself—and this raises the question as to
how many mutations are absolutely unnoticed, affecting no character, or no detectable character, to any appreciable extent at all.
Certainly there must be many such mutations, judging by the frequency with which "modifying factors" arise, which produce an
effect only in the presence of a special genetic complex not ordinarily present.

The Localization of the Change

Certain evidence concerning the causation of mutations has also
been obtained by studying the relations of their occurrence to one
another. Hitherto it has nearly always been found that only one
mutation has occurred at a time, restricted to a single gene in the
cell. I must omit from consideration here the two interesting cases
of deficiency, found by Bridges and by Mohr, in each of which it

seems certain that an entire region of a chromosome, with its whole cargo of genes, changed or was lost, and also a certain peculiar case, not yet cleared up, which has recently been reported by Nilsson-Ehle; these important cases stand alone. Aside from them, there are only two instances in which two (or more) new mutant genes have been proved to have been present in the same gamete. Both of these are cases in *Drosophila*—reported by Muller and Altenburg (1921)—in which a gamete contained two new sex-linked lethals; two cases are not a greater number than was to have been expected from a random distribution of mutations, judging by the frequency with which single mutant lethals were found in the same experiments. Ordinarily, then, the event that causes the mutation is specific, affecting just one particular kind of gene of all the thousands present in the cell. That this specificity is due to a spatial limitation rather than a chemical one is shown by the fact that when the single gene changes, the other one, of identical composition, located nearby in the homologous chromosome of the same cell, remains unaffected. This has been proved by Emerson in corn, by Blakeslee in *Portulaca,* and I have shown there is strong evidence for it in *Drosophila.* Hence these mutations are not caused by some general pervasive influence but are due to "accidents" occurring on a molecular scale. When the molecular or atomic motions chance to take a particular form, to which the gene is vulnerable, then the mutation occurs.

It will even be possible to determine whether the entire gene changes at once, or whether the gene consists of several molecules or particles, one of which may change at a time. This point can be settled in organisms having determinate cleavage, by studies of the distribution of the mutant character in somatically mosaic mutants. If there is a group of particles in the gene, then when one particle changes it will be distributed irregularly among the descendant cells, owing to the random orientation of the two halves of the chromosome on the mitotic spindles of succeeding divisions,[5] but

5. This depends on the assumption that if the gene does consist of several particles, the halves of the chromosomes, at each division, receive a random sample of these particles. That is almost a necessary assumption, since a gene formed of particles each one of which was separately partitioned at division would tend not to persist as such, for the occurrence of

if there is only one particle to change, its mutation must affect all of the cells in a bloc that are descended from the mutant cell.

The Conditions under which the Change occurs

But the method that appears to have most scope and promise is the experimental one of investigating the conditions under which mutations occur. This requires studies of mutation frequency under various methods of handling the organisms. As yet, extremely little has been done along this line. That is because, in the past, a mutation was considered a windfall, and the expression "mutation frequency" would have seemed a contradiction in terms. To attempt to study it would have seemed as absurd as to study the conditions affecting the distribution of dollar bills on the sidewalk. You were simply fortunate if you found one. Not even controls, giving the "normal" rate of mutation—if indeed there is such a thing—were attempted.[6] Of late, however, we may say that certain very exceptional banking houses have been found, in front of which the dollars fall more frequently; in other words, specially mutable genes have been discovered that are beginning to yield abundant data at the hands of Nilsson-Ehle, Zeleny, Emerson, Anderson, and others. For some of these mutable genes the rate of change is found to be so rapid that at the end of a few decades half of the genes descended from those originally present would have been changed. After these genes have once mutated, however, their previous mutability no longer holds. In addition to this "banking house method" there are also methods, employed by Altenburg and myself, for—as it were—automatically sweeping up wide areas of the streets and sifting the collections for the valuables. By these special genetic methods of reaping mutations we have recently shown that the ordinary genes of *Drosophila*—unlike the

---

mutation in one particle after the other would in time differentiate the gene into a number of different genes consisting of one particle each.

6. Studies of "mutation frequency" had of course been made in the *Oenotheras*, but as we now know that these were not studies of the rate of gene change but of the frequencies of crossing over and of chromosome abberrations, they may be neglected for our present purposes.

mutable genes above—would usually require at least a thousand years (probably very much more) before half of them became changed. This puts their stability about on a par with, if not much higher than, that of atoms of radium, to use a fairly familiar analogy. Since, even in these latter experiments, many of the mutations probably occurred within a relatively few rather highly mutable genes, it is likely that most of the genes have a stability far higher than this result suggests.

The above mutation rates are mere first gleanings; we have yet to find how different conditions affect the occurrence of mutations. There had so far been only the negative finding that mutation is not confined to one sex (Muller and Altenburg 1919; Zeleny 1921), or to any one stage in the life cycle (Bridges 1919; Muller 1920; Zeleny 1921), Zeleny's finding that bar mutation is not influenced by recency of origin of the gene (1921), and the as yet inconclusive differences found by Altenburg and myself for mutation rate at different temperatures (1919), until at this year's meeting of the botanists Emerson announced the definite discovery of the influence of a genetic factor in corn upon the mutation rate in its allelomorph, and Anderson the finding of an influence upon mutation in this same gene, caused by the developmental conditions—the mutations from white to red of the mutable gene studied occurring far more frequently in the cells of the more mature ear than in those of the younger ear. These two results at least tell us decisively that mutation is not a sacred, inviolable, unapproachable process: it may be altered. These are the first steps; the way now lies open broad for exploration.

It is true that I have left out of account here the reported findings by several investigators, of genetic variations caused by treatments with various toxic substances and with certain other unusual conditions. In most of these cases, however, the claim has not been made that actual gene changes have been caused: the results have usually not been analyzed genetically and were in fact not analyzable genetically; they could just as well be interpreted to be due to abnormalities in the distribution of genes—for instance, chromosome abnormalities like those which Mavor has recently produced with X rays—as to be due to actual gene mutations. But even if they were due to real genic differences, the possibility has in most cases by no means been excluded (1) that these genic differences were present in the stock to begin with, and merely became sorted out unequally, through random segregation; or (2) that other, invisible genic differences were present which, after random sorting out, themselves caused differences in mutation rate between the different lines. Certain recent results by Altenburg and myself suggest that genic differences affecting mutation rate may be not uncommon. To guard against either of these possibilities it would have been necessary to test the stocks out by a thorough course of inbreeding beforehand, or else to have run at least half a dozen different pairs of parallel lines of the control and treated series, and to have obtained a definite difference in the same direction between the two lines of *each* pair; otherwise it can be proved by the theory of "probable error" that the differences observed may have been a mere matter of random sampling among genic differences originally present. Accumulating large numbers of abnormal or inferior individuals by selective propagation of one or two of the treated lines—as has been done in some cases—adds nothing to the significance of the results.

At best, however, these genetically unrefined methods would be quite insensitive to mutations occurring at anything like ordinary frequency, or to such differences in mutation rate as have already been found in the analytical experiments on mutation frequency. And it seems quite possible that larger differences than these will not easily be hit upon, at least not in the early stages of our investigations, in view of the evidence that mutation is ordinarily due to an accident on an ultramicroscopic scale, rather than directly caused by influences pervading the organism. For the present, then, it appears most promising to employ organisms in which the genetic composition can be controlled and analyzed, and to use genetic methods that are sensitive enough to disclose mutations occurring in the control as well as in the treated individuals. In this way relatively slight variations in mutation frequency, caused by the special treatments, can be determined, and from the conditions found to alter the mutation rate slightly we might finally work up to those which affect it most markedly. The only methods now meeting this requirement are those in which a particular mutable gene is followed, and those in which many homozygous or else genetically controlled lines can be run in parallel, either by parthenogenesis, self-fertilization, balanced lethals or other special genetic means, and later analyzed, through sexual reproduction, segregation, and crossing-over.

Other Possibilities

We cannot, however, set fixed limits to the possibilities of research. We should not wish to deny that some new and unusual method may at any time be found of directly producing mutations. For example, the phenomena now being worked out by Guyer may be a case in point. There is a curious analogy between the reactions of immunity and the phenomena of heredity, in apparently fundamental respects,[7] and any results that seem to connect the two are worth following to the limit.

Finally, there is a phenomenon related to immunity, of still more striking nature, which must not be neglected by geneticists. This is the d'Herelle phenomenon. F. d'Herelle found in 1917 that the presence of dysentery bacilli in the body caused the production there of a filterable substance, emitted in the stools, which had a lethal and in fact dissolving action on the corresponding type of bacteria, if a drop of it were applied to a colony of the bacteria that was under cultivation. So far, there would be nothing to distinguish this phenomenon from immunity. But he further found that when a drop of the affected colony was applied to a second living colony, the second colony would be killed; a drop from the second would kill a third colony, and so on indefinitely. In other words, the substance, when applied to colonies of bacteria, became multiplied or increased, and could be so increased

7. I refer here to the remarkable specificity with which a particular complex antigen calls forth processes that construct for it an antibody that is attracted to it and fits it "like lock and key," followed by further processes that cause more and more of the antibody to be reproduced. If the antigen were a gene, which could be slightly altered by the cell to form the antibody that neutralized it (as some enzymes can be slightly changed by heating so that they counteract the previous active enzyme), and if this antibody-gene then became implanted in the cell so as to keep on growing, all the phenomena of immunity would be produced.

indefinitely; it was self-propagable. It fulfills, then, the definition of an autocatalytic substance, and although it may really be of very different composition and work by a totally different mechanism from the genes in the chromosomes, it also fulfills our definition of a gene.[8] But the resemblance goes further: It has been found by A. Gratia that the substance may, through appropriate treatments on other bacteria, become changed (so as to produce a somewhat different effect than before, and attack different bacteria) and still retain its self-propagable nature.

That two distinct kinds of substances—the d'Herelle substances and the genes—should both possess this most remarkable property of heritable variation or "mutability," each working by a totally different mechanism, is quite conceivable, considering the complexity of protoplasm, yet it would seem a curious coincidence indeed. It would open up the possibility of two totally different kinds of life, working by different mechanisms. On the other hand, if these d'Herelle bodies were really genes, fundamentally like our chromosome genes, they would give us an utterly new angle from which to attack the gene problem. They are filterable, to some extent isolable, can be handled in test-tubes, and their properties, as shown by their effects on the bacteria, can then be studied after treatment. It would be very rash to call these bodies genes, and yet at present we must confess that there is no distinction known between the genes and them. Hence we can not categorically deny that perhaps we may be able to grind genes in a mortar and cook them in a beaker after all. Must we geneticists become bacteriologists, physiological chemists, and physicists, simultaneously with being zoologists and botanists? Let us hope so.

I have purposely tried to paint things in the rosiest possible colors. Actually, the work on the individual gene, and its mutation, is beset with tremendous difficulty. Such progress in it as has been made has been by minute steps and at the cost of infinite labor. Where results are this meager, all thinking becomes almost

8. D'Herelle himself thought that the substance was a filterable virus parasitic on the bacterium, called forth by the host body. It has since been found that various bacteria each cause the production of d'Herelle substances which are to some extent specific for the respective bacteria.

equivalent to speculation. But we cannot give up thinking on that account, and thereby give up the intellectual incentive to our work. In fact, a wide, unhampered treatment of all possibilities is, in such cases, all the more imperative, in order that we may direct these labors of ours where they have most chance to count. We must provide eyes for action.

The real trouble comes when speculation masquerades as empirical fact. For those who cry out most loudly against "theories" and "hypotheses"—whether these latter by the chromosome theory, the factorial "hypothesis," the theory of crossing-over, or any other—are often the very ones most guilty of stating their results in terms that make illegitimate *implicit* assumptions, which they themselves are scarcely aware of simply because they are opposed to dragging "speculation" into the open. Thus they may be finally led into the worst blunders of all. Let us, then, frankly admit the uncertainty of many of the possibilities we have dealt with, using them as a spur to the real work.

References

Blakeslee, A. F. 1920. A dwarf mutation in *Portulaca* showing vegetative reversions. *Genetics* 5:419–33.

Bridges, C. B. 1917. Deficiency. *Genetics* 2:445–65.

———. 1919. The developmental stages at which mutations occur in the germ tract. *Proc. Soc. Exp. Biol. and Med.* 17:1–2.

———. 1921. Genetical and cytological proof of non-disjunction of the fourth chromosome of *Drosophila melanogaster*. *Proc. Nat. Acad. Sci.* 7:186–92.

Emerson, R. A. 1911. The inheritance of a recurring somatic variation in variegated ears of maize. *Amer. Natur.* 48:87–115.

Gratia, A. 1921. Studies on the d'Herelle phenomenon. *J. Exp. Med.* 34:115–26.

d'Herelle, F. 1917. *Compt. Rend. Acad.* 165:373.

———. 1918a. *Compt. Rend. Acad.* 167:970.

————. 1918b. *Compt. Rend. Soc. Biol.* 81:1160.

————. 1919. *Compt. Rend. Acad.* 168:631.

————. 1920. *Compt. Rend. Soc. Biol.* 83:52, 97, 247.

Mavor, J. W. 1921. On the elimination of the X chromosome from the egg of *Drosophila melanogaster* by X rays. *Science* n.s. 54:277–79.

Mohr, O. L. 1919. Character changes caused by mutation of an entire region of a chromosome in *Drosophila. Genetics* 4:275–82.

Muller, H. J. 1920. Further changes in the white-eye series of *Drosophila* and their bearing on the manner of occurrence of mutation. *J. Exp. Zool.* 31:443–73.

Muller, H. J., and Altenburg, E. 1919. The rate of change of hereditary factors in *Drosophila. Proc. Soc. Exp. Biol. and Med.* 17:10–14.

————. 1921. A study of the character and mode of origin of eighteen mutations in the X chromosome of *Drosophila. Anat. Rec.* 20:213.

Nilsson-Ehle, H. 1911. Ueber Fälle spontanen Wegfallens eines Hemmungsfaktors beim Hafer. *Zeit. f. Ind. Abst. u. Vererb.* 5:1–37.

————. 1920. Multiple allelomorphe und Komplexmutationen beim Weizen. *Hereditas* 1:277–312.

Troland, L. T. 1917. Biological enigmas and the theory of enzyme action. *Amer. Natur.* 51:321–50.

Wollstein, M. 1921. Studies on the phenomenon of d'Herelle with *Bacillus dysentariae. J. Exp. Med.* 34:467–77.

Zeleny, C. 1921. The direction and frequency of mutation in the bar-eye series of multiple allelomorphs of *Drosophila. J. Exp. Zool.* 34:203–33.

Artificial Transmutation of the Gene

POPULAR *accounts of the radioactive decay of elements and the immense power released by the conversion of mass into energy were shattering experiences for the world-view of twentieth-century scientists.*

Muller's choice of the term "transmutation" reveals his awareness of the analogy provided by his induced mutations. The immense potential of these artificially altered genes is hinted at, cryptically, with the dismissal that "the time is not ripe to discuss here such possibilities with reference to the human species." His struggle, since 1919, to perfect the genetic stocks to measure mutation rates is also not revealed by Muller's enthusiastic account of his 15,000 percent increase in mutation rate and his experimental proof that the gene is a single or double molecule, rather than a sack full of identical particles. Although the data were presented at the International Congress of Genetics in Berlin in 1927 (See "The Problem of Genic Modification, Verhandlung der V Kongress fur Vererbungslehre," Zeitschrift fur induktive Abstammungs—und Vererbungslehre Supl. Bd. I [1928]: 234–60), this general account reveals how many new features of radiation genetics were encountered in this first tampering with the fundamental units of life.

Most modern geneticists will agree that gene mutations form the chief basis of organic evolution, and therefore of most of the complexities of living things. Unfortunately for the geneticists, however, the study of these mutations, and, through them, of the genes themselves, has heretofore been very seriously hampered by the extreme infrequency of their occurrence under ordinary conditions, and by the generally unsuccessful attempts to modify decidedly, and in a sure and detectable way, this sluggish "natural" mutation rate. Modification of the innate nature of organisms, for more directly utilitarian purposes, has of course been subject to these same restrictions, and the practical breeder has hence been compelled to remain content with the mere making of recombinations of the material already at hand, providentially supplemented, on rare and isolated occasions, by an unexpected mutational windfall. To these circumstances are due the wide-spread desire on the part of biologists to gain some measure of control over the hereditary changes within the genes.

It has been repeatedly reported that germinal changes, presumably mutational, could be induced by X or radium rays, but, as in the case of the similar published claims involving other agents (alcohol, lead, antibodies, etc.), the work has been done in such a way that the meaning of the data, as analyzed from a modern genetic standpoint, has been highly disputatious at best; moreover, what were apparently the clearest cases have given negative or contrary results on repetition. Nevertheless, on theoretical grounds, it has appeared to the present writer that radiations of short wavelength should be especially promising for the production of mutational changes, and for this and other reasons a series of experiments concerned with this problem has been undertaken during the past year on the fruit fly, Drosophila melanogaster, in an attempt to provide critical data. The well-known favorableness of this species for genetic study, and the special methods evolved during the writer's eight years' intensive work on its mutation rate (including the work on temperature, to be referred to later), have finally made possible the finding of some decisive effects, consequent upon the application of X rays. The effects here referred to are truly mutational and are not to be confused with the well-known effects of X rays upon the distribution of the chromatin, expressed by nondisjunction, noninherited cross-over modifications, etc. In the present condensed digest of the work, only the broad facts and conclusions therefrom, and some of the problems raised, can be presented, without any details of the genetic methods employed, or of the individual results obtained.

It has been found quite conclusively that treatment of the sperm with relatively heavy doses of X rays induces the occurrence of true "gene mutations" in a high proportion of the treated germ cells. Several hundred mutants have been obtained in this way in a short time and considerably more than a hundred of the mutant genes have been followed through three, four, or more generations. They are (nearly all of them, at any rate) stable in their inheritance, and most of them behave in the manner typical of the Mendelian chromosomal mutant genes found in organisms generally. The nature of the crosses was such as to be much more favorable for the detection of mutations in the X chromosomes than in the other chromosomes, so that most of the mutant genes dealt with were sex-linked; there was, however, ample proof that mutations were occurring similarly throughout the chromatin. When the heaviest treatment was given to the sperm, about a seventh of the offspring that hatched from them and bred contained individually detectable mutations in their treated X chromosome. Since the X forms about one fourth of the haploid chromatin, then, if we assume an equal rate of mutation in all the chromosomes (per unit of their length), it follows that almost "every other one" of the sperm cells capable of producing a fertile adult contained an "individually detectable" mutation in some chromosome or other. Thousands of untreated parent flies were bred as controls in the same way as the treated ones. Comparison of the mutation rates under the two sets of conditions showed that the heavy treatment had caused a rise of about fifteen thousand percent in the mutation rate over that in the untreated germ cells.

Regarding the types of mutations produced, it was found that, as was to have been expected both on theoretical grounds and on the basis of the previous mutation studies of Altenburg and me, the lethals (recessive for the lethal effect, though some were dominant for visible effects) greatly outnumbered the nonlethals, producing a visible morphological abnormality. There were some "semilethals" also (defining these as mutants having a viability ordinarily between about 0.5 percent and 10 percent of the normal), but, fortunately for the use of lethals as an index of mutation rate, these were not nearly so numerous as the lethals. The elusive class of "invisible" mutations that caused an even lesser reduction of viability, not readily confusable with lethals, appeared larger than that of the semilethals, but they were not subjected to study. In addition, it was also possible to obtain evidence in these experiments for the first time, of the occurrence of dominant lethal genetic changes, both in the X and in the other chromosomes. Since the zygotes receiving these never developed to maturity, such lethals could not be detected individually, but their number was so great that through egg counts and effects on the sex ratio evidence could be obtained of them en masse. It was found that their numbers are of the same order of magnitude as those of the recessive lethals. The "partial sterility" of treated males is, to an appreciable extent at least, caused by these dominant lethals. Another abundant class of mutations not previously recognized was found to be those which, when heterozygous, cause sterility but produce no detectable change in appearance; these too occur in numbers rather similar to those of the recessive lethals, and they may hereafter afford one of the readiest indices of the general mutation rate, when this is high. The sterility thus caused, occuring as it does in the offspring of the treated individuals, is of course a separate phenomenon from the "partial sterility" of the treated individuals themselves, caused by the dominant lethals.

In the statement that the proportion of "individually detectable mutations" was about one seventh for the X, and therefore nearly one half for all the chromatin, only the recessive lethals and semilethals and the "visible" mutants were referred to. If the dominant lethals, the dominant and recessive sterility genes and the "invisible" genes that merely reduce (or otherwise affect) viability or fertility had been taken into account, the percentage of mutants given would have been far higher, and it is accordingly evident that in reality the great majority of the treated sperm cells contained mutations of some kind or other. It appears that the rate of gene mutation after X-ray treatment is high enough, in proportion to the total number of genes, so that it will be practicable to study it even in the case of individual loci, in an attack on problems of allelomorphism, etc.

Returning to a consideration of the induced mutations that produced visible effects, it is to be noted that the conditions of the present experiment allowed the detection of many which approached or overlapped the normal type to such an extent that ordinarily they would have escaped observation, and definite evidence was thus obtained of the relatively high frequency of such changes here, as compared with the more conspicuous ones. The belief has several times been expressed in the *Drosophila* literature that this holds true in the case of "natural" mutations in this organism, but it has been founded only on "general impressions"; Baur, however, has demonstrated the truth of it in *Antirrhinum*. On the whole, the visible mutations caused by raying were found to be similar, in their general characteristics, to those previously detected in nonrayed material in the extensive observations on visible mutations in *Drosophila* carried out by Bridges and others. A considerable proportion of the induced visible mutations were, it is true, in loci in which mutation apparently had never been observed before, and some of these involved morphological effects of a sort not exactly like any seen previously (e.g., "splotched wing," "sex-combless," etc.), but, on the other hand, there were also numerous repetitions of mutations previously known. In fact, the majority of the well-known mutations in the X chromosome of *Drosophila melanogaster,* such as "white eye," "miniature wing," "forked bristles," etc., were reobtained, some of them several times. Among the visible mutations found, the great majority were recessive, yet there was a considerable sprinkling of dominants, just as in other work. All in all, then, there can be no doubt that many, at least, of the changes produced by X rays are of just the same kind as the "gene mutations" which are obtained, with so much greater rarity, without such treatment, and which we believe furnish the building blocks of evolution.

In addition to the gene mutations, it was found that there is also caused by X-ray treatment a high proportion of rearrangements in the linear order of the genes. This was evidenced in general by the frequent inherited disturbances in cross-over frequency (at least three percent were detected in the X chromosome alone, many accompanied but some unaccompanied by lethal effects) and evidenced specifically by various cases that were proved in other ways to involve inversions, "deficiencies," fragmentations, translocations, etc., of portions of a chromosome. These cases are making possible attacks on a number of genetic problems other-wise difficult of approach.

The transmuting action of X rays on the genes is not confined to the sperm cells, for treatment of the unfertilized females causes mutations about as readily as treatment of the males. The effect is produced both on oocytes and early oogonia. It should be noted especially that, as in mammals, X rays (in the doses used) cause a period of extreme infertility, which commences soon after treat-ment and later is partially recovered from. It can be stated posi-tively that the return of fertility does not mean that the new crop of eggs is unaffected, for these, like those mature eggs that manage to survive, were found in the present experiments to contain a high proportion of mutant genes (chiefly lethals, as usual). The practice, common in current X-ray therapy, of giving treatments that do not certainly result in permanent sterilization, has been defended chiefly on the ground of a purely theoretical conception that eggs produced after the return of fertility must necessarily represent "uninjured" tissue. As this presumption is hereby dem-onstrated to be faulty it would seem incumbent for medical prac-tice to be modified accordingly, at least until genetically sound experimentation upon mammals can be shown to yield results of a decisively negative character. Such work upon mammals would involve a highly elaborate undertaking, as compared with the above experiments on flies.

From the standpoint of biological theory, the chief interest of the present experiments lies in their bearing on the problems of the composition and behavior of chromosomes and genes. Through special genetic methods it has been possible to obtain some infor-mation concerning the manner of distribution of the transmuted genes amongst the cells of the first and later zygote generations following treatment. It is found that the mutation does not usually involve a permanent alteration of all of the gene substance present at a given chromosome locus at the time of treatment, but either affects in this way only a portion of that substance, or else occurs subsequently, as an after-effect, in only one of two or more de-scendant genes derived from the treated gene. An extensive series of experiments, now in process, will be necessary for deciding con-clusively between these two possibilities, but such evidence as is already at hand speaks rather in favor of the former. This would imply a somewhat compound structure for the gene (or chromosome as a whole) in the sperm cell. On the other hand, the mutated tissue is distributed in a manner that seems inconsistent with a general applicability of the theory of "gene elements" first suggested by Anderson in connection with variegated pericarp in maize, then taken up by Eyster, and recently reenforced by Demerec in *Drosophila virilis.*

A precociously doubled (or further multiplied) condition of the chromosomes (in "preparation" for later mitoses) is all that is necessary to account for the above-mentioned *fractional effect* of X rays on a given locus; but the theory of a divided condition of each gene, into a number of (originally identical) "elements" that can become separated somewhat indeterminately at mitosis, would lead to expectations different from the results that have been obtained in the present work. It should, on that theory, often have been found here, as in the variegated corn and the ever-sporting races of *D. virilis,* that mutated tissue gives rise to normal by frequent "reverse mutation"; moreover, treated tissues not at first showing a mutation might frequently give rise to one, through a "sorting out" of diverse elements, several generations after treatment. Neither of these effects was found. As has been mentioned, the mutants were found to be stable through several generations, in the great majority of cases at least. Hundreds of nonmutated descendants of treated germ cells, also, were carried through several generations, without evidence appearing of the production of mutations in generations subsequent to the first. Larger numbers will be desirable here, however, and further experiments of a different type have also been planned in the attack on this problem of gene structure, which probably can be answered definitely.

Certain of the above points which have already been determined, especially that of the fractional effect of X rays, taken in conjunction with that of the production of dominant lethals, seem to give a clue to the especially destructive action of X rays on tissues in which, as in cancer, embryonic, and epidermal tissues, the cells undergo repeated divisions (though the operation of additional factors, e.g., abnormal mitoses, tending toward the same results, is not thereby precluded); moreover, the converse effect of

X rays, in occasionally producing cancer, may also be associated with their action in producing mutations. It would be premature, however, at this time to consider in detail the various X-ray effects previously considered as "physiological," which may now receive a possible interpretation in terms of the gene-transmuting property of X rays; we may more appropriately confine ourselves here to matters which can more strictly be demonstrated to be genetic.

Further facts concerning the nature of the gene may emerge from a study of the comparative effects of varied dosages of X rays, and of X rays administered at different points in the life cycle and under varied conditions. In the experiments herein reported, several different dosages were made use of, and while the figures are not yet quite conclusive they make it probable that, within the limits used, the number of recessive lethals does not vary directly with the X-ray energy absorbed but more nearly with the square root of the latter. Should this lack of exact proportionality be confirmed, then, as Dr. Irving Langmuir has pointed out to me, we should have to conclude that these mutations are not caused directly by single quanta of X-ray energy that happen to be absorbed at some critical spot. If the transmuting effect were thus relatively indirect there would be a greater likelihood of its being influenceable by other physicochemical agencies as well, but our problems would tend to become more complicated. There is, however, some danger in using the total of lethal mutations produced by X rays as an index of gene mutations occuring in single loci, for some lethals, involving changes in cross-over frequency, are probably associated with rearrangements of chromosome regions, and such changes would be much less likely than "point mutations" to depend on single quanta. A reexamination of the effect of different dosages must therefore be carried out, in which the different types of mutations are clearly distinguished from one another. When this question is settled, for a wide range of dosages and developmental stages, we shall also be in a position to decide whether or not the minute amounts of gamma radiation present in nature cause the ordinary mutations which occur in wild and in cultivated organisms in the absence of artificially administered X-ray treatment.

As a beginning in the study of the effect of varying other conditions, upon the frequency of the mutations produced by X rays, a comparison has been made between the mutation frequencies following the raying of sperm in the male and in the female receptacles, and from germ cells that were in different portions of the male genital system at the time of raying. No decisive differences have been observed. It is found, in addition, that aging the sperm after treatment, before fertilization, causes no noticeable alteration in the frequency of detectable mutations. Therefore the death rate of the mutant sperm is no higher than that of the unaffected ones; moreover, the mutations cannot be regarded as secondary effects of any semilethal physiological changes which might be supposed to have occurred more intensely in some ("more highly susceptible") spermatozoa than in others.

Despite the "negative results" just mentioned, however, it is already certain that differences in X-ray influences, by themselves, are not sufficient to account for all variations in mutation frequency, for the present X-ray work comes on the heels of the determination of mutation rate being dependent upon temperature (work as yet unpublished). This relation had first been made probable by work of Altenburg and me in 1919 but was not finally established until the completion of some experiments in 1926. These gave the first definite evidence that gene mutation may be to any extent controllable, but the magnitude of the heat effect, being similar to that found for chemical reactions in general, is too small, in connection with the almost imperceptible "natural" mutation rate, for it, by itself, to provide a powerful tool in the mutation study. The result, however, is enough to indicate that various factors besides X rays probably do affect the composition of the gene, and that the measurement of their effects, at least when in combination with X rays, will be practicable. Thus we may hope that problems of the composition and behavior of the gene can shortly be approached from various new angles, and new handles found for their investigation, so that it will be legitimate to speak of the subject of "gene physiology," at least, if not of gene physics and chemistry.

In conclusion, the attention of those working along classical genetic lines may be drawn to the opportunity, afforded them by the use of X rays, of creating in their chosen organisms a series of artificial races for use in the study of genetic and "phaenogenetic" phenomena. If, as seems likely on general considerations, the effect is common to most organisms, it should be possible to produce, "to order," enough mutations to furnish respectable genetic maps, in their selected species, and, by the use of the mapped genes, to analyze the aberrant chromosome phenomena simultaneously obtained. Similarly, for the practical breeder, it is hoped that the method will ultimately prove useful. The time is not ripe to discuss here such possibilities with reference to the human species.

The writer takes pleasure in acknowledging his sincere appreciation of the cooperation of Dr. Dalton Richardson, Roentgenologist, of Austin, Texas in the work of administering the X-ray treatments.

On the Relation between Chromosome Changes and Gene Mutations

ALMOST as soon as Muller's successful induction of mutations was confirmed, criticisms were directed against the two key assertions in this paper: that there were genes at all and that X rays altered genes rather than destroyed segments of chromosomes bearing them. This quest for proof of true gene mutations could not be resolved by the techniques available to geneticists from 1927 to the mid 1950s. Muller's defense of true gene mutations, presented in 1955 at the Brookhaven Symposium on Mutation, is the most detailed theoretical case he attempted. Within two years of its publication the first proofs of molecular substitutions in the nucleotide sequence of DNA, by purine and pyrimidine analogues, were demonstrated in bacteriophage by Seymour Benzer and Ernest Freese ("Induction of specific mutations with 5-bromouracil," Proceedings of the National Academy of Sciences 44 (1958): 112–19). The existence of individual genes and their organization as structural or functional units was also unresolved until molecular analysis demonstrated functional discontinuities in the DNA thread of bacteria and viruses but not physical discontinuities. The organization of genes, physically and functionally, in fruit flies and higher organisms is still a controversial field of contempory interest.

Lying implicit in my topic there are two basic questions, both as old as genetics but still warmly disputed. First, have we a right to speak of individual genes as separable bodies rather than only as convenient mental isolates, conceptually cut out of an uninterrupted genetic material, or chromosome, of dimensions far larger than they? Second, if the expression "the individual gene" does correspond to a material reality of about the order of magnitude which it has been conceived to have, do we have a right to regard any, or many, of the Mendelian differences with which we deal in genetics as representing changes, chemical in nature, within these individual genes; or are these differences caused only by decreases and increases in number and possibly in size (i.e., in number of identical parts), and by changes in mutual arrangement, of genes that themselves remain essentially unchanged, or even unchangeable? A variant of this supposition that there are no qualitative intragenic mutations is the view that although they occur they are not dealt with by geneticists, being either too rare or too small in their visible effects to be detected by our crude means, or that at any rate they are not found in experiments with ionizing radiation, which is too lacking in subtlety to induce them.

Do Genes Exist as Separate Units?

Turning to the first question, that of whether the genes are discrete, it may be noted that only *some* of the earlier students of chromosomes, among them of course W. Roux, A. Weismann, E. Strasburger, T. Boveri, E. B. Wilson, and F. A. Janssens, believed that the chromosomes were compounded of many diverse parts, each capable of self-reproduction even if separated or rearranged with respect to the others. For example, it may be recalled that in 1919 W. E. Castle spoke of the whole chromosome as one molecule, whereas at the opposite extreme Belling in 1928 thought of the genes as cytologically visible and countable chromomeres separated from one another, at least at interphase, by relatively long fibers of nongenetic material.

Although it is probable that few geneticists would follow Belling today in believing the genes to be widely separated, the question remains important, even if they are in direct contact (as seems more probable), whether or not the chromosome has a fundamentally segmental structure at all: that is, a structure made up of subdivisions of an order of magnitude which is several times that of the ultimate component nucleotide and amino acid groups. For, if the chromosomes are not thus segmented, there is no essential distinction between structural changes of chromosomes and what have been called point or gene mutations. In that case, *all* these changes are chemical changes involving virtually identical bond substitutions, and it is to be taken for granted that such changes in the positions of parts would have phenotypic effects. Moreover, the breaks both of crossing-over and of structural change would in that case not be confined to specific positions, of the order of some thousands to a chromosome of ordinary size, but they might take place almost anywhere along the chain of ultimate components. In crossing-over, this situation would require a far higher order of accuracy for the avoidance of deficiencies and duplications than would be necessary for a chromosome segmented into a thousand to several thousand genes, within any one of which exchange did not ordinarily occur.

The idea that seeming point mutations might only be small structural changes acquired plausibility when it was found that the same agent—ionizing radiation—which induced point mutations in abundance also induced structural changes of all known types. It remained, however, for A. S. Serebrovsky, in 1929, to propose and advocate this view publicly, although he did not tie it with a denial of gene discreteness. The idea of interstitial rearrangements on a minute scale received its first proof with the demonstration, in 1933 and 1934, through the observation of salivary chromosomes by T. S. Painter and O. Mackensen, that the deficiencies of *Drosophila* really represent absences of tiny sections within chromosomes, and the finding in 1934 and 1935, by the group of research workers with whom I was associated in Russia (Muller and Prokofyeva 1934; Muller et al. 1934, 1935a, 1935b, 1936; Kossikov and Muller 1935; Muller 1935a, 1936) of similarly tiny interstitial inversions (scute 10, scute J1), transpositions (scute 19, Pale), and duplications (Bar and those derived from the transpositions). At the same time, our group and N. P. Dubinin's (Dubinin and Sidorov 1934) had both accumulated evidence of the *general* existence in *Drosophila* of positional influence between parts of chromosomes, a phenomenon which Sturtevant had discovered for Bar eye in 1925. This led us in 1934 and the years following (cf. Muller 1937) to point out that these minute structural changes would in many cases be indistinguishable from gene mutations and that, with their distinguishing criteria thus obscured, the very concepts of gene mutation and of the gene as a unit would be subjected to further attack. It was not long before Goldschmidt (1937, 1938) launched just this attack.

The "Left-Right Test" of Breakage Position

The case for a segmented chromosome had, however, been somewhat fortified in the meantime by a series of intensive genetic analyses which I had conducted, mainly from 1931 to 1936 (Muller and Prokofyeva 1934; Muller et al. 1934, 1935a, 1935b; Muller 1935a, 1932, 1935b; Raffel and Muller 1940), but continued to some extent over the past 25 years, on mutations of varied kinds involving a narrowly limited chromosome region. The region chosen was that extraordinarily suitable one, near the left end of the X chromosome of *Drosophila,* which is subject to changes, both of the position effect and of the subtraction-addition types, affecting the phenotypes known as scute, achaete, and yellow. The earlier results of the genetic tests of mutants involving this region, supplemented by cytological observations of the same cases by Prokofyeva, were summarized by us in 1934 in our paper entitled "Continuity and discontinuity of the hereditary material." Since except for this early condensation only fragmentary data on this series of studies have been published (e.g. Raffel and Muller 1940 and notes in *Drosophila Information Service*), a brief sketch of them may be given here.

   The chief objective of the study was to obtain evidence concerning the relative positions of breakage of the chromosome in mutations in which structural change had occurred. Some three dozen radiation-induced mutants of the types in question, obtained in the work of Serebrovsky, Dubinin, and their coworkers and that of my own groups of coworkers, were subjected to preliminary genetic tests. The great majority could be proved to involve structural change, either gross or minute; in fact, it was in this study, when supplemented by the cytological observations, that the first cases of minute inversion and insertion were demonstrated. However, in not much more than a dozen cases were the structural changes of types suitable for the determination, by the genetic techniques used, of the precise position of the break or breaks in the given region relative to the positions of the breaks in the other cases.

The essence of the technique lay in the construction, through crosses between the different mutants and appropriate recombining operations, of zygotes that contained the left-hand portion of the X chromosome of, say, case A, extending up to the break in the given region, and that containing at the same time the right-hand portion of the X chromosome of case B, extending from the corresponding break of case B rightwards. As a complement to each of these types of zygotes the reciprocal type also was constructed, which contained the left-hand portion of the X chromosome of case B, up to its break, and the right-hand portion of the X of case A, from the corresponding break rightwards. If, now, the break of case A in the given region were to the left of that of case B, the first mentioned type of recombinational zygote would have a deficiency and, in the hemizygous male at least, might be expected to show evidence of this by lethality or phenotypic abnormality, whereas the second type of recombinant, having an overlapping representation of the small region between the two breaks, would show little if any disturbance. If, on the other hand, A's break were to the right of B's the situation would be reversed and the recombinant with the left portion of A and the right portion of B would have the overlap and the other recombinant the deficiency. Finally, in the event that the breaks in question in cases A and B were in identical positions, neither of the two complementary types of recombinational zygotes would have a deficiency in the given region, and neither would show any greater abnormality with respect to phenotypes dependent upon this region than that shown by the original unrecombined mutants of either of these types.

It may be mentioned that in many cases the carrying out of this "left-right test," as I have called it, was by no means simple. For, all recoverable cases of structural change involve at least two breaks, so that a recombinant which is suitably constructed with regard to the breaks in the region under study (here the yellow-achaete-scute region) may have a considerable deficiency or overlap (duplication) with regard to some other region or regions. Only where the other region of breakage in both cases being compared lies in the heterochromatic portion of the same chromosome arm can the resultant aneuploidy be neglected. Since the cases studied with reference to each other included diverse translocations, as well as inversions of which several had their right-hand break in some euchromatic region, and a transposition, varied genetic manipulations, such as the provision of extra chromosome fragments, had to be resorted to in order to overcome sufficiently the aneuploidy caused by the nonmatching of the breaks outside the region under study. In some cases this required the production of needed types of aberrations by further irradiation operations. It would take us too far afield to go into any of these details here.

In all, sixteen breaks were found to have taken part in rearrangements of a type that made it possible to determine their positions with relation to one another by the left-right test. Considering these breaks in order from left to right, two, here denoted as A, were in sensibly the same position just to the left of the yellow-determining locus or subregion, and therefore just to the left of all that portion of the chromosome which was being studied. Two more, denoted as A', were either in the same position as these first two or else just to the right of the yellow locus or subregion but to the left of that of achaete. The reason their position with reference to yellow was indeterminable was that they were associated with a completely yellow phenotype caused by either loss or position effect. Three breaks had taken place between achaete and scute in positions sensibly identical with one another, which will be noted as position B. Three other breaks, occupying position C, were just to the right of the scute-determining subregion. Finally, six were still farther to the right in positions which again were sensibly identical with one another and which will therefore be designated as D. Absence of the subregion between breaks A and B results in an extreme yellow achaete phenotype, without lethality; absence of that between B and C results in an extreme scute phenotype that is nearly but not always lethal in the hemizygous condition; and absence of that between C and D results in a lethality not allelic to that of the scute (B–C) deficiency.

The striking fact is that all these sixteen breaks fell into the limited number of positions that we have noted. There was no suggestion of any positions intermediate between them. For, when recombinants were produced involving any two cases having breaks here attributed to the same position, both complementary classes of recombinants appeared to be as viable, fertile, and on the whole as phenotypically normal as that unrecombined original type whose positionally "mutant" locus they carried (see, for instance, Raffel and Muller 1940). In view of the not wide diversity in numbers of breaks at the different positions, it seems likely that in the region under study breakage did occur at the majority of positions at which it could occur. If, as also seems likely, yellow and achaete will prove in further work to be definitely separable, this would mean that there are in this region at least four segments, or genes, separable by breakage, but that there are probably not many more than four. In this connection it is of interest to note that at the time our paper (Muller and Prokofyeva 1934) was published, when only eight breaks had yet been located with reference to each other, all four of the above positions of breakage had already been ascertained. That is, in the twenty years since that time, during which another eight breaks have been located genetically, no further positions of breakage have been found.

It may be recalled that exactly this entire region, and no more, is comprised in the scute-19 transposition (deletion-insertion), the left break of which is at A and the right at D. Prokofyeva's cytological examination showed that in the normal X chromosome this region occupies slightly more than half of the large band, usually appearing as a double band, which was later designated as B1–4 in Bridges' standard salivary X chromosome map of 1938. Its total length in this map of the stretched (414 μ long) salivary chromosome is only about half a micron. This gives a maximum of $\frac{1}{8}$ μ per segment. However, in a less highly chromatic region the length might be several times as great if, as seems likely, the deeper chromatization expresses relatively denser supercoiling on the part of the nucleotide chains. These results have allowed us to derive a maximum estimate for gene size in *Drosophila* of about 1/30 μ, cubed, and a minimum for gene number of about 10,000 (Muller 1935c). Considering the sources of error, these estimates agree surprisingly closely with those arrived at by the other two entirely different methods which I have proposed: the method based on the minimum typical frequency of crossing-over, and that based on the relative frequency of allelically acting mutations, especially if the last estimates are doubled to allow for pseudoalleles. Whether pseudoalleles or subgenes will bring us to a still finer state of subdivision in our material is a point still to be settled, but if so it may prove to be subdivision of a somewhat different category.

No claim is made that these results are entirely decisive in proving the main point at issue, that of the segmentation of the chromosomes, because it is conceivable that the breaks classed as being in the same position were really in somewhat different positions, but that a deficiency for the small region between them had too insignificant an effect either to be lethal or evident by mere inspection of the phenotype. This assumption would seem to be made more plausible by the fact that in many cases the phenotype had already been affected, in the direction in which such a deficiency might be expected to operate, by reason of the hypomorphically mutant appearance of one or both of the original types, prior to their becoming recombined in the left-right test. However, the assumption that deficiencies are so often without any detectable effect is not easily reconciled with our knowledge of the exceedingly great complexity, not only morphological but more especially biochemical, of every higher organism (and, for that matter, even of known unicellular organisms, only excepting some viruses). To reinforce this conclusion we have the evidence in L. J. Stadler's work that even the minutest presumptive deficiencies induced by X rays had a markedly detrimental effect on pollen tube growth.

Modern evidence supports the conception of a linear arrangement of the genetic material all the way down to its ultimate components, the nucleotides. Surely, in the so-called "code" of these units that determines the production of the superlatively intricate organization of the whole finished body, and of all features of the life cycle, there must be more than ten thousand different specifications of such importance that their omission would result in death or visible abnormality. But if this is true, then a deficiency of a smaller part than one of our inferred segments or genes would still, in many cases, have given a result detectable by our methods, if such a deficiency would have been brought about. At the same time, a deficiency of a whole segment might be expected usually to be pleiotropic in its final effects, as does in fact appear to be the case. In the light of these considerations, the present results take on more cogency in their support of the idea of chromosomal segmentation, that is, of discontinuous genes.

We can at least say that if there are not segments defined by a type of bond between them essentially different from those within them, then those bonds lying at the junctions we call intergenic are more subject to breakage involving substitution than are the other bonds, or else there are, making up a so-called locus, comparatively long outlying regions of relative genetic unimportance and, sandwiched between them, short essential regions that despite their relatively small size are able to perform the critical operations characteristic of that region, though perhaps in a somewhat restricted way when without their outlying wings. Thus the structure would be segmental in a certain functional sense even if not from a narrower chemical viewpoint. In using the words segment or gene, we do not imply that we know the answer to these finer questions.

Other Evidence of Chromosome Segmentation

A related kind of evidence for segmentation is provided by the fact that in most organisms in which structural changes have been found—*Diptera* and molds, with their evidence of abundant position effects, necessarily being exceptions—it is usually possible to obtain these structurally changed chromosomes in homozygous condition without killing or obviously damaging the organisms (e.g., Carter et al. 1955). If, however, breaks usually occur within instead of between internally integrated organizations of genetic material, such as chains of nucleotides must be, the functions of these complexes must often be greatly disturbed. Moreover, the formation of chemical junctions between previously separated parts would likewise tend to give abnormalities. In fact, even in

Drosophila, when one makes allowance for the numerous position effects that are induced at an appreciable distance from the point of breakage and recombination, it turns out that there is a surprisingly large number of cases in which the structural change was relatively innocuous, as compared with what one might expect if every structural change were equivalent to the breaking of a gene. If the breaks are between genes, all this is understandable.

In the hands of Bernstein and Mazia (1953a, 1953b), a biochemical approach has recently led to the interesting finding that when the chromosomes of sea urchin spermatozoa are subjected to decalcification by a chelating agent, and then placed in a solution of low ionic strength to increase the electric repulsions between particles, the chromosomes come apart into numerous small rod-like pieces measuring roughly .4 by .025 μ as seen with the electron microscope. This is a value of the same order of magnitude as that above estimated for the segments of *Drosophila* chromosomes, as found by our right-left technique utilizing radiation breakage. It was further shown by Mazia (1954) that salivary chromosomes of *Drosophila* and condensed chromosomes of a grasshopper likewise go to pieces if subjected to decalcification and low electrolyte concentration. Capping this, it has been reported by Steffensen (1955) that in *Tradescantia* growth under conditions of abnormally low calcium concentration greatly increases the frequency of both spontaneous and radiation-induced chromosome breaks. This finding tends to bridge the gap between Mazia's in vitro studies and our own studies on breaks at the scute locus, and renders it probable that the breaks studied in both cases are similar in type. Thus support is given to the conclusion that breakage between chromosome segments is a different sort of thing from that within them.

A less direct argument for segmentation is to be derived from the fact that whatever the nature of the genetic material itself may be, its functional products are almost certainly in the form of discrete molecules, not larger than those of ordinary proteins and capable of diffusion through the nuclear and probably through the cytoplasmic medium. If the popular notion is correct that the immediate products are modified replicas of the genetic material, then this particulateness of the products points directly to a segmental structure of the genetic material. But even if they are in no sense replicas, their own discontinuity and the standardization of structure which we must infer them to have would point to the existence of numerous *functionally* circumscribed regions of the chromosome thread, and it would be strange if this functional delimitation were not aided by structural boundaries in the genetic material, i.e., by some corresponding type of segmentation.

It is true that the existence of position effects shows clearly that even in their more immediate functionings the inferred segments are influenced by their neighbor segments and that in this sense the discontinuity of the genetic units is not complete. Such completeness of separation, however, was not the matter in question. What was sought was evidence as to whether there is a periodic structure in the chromosome, of a considerably higher order of magnitude than that of the nucleotides, which would allow us to distinguish between intragenic and extragenic phenomena. The various lines of evidence reviewed, when taken together, strongly indicate this to be the case.

At the same time, we must beware of jumping to the conclusion that the unit as defined by the test of the breakages occurring in structural changes necessarily coincides with that which might be defined by the most refined possible crossing-over test, on the one hand, or by the test of apparent allelism, on the other hand. It seemed very likely, both a priori and on the basis of the scant direct evidence that exists in the scute region, that the breakage gene and the cross-over gene would coincide, but definitive tests of this point have been lacking. On the other hand we already know that the regions defined by the phenotypic expressions of allelism are often larger. Moreover, by no means can we be sure that genes are entirely indivisible, in the sense that by special means they might be separated into two or more parts each of which was still capable of self-reproduction. It is quite possible that there are segments within segments, of several ranks.[1] But

1. The exemplary results of Benzer (1956), announced at this Symposium, which show what minute parts are subject to crossing-over in his phage material, were not known to the writer when the above was written.

even if this were true, it would not destroy the validity of units of a given rank defined by a particular operational criterion. Of these criteria, the most useful to date has been breakage.

What, If Any, Mutations Are Intragenic?

Accepting now, for purposes of further discussion at least, the segmentation of the chromosome into genes definable in our material by the test of breakage that can be followed by structural change, the question must be faced: are all mutations of this structural change character, involving only breakages between the genes and the resulting subtractions, additions and rearrangements of whole genes, or are some mutations purely intragenic?

Intragenic Mutation Required by Evolution

Put in this form, the question is little more than a rhetorical one, provided we accept both the theory of evolution and the theory that species differences are referable to the differences between the sets of genes that the species contain. It is true that Bateson and Punnett tried to represent Mendelian differences on a presence/absence basis. However, mutation involving the origination of genes *de novo* has proved to be a mirage. And evolution brought about entirely by the loss of primordial genes, and by the recombination of these losses through crosses, as pictured by J. P. Lotsy and later by E. E. Just, who thought of such losses as the removal of nuclear inhibitors of the omnipotent cytoplasm, is a *reductio ad absurdum*. Allowing additions of genes to arise as duplications, i.e., by the formation of repeats, does not help significantly either, if the repeated sections are unable to undergo subsequent intragenic differentiation from one another.

Even the invocation of position effects is inadequate to provide a basis for long continued, progressive evolution, if the structural

---

Possibly in higher organisms these finer subdivisions are relatively less subject than the larger subdivisions to breakage of either a crossing-over or a structural change type.

changes responsible for the position effects are purely intergenic. Enough is known about position effects in *Drosophila* to show that even in this group of organisms, in which such effects are commoner and more pronounced than in most forms, the effects on any one locus or, if one prefers to call it so, region, usually extend over a short distance only and are very limited in their types. Since the limitation in distance allows only a small number of genes or, at any rate, a small number of genes of euchromatic regions to participate at any one time in the position effect on any given gene, and since the individual effects themselves are limited in type, no amount of this permutation and combination of genes can result in an indefinitely continued, progressive evolution of the potentialities of these circumscribed groups of loci, and, consequently, there will be a severe limitation on the evolutionary potentiality of the set of genes as a whole.

This is in contrast to the situation for intragenic mutations. For, even though any given gene is obviously limited in regard to the types of mutant alleles that it can give rise to by any single mutational step, it should theoretically be capable, by an indefinitely continued succession of steps, of departing further and further, and ultimately in the most diverse directions, from whatever "starting point" we happened arbitrarily to assume for it. It is to be admitted that no one has ever demonstrated this to hold for intragenic mutations. It is simply a necessary extrapolation from evolution theory, as seen in the light of genetics, and it raises no real difficulties, if only it is admitted that intragenic mutation is possible at all.

In other words, our best evidence for intragenic mutation does not consist of this or that case, studied in breeding tests. It consists of the evidence in all its great sweep and diversity for the theory of evolution itself, taken in conjunction with the evidence for the existence of individual genes. So long as we retain both concepts we must admit that at bottom evolution has been built up out of intragenic mutations, together with some superstructure of intergenic structural changes that worked only by utilization of the gene differences brought about by the intragenic mutations. This does not mean, however, that we can point to a given case and say: this case surely represents an intragenic mutation.

Have Intragenic Mutations Been Observed to Arise?

Because of this dearth of adequate criteria for gene mutations, i.e., for intragenic alterations, it is even possible to maintain that although they do form the building blocks of evolution, nevertheless, the mutations which have been observed to arise in the experiments of geneticists are not of this nature, but only intergenic *hoaxes*. I am reminded here of the taunts long ago hurled at *Drosophila* workers by some paleontologists and other biologists in nongenetic fields. They stressed the pathological character of the mutants and their obvious unfitness to live. They used this unfitness as an argument against their being representatives of the changes out of which evolution was built, forgetting that it is just the sort of thing to be expected of the more conspicuous changes if their direction has been unplanned and if selection of mutations has played the guiding role in adaptation.

Even in the nineteenth century, however, it was recognized by Darwin himself that the smaller changes are less likely to be detrimental and thus more likely to become established in evolution. To make his work practicable, the geneticist has of course chosen to deal, in most cases, with the more conspicuous and therefore more pathological changes, but when he looks into the matter he finds convincing evidence of a graded series, with the lesser grades not merely less detrimental but also more numerous, as I pointed out in papers of 1918 to 1923 (Muller 1918, 1920, 1923). This is not to say that in any given series of alleles the lesser changes are more frequent—in fact, they are often rare— but only that in the case of any given character there are more loci with changes likely to affect that character slightly than those likely to affect it drastically. These facts give no ground whatever for making any distinction in their basic nature or in the manner of origination between the smaller changes and the larger ones. Thus it would be quite arbitrary to suppose that the true intragenic mutations are in general too small for us to find, and that those we find are therefore intergenic. There should be some more positive evidence of such a view before it is held to be plausible. Hence, if we admit intragenic changes for evolution, it seems to me probable that they have not been absent from the material dealt with in our crosses.

It is to be noted that, in such analytical crosses as can be made between organisms of groups that have differentiated from one another in natural evolution, evidence has been obtained of the existence of numerous basically Mendelian differences, usually small ones, even though the picture may also be complicated by structural changes. There is nothing in principle, so far as we have any evidence, to distinguish between these differences and those found in the laboratory, except that the former have passed through the sieve of selection. In the latter respect an intermediate situation is occupied by gene differences found in the field between individuals of the same population; they are more likely than the group differences but less likely than those freshly arising in the laboratory to include mutants of a conspicuous, detrimental type. All this is simply to be expected if the spontaneous mutations of the laboratory are representative of those in nature.

In considering the suggestion that genuine intragenic changes of evolutionary potentiality are below the threshold in size but of relatively frequent occurrence so that, while not graspable by the geneticist, they may accumulate and thus acquire importance in the course of time, it may be recalled that just this kind of possibility was in fact in the center of attention four and five decades ago and was put to rather critical tests. I refer in the first place, of course, to the experiments of Johannsen (Johannsen and Fischer 1909), and to some related work by others, in which every opportunity was given for such so-called continuous hereditary variation to express itself if it existed in so-called "pure lines," by allowing a gradual shifting of the phenotypic mode under the influence of selection. Instead, only rare, discrete mutations were obtained.

For those who might object that pure lines provide too limited a setup and that crossbreeding in some manner provides a stimulus to such variation over and above the variation resulting from Mendelian recombination itself, we may recall a number of extensive studies on *Drosophila*, more especially those by Altenburg and myself on truncate wings (Altenburg and Muller 1920;

Muller et al. 1923), followed by Sturtevant's work (1918) on dichaete bristles. In these studies it was possible to reach the same conclusions as Johannsen's despite the fact that the material here studied was heterozygous for many loci. The technique involved the use of linked marker genes to tag the chromosomes. Given a certain chromosome combination as shown by the markers, neither plus nor minus selection, continued over many generations, availed to change the phenotypic average, even though these phenotypes were proved to be especially labile in responding both to environmental and to genetic differences. In other experiments (Marshall and Muller 1917; Muller 1951), recessive genes have been kept in heterozygous condition for scores and even hundreds of generations, during which time, since they were largely protected from selection, they should have been subject to considerable drift in their potential expression if subliminal mutations are relatively frequent, yet when finally allowed to become homozygous or hemizygous they have exhibited no noticeable change in phenotype. In the light of these results, the onus of proof for the idea of a creeping variation of genes as the basis of selection would seem to lie with those who advocate this doctrine.

This argument should by no means be construed, and was never intended, as a denial of the occurrence of below-the-threshold changes in the genes. By the devices of lowering the threshold by means of especially sensitizing genes (so-called "chief factors"), as well as by forming compounds with more extreme alleles, and by controlling environments, it has been abundantly shown (as in the cases of Truncate, Beaded, Bar, eosin, vestigial-nick, ebony, and other mutants in *Drosophila)* that many spontaneous mutations are subliminal in their effects. (Muller 1918; Altenburg and Muller 1920; Zeleny 1922; Bridges 1919; Bridges and Morgan 1919; Stern 1926). However, no basis has appeared for distinguishing the smaller from the larger so far as their manner of origination is concerned, and it would be arbitary to assume such a basis. After all, the position of the threshold is determined by the nature of the processes of expressions and observation, which differ according to the character studied. Moreover, when we confine our attention to some given locus, suitable for the detection of alleles over a considerable quantitative range of phenotype, we do not

ordinarily find the principle observed that the smaller the mutation is, the more frequently it occurs. This was pointed out more
than 35 years ago (Muller 1918, 1920), in response to some com-
ments by Jennings (1917) on the seemingly high variability of the
white locus in *Drosophila:* that is, there is no tendency for the
variation to follow a normal curve, but, instead, all are similarly
rare, sudden, and discrete, as though they arose by similar
processes. This as well as other considerations (Muller 1918) makes
unlikely the idea of a heritable variation in gene size, that is, in
the number of identical units, except of course by linear rearrangement of duplicational and deficiency type.

Does Radiation Produce Intragenic Mutation?

Turning now from spontaneous mutations to those induced by
ionization radiation, we do indeed find some important differences
which are, however, far more prominent in some kinds of organisms than in others. Certainly the work of Stadler and his associates has made it clear that in X-rayed maize, and probably in
other cereals, the great majority, if not all, of the seeming point
mutations arising at certain intensively studied loci or, rather,
groups of loci, are multigene deficiences rather than intragenic
changes. Moreover, as mentioned earlier, there is no doubt that
in X-rayed *Drosophila* also, at least when the irradiation is applied
to condensed chromosome stages, such as those of spermatozoa,
deficiencies as well as other demonstrable structural changes arise
with much higher frequency, relative to changes that appear to
involve but one gene, than they do without treatment. Hence the
question must be faced: is there any good reason to believe that
ionizing radiation produces intragenic changes at all?

The best answer we have to this question lies in the mass of
data obtained in X- and gamma-ray experimentation on *Drosophila*
which shows that despite the production of clear-cut deficiencies
and other structural changes a very large proportion of the seeming point mutations, and especially of those induced in stages
with extended chromosomes (Muller 1941; Muller et al. 1950), are
in no known way distinguishable from the mutations that have
arisen spontaneously. In fact, experience shows that every spon-

taneous mutant of *Drosophila* can, if thoroughly searched for, also be found after X-ray treatment. In the case of multiple-allele series, mutants of intermediate degrees of expression, including those deviating only slightly from the normal and those of more restricted rather than pleiotropic expression, as well as the more extreme and the more pleiotropic mutants, are produced by ionizing radiation, unlike what Stadler and his coworkers found in the case of the loci examined by them in maize. The same is true of partial and of complete reverse mutations, that is, they arise in both treated and untreated material, even though for most loci they are in both types of material much rarer than the abnormal mutations (Patterson and Muller 1930; Giles 1956).

It has been granted that in the case of any individual mutant, whether arising as a result of radiation or spontaneously, it is possible to construct a plausible hypothesis that will interpret it as an intergenic change, that is, as involving only a loss or duplication of a gene or genes or one or more position effects caused by intergenic rearrangement. Yet, if we accept the arguments previously given for the conclusion that, in addition to such phenomena, truly intragenic changes are included among the mutations which have arisen spontaneously in our laboratory and field material, then the above-mentioned extraordinary congruence between the bulk of our results on irradiated and on untreated *Drosophila* material leads us almost irresistibly towards the conclusion that the radiation mutations also include a considerable intragenic contingent.

The only escape from this conclusion, provided that we accept the intragenic nature of many of the spontaneous mutations at least, is by way of the ad hoc assumption that practically any intragenic mutation can have its observable effects imitated by a minute intergenic structural change or loss involving the same locus. This is stretching hypotheses pretty far, unless we consider the gene as defined by tests of phenotypic allelism to be divided up into many more actual genes—the Russians had a word for it: "subgenes"—than the evidence already reviewed, and that to be reviewed, indicates the existence of. Yet, as we shall see, even the subgene or finely divided multilocus view would not explain, without intragenic mutation, how the supposed condition of numerous related but differentiated neighboring units had come into existence.

Outside of *Drosophila* and its relatives, the animal that has had its radiation mutations most intensively studied so as to allow locus-by-locus comparison with its spontaneous mutations is the mouse, in the notable recent studies by Russell (1954, 1956, personal communication). The results obtained by him thus far point strongly to the conclusion that the mutations induced by X rays in gonia of the mouse, like those of *Drosophila*, resemble the mutations arising spontaneously. For, the induced mutations acting as alleles of a given locus include both less extreme and more extreme types, associated with different amounts of effect on viability, and some of the alleles are indistinguishable from or very similar to known spontaneous ones. Obviously the mouse and *Drosophila* fall into the same class in regard to the point mutations induced in their interphase cells and differ in this respect from maize pollen.

In attempting to find an interpretation for the existence of such a difference, attention should be called to the fact that if we had taken for comparison with the maize findings the results derived from the irradiation of mature *Drosophila* spermatozoa instead of from the gonia of *Drosophila* or the mouse the difference, although still a marked one, would not have been as extreme. For, in this case a much larger group of small deficiencies, duplications, and other demonstrable but minute structural changes would have been included in the class that was inherited like point mutations (i.e., those showing no appreciable change in cross-over frequencies), and in addition there would have been an abundant class of gross structural changes. Moreover as Lüning (1952a, 1952b) has shown, immature spermatozoa of *Drosophila* when irradiated produce many more structural changes, both gross and minute, in relation to seeming gene mutations than do even the mature spermatozoa. Not only different developmental stages but also different treatments associated with the ionizing irradiation can affect the frequency of demonstrable structural changes differently from that of mutations of an apparently Mendelizing kind. This has been shown in *Drosophila* for both infrared and ultraviolet (Kaufmann et al. 1946; Kaufmann and Hollaender

1946; Kaufmann and Gay 1947, 1948), although their affects on X-ray mutagenesis are very divergent. It has been shown still more strikingly in experiments on irradiated barley seeds carried out by D'Amato and Gustaffson (1948), using KCN, by Kaplan (1950, 1951), using either NH_4OH or CO_2, and by Caldecott and Smith (1951, 1952) using heat shocks. In some of the experiments cited, structural changes were decreased in frequency while seeming gene mutations were increased, and in others the reverse pair of effects was produced. If such great differences of this kind can exist between different cells of the same organism under different conditions or in different stages, there may well be an even more marked difference of the same sort between two organisms as unlike as *Drosophila* and maize.

It may be recalled that even gross and minute structural changes do not run parallel in their frequencies in different cell stages. A pertinent example is provided by the fact that mature spermatozoa have a far higher frequency of radiation-induced gross structural changes than is found in nearly mature oocytes, but only a slightly, if at all, higher frequency of minute structural changes (Muller et al. 1950; Glass 1956). Such differences are still more to be expected in a comparison of structural changes in general, or of minute structural changes in particular, with gene mutations.

That the chromosomes of maize and related plants have a far higher frequency of structural changes induced in them by a given dose of ionizing radiation than the chromosomes of *Drosophila* is clear. It is true that the plant chromosomes appear larger, but it would be strange, in view of the economy of organization of living things, if maize has so many more genes than *Drosophila* as to explain on this basis alone the so very much greater susceptibility of its chromosomes to structural change. At any rate, the induced structural change frequency of maize is so high that only doses of X rays can be used in genetic experiments with maize that, if used in *Drosophila,* would result in a production of point mutation so low as to be within the frequency range attained by spontaneous mutations in some of the more frequently mutating lines. Thus, if maize were like *Drosophila* in its frequency of induced gene mutations, not many mutations would have been expected in the X-ray experiments that have been carried out, even though many obvious deficiencies and gross structural changes have been produced. Yet, in view of the experiments which we have cited showing the lack of parallelism between structural changes and seeming gene mutations, it is entirely possible that in maize pollen, X-ray-induced gene mutations are produced with a *lesser* frequency, by a given dose, than in *Drosophila* spermatozoa. This very small assumption, then, would explain the main discrepancy in results between these organisms.

"Nests" of Genes as Evidence for or against Intragenic Mutation

In the discussion of multiple-allele series as evidence for intragenic changes given in the first edition of *The Mechanisms of Mendelian Heredity* (Morgan et al. 1915), the alternative interpretation of them as involving losses or inactivations of different members of a closely linked group or "nest" (as we later termed the idea) of functionally interrelated genes was rejected on several grounds that we now know to be mistaken. For one thing, the evidence then existing was taken to indicate that the genes were arranged in line in a random manner, so far as their functions were concerned. However, we now know this to be true only on a large-scale view, not on the small scale one on which the existence of position effects and of minute repeats becomes evident.

Second, the simultaneous loss of two or more members of the nest, an assumption which we took to be necessary (on the nest view) to account for the fact that the members having somewhat different expressions acted phenotypically as alleles in compounds, was thought to be very improbable. However, we now know that not only do small groups of contiguous genes become lost, in the occurrence of minute deficiencies, but that on occasion ionizing radiation can cause the loss or mutation of nearby genes at positions far enough apart to allow a small amount of crossing-over between the affected loci. One example of this was the simultaneous scarlet and lethal mutation, showing about .1 percent crossing-over between them, reported by me in 1932 and the other is the simultaneous Contrabithorax and postbithorax, showing about .02 percent crossing-over, reported by Lewis (1954). The most probable interpretation of these cases is that two ionizations of the same delta-ray cluster or primary electron track tail both chanced to be mutagenic. The same sort of thing seems to occur in much greater relative abundance with neutron treatment (Muller and Valencia 1951a, 1951b; Muller 1954a), as is to be expected on this interpretation. It would be interesting to know whether it also happens in mutagenesis by chemicals.

Third, in 1915 it was thought to be very unlikely that recessive mutations at two different, even though nearby and functionally related, loci could give rise, in compound with one another, to the mutant phenotype. However, the discovery of repeats in the normal organisms, and more especially the discovery of the generality of position effects in *Drosophila*, changed this expectation. As Offermann (1935) pointed out in his fundamental paper on position effect, it could be deduced from this phenomenon that mutations of two nearby loci, separable from one another by crossing-over, would each give rise to an effect like that of mutation of a given one of these loci. It is also possible for this sort of effect, now termed "pseudoallelism," to occur without any position effect at all, where there are repeats whose genes are (or have become) weak enough in their action to cause two doses of the normal locus to have a different phenotypic expression than four. Whichever of these two explanations may hold true in any given case, abundant instances of these so-called "pseudoalleles" are now known, thanks largely to the work of Lewis (1954, 1952, 1955), of Green (1955), and of Laughnan (1955a, 1955b).

This proof of gene nests, of the capacity of different loci within them to give phenotypic allelism, and of their capacity to undergo simultaneous mutation, has made it abundantly possible to get series of diversified multiple alleles that originate only by loss, and of others that involve only rearrangement of loci or loss, that is, purely intergenic changes. But this by no means signifies that all multiple allele series actually are of this nature, or that no evidence for intragenic change can be derived from any of them.

The studies of MacKendrick and Pontecorvo (1952) and of MacKendrick (1953) on the white allele series of *Drosophila* have shown that, although there are two separable loci, about a fortieth of a map unit apart, giving allelically acting reductions of eye color, and it is possible that there is a third locus, nevertheless four and probably five different mutants (coral, apricot "Cal Tech," eosine, ivory, and probably blood) all have failed to give cross-overs with one another, in a total count of 145,000 as though they all occupied one locus, whereas two others (white and apricot "Edinburgh") behave as though they were both at the other locus. Short of postulating separate genes the linkage between which is inordinately (at least one order of magnitude) stronger than that binding the members already known to be separate (a view of which would itself imply a type of segmentation), we are thereby led to conclude that at each of these two loci a series of diverse mutations has occurred. It may be recalled, moreover, that the phenotypic differences between them are much more diverse than in mere amount of pigment. Not only the type of color, but also the response to dosage compensators and other modifiers are involved, as well as differential effects on spermatheca shape (Dobzhansky 1927) and on fertility and viability (Timoféeff-Ressovsky 1933).

In the case of most pseudoallelic loci, it has not yet been possible to obtain decisive evidence whether the two or more loci are functionally related only through position effects or whether in addition, or instead, they are derived from a common ancestral locus by a repeat formation that occurred in the relatively recent evolutionary history. More critical evidence that two nearby genes whose mutations have given rise to similar phenotypes are really related in origin is obtained (1) by the test of synaptic affinity, as shown by cytologically visible association or by unequal crossing-over, or (2) by the test of their ability still to produce their characteristic phenotype, to some extent at least, even when they have become separated from one another by a structural change such as translocation, inversion, deletion, or unequal crossing-over. It has not yet, so far as I am aware, been possible to apply the first test in Drosophila except in the case of Bar eye and other duplications that have arisen in laboratory material. The second test has thus far given results in the case of several locus groups of Drosophila, including that of achaete-scute, that of the sperm-motility genes of the Y chromosome, and that of forked bristles. In all these cases there is evidence of the existence of more than one locus, each capable, when far removed from or in the absence of the other locus or loci, of producing a part at least of the phenotypic effect in question. In fact, for the sperm-motility genes Neuhaus (1939) showed that there are probably at least fourteen of them.

Now the point of special interest about the two best studied of these cases of repeated genes, those involving scute-achaete and the sperm-motility genes, is the fact that despite their having presumably been derived from a common ancestral gene they are by no means identical in their mode of functioning at the present time. In fact, they do not even act as pseudoalleles on crossing, except perhaps to a very minor degree. Hence, if we concede their common ancestry we must also concede that since the time of the repeat formation they have diverged in a qualitative manner, as I pointed out concerning the scute region in my discussions of 1935 (1935a, 1935b). Thus the originally duplicate genes have come to have more or less complementary specialized roles in the production of that character complex for the determination of which the ancestral gene had already become highly organized, and in addition they may have taken on functions more or less new to them.

Evidence for exactly the same kind of a story, but with a far greater wealth of details, was recently brought forward by Laughnan (1955a, 1955b) for the group of loci of the A series in maize, and we have a fascinating account of such cases in *Neurospora* by Giles (1956). In the case of maize it was not gross rearrangement but unequal crossing-over which affected the separation of the loci and thereby provided evidence of their ability, when separated, to exert the type of phenotypic influence in question. Presumably, it was also by unequal crossing-over that the repeats had long ago arisen. But the important point for us here is the evidence that since that time they have differentiated qualitatively and that in different varieties this differentiation has taken varied forms. Any attempt to explain this other than by intragenic mutation, i.e., mutation within the region having the given function, encounters great difficulties unless we virtually abandon the concept of chromosome segmentation. This, however, is "where we came in." All in all, then, the gist of the work on long-established duplications is to support the thesis of intragenic mutation. In fact, it gives us that very picture, lacking in our ordinary genetic work on the single mutational steps that have occurred under our observation, of what happens to genes as a result of the accumulation of a series of selected mutational steps, which have caused them to diverge relatively far from some common ancestral "starting point." This can take us a long way indeed beyond the point at which we came in.

Further Considerations Concerning the Relation Between Structural Changes and Gene Mutations

The question of why rearrangements of genes should often give effects similar to those of gene mutations—the question, that is, of the nature of position effects (Muller 1935d, 1938) is one which limitations of time and space preclude discussion of here.[2] We may pause only for one other point regarding position effects, a usually neglected one that was well brought out in Offermann's paper of 1935 on this general subject. As Offermann pointed out, despite the existence of certain additional opportunities for biochemical organization afforded by position effects, there is a great long-term advantage in having these position effects limited, in the main, to very short range influences. These are found usually to be of an order of magnitude hardly greater, in the euchromatin at any rate, than that of the genes themselves. For, this situation allows a much higher degree of specialization of the local regions of the chromatin. It gives them a relative independence of one another in functioning that allows a higher degree of genetic adaptability in undergoing evolutionary change than would exist if a change in any part of the genetic material were likely automatically to carry with it changes in the mode of action of many other widely separated and functionally very different parts.

In other words, for an organization that is not perfect or static but is ever subject to improvement, too much holism is bad for

2. The paper by the Demerecs (1956), presented at this Symposium, reports results which show conclusively that, in their bacterial material at any rate, position effects are produced as a result of interaction between products of gene activity highly localized near their genes of origination.

the whole by depriving the components of some of the opportunities for progress that individual initiative brings. Perhaps that
is one reason why in many higher organisms the position effects
seem so restricted. It would be a reason why chromosomes tended
to become or to remain segmented, and to have their spontaneous mutations usually confined within these segments. For, on
the whole, narrowly limited changes have a much better chance
of not upsetting the apple cart.

Another question which would logically be included under our
title is that of whether gene mutations, or at least those produced
by ionizing radiation, usually arise in connection with breaks of
chromosomes. This possibility, which I rashly suggested in 1941
on becoming aware that the great majority of breaks induced in
spermatozoa undergo restitution, has receded in its plausibility in
more recent years. As I undertook a rather extended discussion of
this matter not long ago (1954b), I will not go into the details
here of the grounds for concluding that most gene mutations,
even if induced by radiation, do not arise in association with
chromosome breaks, or at least not with those of the type which
cause structural changes. On the other hand, since as we have
seen induced point mutations themselves sometimes arise in clusters, probably as a result of the clustering of the mutagenic
ionizations, and this is true also of the breaks that form minute
rearrangements, it is to be expected that there would *sometimes*
be, in like manner, a tendency for a break and a gene mutation
to be produced in the close neighborhood of one another.

In making this inference we are, of course, taking it for granted
that an ionization or group of ionizations or, more generally speaking, of activations, represents the start of the chain of events in
mutagenesis by ionizing radiation, and that this ionization somehow, even though indirectly, produces its mutagenic effect in
rather close proximity, usually, to its own site of origination, no
matter whether that effect be a chromosome break or a gene
mutation. This is not the place to discuss the possible details of
this mutagenic mechanism, but one point here implied is of importance for our theme. This point is the implication that the same
basic mechanism can lead to either one of the two phenomena
we are considering: chromosome breakage or gene mutation. This

conception becomes reinforced when we consider that it is not ionizing radiation only which provides a basis for both breakage and gene mutation but also (if we base our judgment of the production of these phenomena on the same kind of grounds as with ionizing radiation itself) every other primary mutagen that has this far been studied with reference to this question. These agents include ultraviolet, the mustard group, urethane, triazine, formaldehyde and some other chemical mutagens tested, and even mutator genes.

It is true that in most of the chemical cases the analysis has not yet been pushed far enough for our conclusions concerning the production of gene mutations to be well enough based. Nevertheless, the apparent parallelism in both kinds of mutagenesis in this series of cases is so impressive as to indicate that the two kinds of changes have much in common. The problem of the nature of this common basis is ultimately a chemical one, dealing with the nature of the bonds involved. For one thing, it is probable that in both cases the bonds can be attacked by oxidation reactions, but that in itself is so commonplace that, alone, it does not seem very helpful.

On the other hand, there are, as we have noted, many conditions accessory to irradiation which have very different grades of effect, and are sometimes even opposite in their influence, on structural change and on gene mutation, respectively. In part, this divergence is caused by the fact that the frequency of structural change depends on the type of union that follows breakage as well as on the frequency of breakage itself. Since there has been much uncertainty as to whether a given condition that influences the production of structural changes by radiation is chiefly affecting the process of breakage or of union, we are seldom in a position definitely to compare the mode of influence of a given condition on the primary processes, those of breakage and of gene mutation, and thus to gauge the extent of their parallelism.

One specific result of interest in this connection may be mentioned here, however. That is the recent evidence obtained by a number of different investigators working separately (Muller 1954a; Baker and Von Halle 1954; Conger 1954; Kirby-Smith and Swanson 1954; Mickey 1954; Russell et al. 1954; Ives et al. 1954) of a higher mutagenic effectiveness of neutrons than of X rays in the production not only of chromosome breaks but also of point mutations. In some of the work there was evidence that these point mutations in all probability comprised, in the main, gene mutations. For broken chromosomes, evidence of the higher effectiveness of neutrons had in fact been found earlier, as by Marshak (1942) and Giles (1943), but the work on point mutations, or rather lethals, had not led to a similar conclusion, probably because of faulty dosimetry. Assuming, now, that the more recent results are correct and really apply to both breakage and gene mutation themselves (and not merely to structural changes, in the production of which the propinquity of different breaks to one another is known to be a factor), to what conclusions do they lead us? It seems evident that the primary inference to be drawn is that different *neighboring* ionizations (or other activations) somehow cooperate with one another in the production of a break, and that the same is true in the production of a gene mutation, although perhaps not as markedly so since the ratio of neutron to X-ray effectiveness seems in the latter case to be not quite as high as in the former. That this can be true despite the sensibly linear relation between the X-ray dose and the frequency of both types of effects (Muller 1954b) and despite their independence of radiation intensity, shows that only those activations cooperate that are closer together than the ones arising in the course of independent ionization tracks, even when the highest practicable doses and intensities are used. In other words, the ionizations in question belong to the same natural cluster. A mechanism for this cooperation on the level of ordinary (small-molecule) chemistry seems less likely here than one on the somewhat larger scale level of chemo-biological organization.

According to this viewpoint, an intergenic break is more likely to escape restitution, and so is an intragenic displacement, if there have been two nearby displacements, that is, if there has been a kind of shattering. This might consist of two or more breaks or lesser displacements located close to one another along the very same genetic chain. Or, more likely, it might consist of breaks or displacements close to one another in parallel chains. As was pointed out in a recent discussion of the greater effectiveness of more densely ionizing radiation in causing chromosome breaks (Muller 1954b), this doubleness could have resulted from the chromosomes having consisted of two adjoining chromatids. For, after only one break, the unbroken thread would have tended to act as a splint to hold together the broken one until it had rejoined. Now I should like to adapt the same idea to the finding that neutrons are more efficient in breaking even chromatids, and also in causing gene mutations. In making this adaptation, we are led to the conception that the genetic chain, even at its most elementary level, is not single. Thus we arrive at a conclusion in harmony with the model that has been presented to us by Watson and Crick (1953a, 1953b). How ultraviolet may fit into this picture is another question, the consideration of which at the moment would take us too far afield.

As demonstrated by the 14 May 1955 issue of *Nature* (Feughelman et al. 1955), with its announcement of sensational progress in the unraveling of the ultimate structure of the genetic material, the day is already dawning in which the distinction between the biological, the chemical, and the physical will fade and become a convenience of technique only. We will not then see the gene disappear, however, or see the distinction between intra- and intergenic obliterated. The biological facts are in their way no less real than the chemical, and it is after all the theory of the gene that has led us finally to the point where we know at what to direct these newer methods and how to judge their meaning in relation to the larger but just as important aspects of life. It is a rich new world into which this convergence of biochemistry and biophysics on genetics is leading us, even though it is no more revolutionary, for its day, than the world which the coalescence of cytology and genetics opened up to us. In the course of that development, the cell and the chromosome did not disappear. Neither will the gene and gene mutation disappear. They have enlarged to become the gateway to the playground of the new generation of explorers, those whose road leads to the understanding of, yes, and the mastery over, the gene.

References

Altenburg, E., and Muller, H. J. 1920. *Genetics* 5:1.

Baker, W. K., and Von Halle, K. 1954. *Science* 119:46.

Belling, J. 1928. *Univ. Calif. Pub. Botany* 14:307.

Benzer, S. 1956. *Brookhaven Symp. Biol.* no. 8:3–5.

Bernstein, M. H., and Mazia, D. 1953a. *Biochim. et Biophys. Acta* 10:600.

————. 1953b. *Biochim et Biophys. Acta* 10:59.

Bridges, C. B. 1919. *J. Exp. Zool.* 28:337.

————. 1938. *J. Heredity* 29:11.

Bridges, C. B., and Morgan, T. H. 1919. *Pub. Carneg. Inst.* no. 278:123.

Caldecott, R. S., and Smith, L. 1951. *Rec. Genet. Soc. Amer.* 20:94.

————. 1952. *Genetics* 37:136.

Carter, T. C.; Lyon, Mary F.; and Phillips, Rita J. S. 1955. *J. Genet.* 53:154.

Castle, W. E. 1919. *Proc. Nat. Acad. Sci.* 5:25.

Conger, A. D. 1954. *Science* 119:36.

D'Amato, F., and Gustafsson, A. 1948. *Hereditas* 34:181.

Demerec, M., and Demerec, Z. 1956. *Brookhaven Symp. Biol.* no. 8:75–87.

Dobzhansky, Th. 1927. *Z indukt. Abstamm. -u. Vererb. Lehre* 43:330.

Dubinen, N. P., and Siderov, B. N. 1934. *Amer. Natur.* 68:377.

Feughelman, M.; Longridge, R.; Seeds, W. E.; Stokes, A. R.; Wilson, H. R.; Hooper, C. W.; Wilkins, N. H. F.; Barclay, R. K.; Hamilton, L. D. 1955. *Nature* 175:834.

Giles, N. H. Jr. 1943. *Genetics* 28:398.

———. 1956. *Brookhaven Symp. Biol.* no. 8:103–25.

Glass, H. B. 1956. *Brookhaven Symp. Biol.* no. 8:148–70.

Goldschmidt, R. 1937. *Proc. Nat. Acad. Sci.* 23:621.

———. 1938. *Sci. Monthly* 46:268

Green, M. M. 1955. *Amer. Natur.* 89.65.

Ives, P. T.; Levine, R. P.; Yost, H. T. Jr. 1954. *Proc. Nat. Acad. Sci.* 40:165.

Jennings, H. S. 1917. *Amer. Natur.* 51:301.

Johannsen, W. 1909. *Elemente der exakten Erblichkeitslehre* Jena: Carl Fischer.

Kaplan, R. W. 1950. *Naturwiss.* 37:546.

———. 1951. *Z. indukt. Abstamm. -u. Vererb. Lehre* 82:347.

Kaufmann, B. P., and Gay, H. 1947. *Rec. Genet. Soc. Amer.* 16:39.

———. 1948. *Genetics* 33:112.

Kaufmann, B. P., and Hollaender, A. 1946. *Genetics* 31:349.

Kaufmann, B. P.; Hollaender, A.; Gay, H. 1946. *Genetics* 31:349.

Kirby-Smith, J. S., and Swanson, C. P. 1954. *Science* 119:42.

Kossikov, K. V. and Muller, H. J. 1935. *J. Heredity* 26:305.

Laughnan, J. R. 1955a. *Proc. Nat. Acad. Sci.* 41:78.

———. 1955b. *Amer. Natur.* 89.91.

Lewis, E. B. 1952. *Proc. Nat. Acad. Sci.* 38:953.

———. 1954. *Caryologia* Vol. Suppl.: 100.

———.1955. *Amer. Natur.* 89:73.

Lüning, K. G. 1952a. *Acta Zool.* 33:193.

———. 1952b. *Hereditas* 38:321.

Mackendrick, M. Elaine. 1953. *Drosophila Information Service* 27:100.

Mackendrick, M. Elaine, and Pontecorro, G. 1952. *Experientia* 8:390.

Mackenson, O. 1933. *Rec. Genet. Soc. Amer.* 2.

———. 1934. Amer. Natur. 68:76.

Marshak, A. 1942. *Proc. Nat. Acad. Sci.* 28:29.

Marshall, W. W., and Muller, H. J. 1917. *J. Exp. Zool.* 22:457.

Mazia, D. 1954. *Proc. Nat. Acad. Sci.* 40:521.

Mickey, G. H. 1954. *Amer. Natur.* 88:241.

Morgan, T. H.; Sturtevant, A. H.; Muller, H. J.; Bridges, C. B. 1915. *The Mechanism of Mendelian Heredity*. New York: Henry Holt and Co.

Muller, H. J. 1918. *Genetics* 3:422.

———. 1920. *J. Exp. Zool.* 31:443.

———. 1923. *Genetics, Eugenics, and the Family* 1:106.

———. 1932. *Proc. 6th Int. Congr. Genet.* 1:213.

———. 1935a. *Genetica.* 17:237.

———. 1935b. *J. Heredity* 26:469.

———. 1935c. *Amer. Natur.* 69:405.

———. 1935d. *in Sum. 15th Int. Physiol. Congr., Leningrad,* pp. 286–89.

———. 1936. *Science* 83:528.

———. 1937. *Reunion int. phys. -chim. -biol. Act. Sci. et. Ind.* no. 725: 477–94.

———. 1938. *in Proc. 15th Int. Physiol. Congr., USSR* 21, no. 5–6:587.

———. 1941. *Cold Spring Harbor Symp. Quant. Biol.* 9:151.

————. 1951. *Genetics in the Twentieth Century.* New York: Macmillan, Pp. 77–99.

————. 1954a. *Genetics* 39:985.

————. 1954b. *in Radiation biology.* ed. A. Hollaender. New York: McGraw-Hill. Vol. 1, pp. 475–626.

Muller, H. J., and Prokofyeva, A. A. 1934. *Dokl. Akad. Nauk SSSR,* n.s. (Russ./Eng.) 4:74. Revised edition 1935 in *Proc. Nat. Acad. Sci.* 21:16.

Muller, H. J.; Prokofyeva, A. A.; Kossikov, K. V. 1936. Compt. Rend. (Doklady) Acad. Sci. U.R.S.S., n.s. (Russ./Eng.) 1 (10):83.

Muller, H. J.; Prokofyeva, A. A.; and Raffel, D. 1934. *Rec. Genet. Soc. Amer.* 3:48.

————. 1935a. *Amer. Natur.* 69:73.

————. 1935b. *Nature* 135:252.

Muller, H. J., and Valencia, J. I. 1951a. *Rec. Genet. Soc. Amer.* 20:115.

————. 1951b. *Genetics* 36:567.

Muller, H. J.; Valencia, R. M.; and Valencia, J. I. 1950. *Genetics* 35:126.

Neuhaus, M. E. 1939. *Genetics* 37:229.

Offermann, C. A. 1935. *Bull. l'Acad. Sci. de l'URSS* 89, no. 9: 129.

Painter, T. S. 1933. *Science* 78:585.

Patterson, J. T., and Muller, H. J. 1930. *Genetics* 15:495.

Raffel, D., and Muller, H. J. 1940. *Genetics* 25:541.

Russell, W. L.; Russell, Liane B.; and Kimball, A. W. 1954. *Amer Natur.* 88:269.

Serebrovsky, A. S. 1929. *Amer. Natur.* 63:374.

Stadler, L. J. 1954. *Science* 120:811.

Steffensen, D. M. 1955. *Proc. Nat. Acad. Sci.* 41, no. 3:155.

Stern, C. 1926. Z. indukt. Abstamm. -u Vererb. Lehre 41:198.

Sturtevant, A. H. 1918. *Pub. Carneg. Inst.* no. 264.

————. 1925. *Genetics* 10:117.

Timoféeff-Ressovsky, N. W. 1933. z. indukt. Abstamm. -u. Vererb. Lehre 65:278.

Watson, J. D., and Crick, F. H. C. 1953a. *Nature* 171:737.

————. 1953b. *Nature* 171:964.

Zeleny, C. 1922. *Genetics* 7:1.

Questions from the Audience

Why does maize seem to be so different not only from Drosophila *but apparently from all the microorganisms, where you get apparent mutations by the use of ionizing irradiation, or is, perhaps, our technique not sufficiently refined to detect these? We do have cases, and we have had cases, in which there was no detectable cytological change, and, of course, that is an argument for there being an intragenic change. But why should maize be in a class by itself?*

Muller: I don't think I would be rash enough to attempt an interpretation of the reason for it, and all I can do is to repeat the fact that materials do differ a lot, and this differs more.

What analysis can presently be made to distingusih between intragenic mutations and mistakes in the duplication process of genes?

Muller: I was not trying to distinguish between these. This is a matter, of course, that concerns the mechanism by which the mutations come about. It is true that we can conceive of an intragenic change coming about either by a mistake in the building of the daughter gene or a change in the gene already present and, in any individual case, we seldom can tell which process actually occurred. However, there is good reason to infer that we do have changes in the old gene when, in *Drosophila*, we irradiate mature spermatozoa and get effects like gene mutations involving a visible character like yellow body color, that can be seen over a large part of the body. The inference that the old gene was changed can be drawn when we see that the given character gives every evidence of involving the whole body, that is, all the parts that we can see, rather than only about half of the body. We do occasionally get a half, but much more often the whole, in such a case. If there had been a mistake in the building of the daughter gene, it should have been merely a half of the body that the daughter gene went to. Doubtless, mistakes in gene reproduction do occur sometimes. But at least the whole body mutations give us evidence that the old gene can mutate.

Now, there is other evidence that mistakes may happen in the building of the daughter gene, but this evidence is less direct, being based on the fact that in some material one gets spontaneous mutations more frequently at stages at which there is more gene building. We don't actually know whether in such cases the higher frequency of gene reproduction leads to more mistakes in daughter gene construction or whether more changes are induced in already existing genes as a result of a higher metabolism or for some other reason, but there is that correlation. On the other hand, we also find mutations rather frequently in certain stages that do not involve any gene building, such as mature spermatozoa. Hence, I feel it is very likely that mutations occur both ways.

How Radiation Changes
the Genetic Constitution

T HE artificial transmutation of the gene in 1927 was, like so many scientific discoveries, a source of optimistic speculation and realistic despair. Muller knew, as he reported in his "fourteen-point analysis" of mutation, that most newly arising mutations were harmful. This was borne out for X-ray mutations, too. Added to this expected property was the high incidence of chromosome breakage which characterized all ionizing radiations. Muller and his colleagues showed that the major expression of radiation damage to the individual's body arose from these breakages. The study of gene mutations in the population led Muller to the concept of the mutational or genetic load which is a measure of the number of deleterious genes carried, on the average, by an individual. This essay shows how far the field of radiation genetics had progressed since 1927 and how inescapable were the social consequences of the use and abuse of ionizing radiation.

Muller prepared this paper for presentation at the First Atoms for Peace Conference, Geneva, Switzerland, but was not permitted to present it by a decision of the U.S. Atomic Energy Commission. The subsequent publicity over the incident led to an apology from AEC Commissioner Lewis Strauss and a widespread interest in the genetic effects of radiation.

The changes in the genetic constitution produced by ionizing radiation may for convenience be classified into two major groups: *chromosome aberrations* and *point mutations*.

The chromosome aberrations consist of losses and additions of

74587

whole chromosomes or chromosome parts and or alterations, called structural changes, in the alignment of chromosome parts. Structural changes are caused by the breakage of one or more chromosomes at two or more points, followed by the junction of the fragments at their broken ends, so as to form a new arrangement: that is, a new linear sequence of their component hereditary particles or genes (Muller 1940).

Point mutations are changes confined to regions of the chromosomes so small that no loss or addition or change in arrangement of genes can be demonstrated by microscopic examinations or breeding tests. Since structural changes range from "gross" to those so minute as to be at the limit of being detectable as such, there are doubtless other cases of substantially the same kind, but below that limit of size, which become included among the point mutations. However, there is reason to infer that many of the point mutations produced in animals by radiation are not of this kind, but involve changes within the individual genes, and are therefore to be considered as "gene mutations." By this it is meant that these changes are restricted to genetic elements too small to be divided either by the process of normal hereditary recombination (crossing-over) or by that of gross structural change. This seems to be true also of the great majority of genetic differences that exist naturally between individuals of the same species: that is, they appear to have arisen as gene mutations.

Chromosome Aberrations

The chromosome aberrations produced by radiation in the cells of somatic tissues that replenish themselves by proliferation cause necrosis in much of the tissue descended from these cells and abnormality in much of the surviving descendant tissue. This constitutes a major source of delayed radiation damage, some of it never repaired, in the exposed individual himself. The same series of events, occurring among the immature germ cells of the exposed individual, can result in partial or complete sterility. Among mature and nearly mature germ cells, especially spermatozoa, there is a much higher incidence of induction of these chromo-

some changes, for any given dose of radiation, than among immature germ cells or somatic cells.[1] Recent evidence (Oster 1954)
confirms the inference (Muller 1940) that this peculiarity depends
upon the chromosomes being in a condensed (tightly spiralized)
condition and that it therefore applies also to cells that are in
mitosis at the time of irradiation.

Mature sperm or eggs in which chromosome aberrations (actual
or potential) have been induced, function in fertilization, but
many of the resulting embryos die in consequence of their abnormal chromosome content. Other embryos, in which there has
been gross structural change without excess or deficiency of
chromosome parts, develop into normal adult individuals. However, when these seeming normals reproduce, recombination occurs between the structurally changed chromosomes derived from
one parent and their normal homologues derived from the other
parent. In consequence of the nonmatching linear arrangement of
the genes from the two parents, about 50 percent of the germ cells
now produced have excesses and deficiencies of chromosome
content. These germ cells usually function but give rise to embryos (of the second generation after exposure) which die in utero
at an early stage (Hertwig 1940; Koller 1944; Snell 1934). This
mortality of embryos tends to be repeated over an indefinitely
long series of generations. For half of the surviving embryos of
such a line of descent, although not themselves containing the
lethal excesses or deficiencies, have the grossly changed linear
arrangement of genes that, by recombination, again gives rise to
these effects.

1. However, some immature germ-cell stages are much more susceptible
to chromosome alteration than they appear to be when judged by the
frequency with which such alterations are found later, on analysis of offspring derived from the cells that had been exposed while immature. This
is because the descendant cells derived from those immature germ cells
in which the chromosomes had been altered so often die out and have
their places taken by compensatory multiplication of descendant cells
derived from those immature germ cells in which the chromosomes had
not been altered. This consideration does not apply in the case of point
mutations. (Note added 5 October 1955.)

In modern human populations, there is a tendency to compensate or even overcompensate for reductions in the frequency of viable births, by purposely increasing the number of pregnancies (Glass 1950). Hence damage of this kind, once induced, does not tend to die out rapidly but may even spread.

Fortunately there are several factors which serve to limit the frequency with which these cases of inherited abortions are produced. One is the fact that the period spent by male germ cells in a mature or nearly mature state averages, at the very most, a few months, whereas they usually spend some 25 years or more—well over 100 times as long—as immature germ cells, relatively insusceptible to the induction of chromosome aberrations. Although the relative lengths of the corresponding periods for female germ cells are not well established, the germ cells are, even when nearly mature, much less susceptible than spermatozoa to the induction of the gross aberrations that cause inherited abortion (Snell and Ames 1939). It may be concluded that more than 99 percent of the germ cells which function after a given exposure of limited duration (comprising only a few days or weeks) were at the time of that exposure in an immature stage, relatively insusceptible to the induction of chromosome aberrations. In them, aberrations of all kinds were induced with far lower frequency than point mutations.

Even in the less than one percent of germ cells that are exposed to radiation of beta or gamma type during their susceptible stage, gross structural changes of chromosomes will be produced at a low frequency, relatively to point mutations, unless the total dose of radiation received in that period is fairly high, of the order of a hundred or more r (roentgen) units. This is because the production of these aberrations requires at least two chromosome breaks, and these are usually produced independently, by the tracks of different fast particles. On account of being in this sense double or multiple events, these aberrations vary in their frequency according to an exponent of the dose of radiation higher than one (commonly, about 1.5) (Muller 1940). On the other hand, the point mutations vary as single events, according to the dose itself. Thus, as the dose is diminished, they do not drop off as fast as the structural changes do, and the latter become rare, relative to the former.

It follows from the above considerations that inherited abortion caused by structural change is a relatively insignificant danger even in the case of a large dose of beta or gamma radiation that has been received in small fractions of not more than a few r per month. If the amount received in any month is higher than this, however, measures should be taken to avoid this damage. These measures would consist in the prevention or avoidance of conception until the passage of several months after the high exposure. With a very high dose, however, all but the first month of this period would be sterile anyway.

When the exposure has been alpha or neutron radiation, the production of gross structural changes tends to vary with the dose itself instead of with a higher exponent (Catsch et al. 1944; Giles 1940, 1943; Muller 1954a; Muller and Valencia 1951a, 1951b). This is because both the breaks participating in such an aberration are usually produced by activations arising from the track of the same fast atomic nucleus. In consequence both of this proportionality of the frequency of structural change to dose with this type of radiation and of the fact that the more densely crowded activations from such radiation are actually more efficient in breaking the chromosomes, much lower doses, in reps (roentgen equivalent physical), of neutrons or alpha rays than of gamma, beta, or X rays give significant numbers of structural changes. Hence, the rule of not reproducing within some months after exposure should be applied in the case of much lower doses when the radiation has been of these types. In order to gauge how low this limit should be placed, it should be taken into consideration that even five reps of neutrons, applied to spermatozoa, may be estimated to induce inherited abortion, based on gross structural change in some one to six among every thousand viable individuals derived from these spermatozoa (Snell 1939).

The frequency of natural occurrence of gross structural changes giving inherited abortion has not been studied extensively in mammalian populations, but it is known to be low. The highest recorded figure (Hertwig 1938, 1940), is about 6 percent. Among offspring from spermatozoa treated with 500 r X rays, 25 percent have been reported by two observers (Russell 1954).

Characteristics of Natural-Point Mutations

Among the genetic changes induced by exposure to radiation from artificial sources, the point mutations are far more frequent and significant than the chromosome aberrations. Among the genetic changes that arise from natural causes (those somewhat misleadingly referred to as "spontaneous"), the point mutations are still more frequent and important, as compared with the chromosome aberrations. Any ordinary population contains a large accumulation, or "load," of these natural-point mutations, which have arisen in the course of many past generations. If any new point mutations are induced by radiation these are added to this already existing load of mutations. They thereupon become lost to view among the latter, in the sense that, with rare exceptions, the origin of any individual point mutation cannot be traced to the radiation. Thus, in order that radiation mutations may be viewed in due perspective, certain salient facts about the natural mutations should first be passed in review.

Natural point mutations occur sporadically. They are not individually controllable. Any such mutation may be thought of as resulting from an accidental ultramicroscopic encounter between a gene and some atom group, particle, or photon to which the gene happens, under the circumstances, to be vulnerable. It is probable that, on occasion, instead of the original or "mother-gene" becoming altered, the accident causes a misstep in the construction of the "daughter-gene," but the effect is much the same as if the old gene had itself mutated. In either case, point-mutational changes are permanent. This implies that the changed gene tends to be very stable, as the original gene was, and that in reproducing it continues to give rise to daughter genes like itself, that is, in this case, of the new type. Thus it "copies itself" through an indefinite succession of generations (Muller 1921, 1918, 1920, 1922, 1923, 1928).

The frequency of mutations in general is influenced, however, by many conditions. Thus, cells in certain developmental stages have mutations occurring more frequently in them, in other stages less frequently (Muller 1946a, 1946b, unpublished data). There is some evidence that markedly detrimental disturbances in the cellular biochemistry, of whatever nature, tend to favor the occurrence of mutations, while the functioning of the cell within its normal range is associated with a low mutation frequency. Certain special substances, such as the mustard gas series, some organic peroxides and epoxides, and triazine are so conducive to mutation that they have been termed "mutagens" (Auerbach 1952; Auerbach and Robsen 1946; Bird 1952; Demerec et al. 1951; Jensen et al. 1952; Rapoport 1946a, 1946b, 1948; Wyss et al. 1948). Some of them can in fact be used to induce mutations at about as high a frequency as with radiation. When the distribution of relative frequencies of the different types of mutations induced by one mutagenic agent is compared with that induced by another, or with that of spontaneous mutations, considerable differences are often found, even though most types of mutations produced by one agent are also produced to some extent by any other and also arise spontaneously but at a lower rate (Demerec 1954).

The partial selectivity of action of mutagens does not give evidence of being of such a nature as to result in the mutations produced by a given agent, or under given conditions, being better adapted, as a group, for life in the presence of that agent, or under those conditions, than are the mutations which arise under other circumstances. That is, mutations arising independently of radiation like those produced by radiation are, so far as the organism is concerned, accidents, not adaptive responses. There is evidence indicating that the organism has, through a long period of evolution, been selected for the maintenance of biochemical operations which give it as low a frequency of "natural" mutations as can practicably be attained, just as it has been also selected to react in such ways as to minimize the occurrence of other accidents (Muller 1918; Sturtevant 1937).

It is entirely in line with the accidental nature of natural mutations that extensive tests have agreed in showing the vast majority of them to be detrimental to the organism in its job of surviving and reproducing, just as changes accidentally introduced into any artificial mechanism are predominantly harmful to its useful operation (Muller 1921, 1918, 1920, 1922, 1923, 1928). According to the conception of evolution based on the studies of modern genetics, the whole organism has its basis in its genes. Of these there are thousands of different kinds, interacting with great nicety in the production and maintenance of the complicated organization of the given type of organism. Accordingly, by the mutation of one of these genes or another, in one way or another, any component structure or function, and in many cases combinations of these components, may become diversely altered. Yet in all except very rare cases the change will be disadvantageous, involving an impairment of function.

It is nevertheless to be inferred that all the superbly interadapted genes of any present-day organism arose through just this process of accidental natural mutation. This could take place only because of the Darwinian principle of natural selection, applying to the genes. That is, on the rare occasions when an accidental mutation did happen to effect an advantageous change, the resultant individual, just because it was aided by that mutation, tended to multiply more than the others. By the continuance and repetition of this process, the type that had been normal became supplanted by other types, that were at least better adapted for life in certain particular environments, or in certain ways. Thus, the mutant gene of the previous era became the normal gene of today, and the whole system of genes of the species tended to become ever more differentiated and highly organized. Yet at each stage the great majority of new mutations, if examined before being put through the sieve of selection, must have been detrimental to life or to reproduction, as they are today in all species studied, no matter what the degree of advancement of the species.

As important for the survival of a species as the differential multiplication of the few better adapted mutants is the reduction in number and eventual dying out, in competition with the "normal" type, of the much more numerous mutants that are less fit than the normals. Since each generation supplies a fresh crop of these mutations, to be added to those inherited from earlier generations, it is obvious that without this negative selection the system of genes would undergo continued decay. Thus after a time it would become completely heterogeneous, disorganized, and degenerate (Muller 1921, 1918, 1920, 1922, 1923, 1928). In the past, only natural selection has saved it. This selection makes it practically inevitable that any detrimental mutation, no matter how small its harmful effect, will in the long run become limited by tipping the scales against some descendant who carries it, causing his premature death or failure to reproduce.

However, this dying out of the unfit mutants is in most cases rather long delayed. One reason for this delay is the fact that mutant genes are in the great majority of cases heterozygous, that is, present in individuals who have received the corresponding normal gene from their other parent, and that in such a situation the normal gene usually produces most of the effect. The normal gene is for this reason said to be "dominant," and the mutant gene "recessive," even though the mutant is seldom completely without expression when heterozygous.

Another reason for the delay in the dying out of mutant genes lies in the fact that even in those relatively rare individuals who are "homozygous" for a given mutant gene, by reason of having inherited that same gene from both parents, the amount of abnormality is often not very great. Hence, even in this situation the gene usually confers a much less than 100 percent risk of premature death, or of failure to reproduce. It may be noted in this connection that the idea that most mutations are monstrosities or freaks is a popular misconception. In fact, only a tiny minority of mutations cause very conspicuous visible abnormalities.

Calculation of Natural Mutations Present in a Population

The total number of point mutations (or, more correctly, of point-mutant genetic conditions) present in any population at a given time is a product of two interacting numerical factors. The first factor, a, is the total number of new point mutations that arise in one generation. The second factor, b, to be multiplied by the first, is termed the persistence. It represents the total number of individuals of successive generations by whom, on the average, any given mutation, present at first in one individual, comes to be inherited (Muller 1950a; Muller and Campbell unpublished data). This same relation holds for mutations of any particular type as well as for the totality of mutations.

Obviously b, the persistence, depends upon the ability of the individuals carrying the mutation to live and breed, as compared with normal individuals. If, for simplicity, we assume the whole population to be of stable size, then b, for the average mutation, or for any given type of mutation, is the reciprocal of c, the average chance that an individual who has inherited it will be killed prematurely, or will fail to reproduce, as a result of the one or more functional impairments occasioned in him by that mutation. In getting this average chance of elimination, c, we must estimate the relative frequences of individuals heterozygous and homozygous for the mutation, and multiply the chance of elimination of each of these types, taken separately, by its relative frequency. When this is done it is found that usually, despite the much smaller detrimental effect in the heterozygous individuals, their relatively large numbers cause most of the eliminations, and most of the total genetic damage to the population, to occur in this group. Thus, in most cases, the homozygous group can for practical purposes be ignored (Muller 1950a; Muller and Campbell unpublished data).

In order to apply this method of calculation to human populations we must first have estimates of a and b. At present such estimates are very indirect, and serve only to indicate a broad range, within which, somewhere, the actual value is probably located. The fruit fly Drosophila has thus far been the only organism in which anything like a direct approach has been made to an observed value for either a or b, and even here the results are subject to very large errors. In this material it can be estimated that, in a population of a hundred million, a, the number of new mutations arising naturally per generation that becomes transmitted to the next generation, is on the average at least eight million, and that b, the persistence or average number of individuals of successive generations which finally come to inherit any given mutation, is considerably more than 20 and probably more than 40. This makes ab, the number of mutations carried by the population of a hundred million in any given generation, probably more than 320,000,000, that is, probably more than three per individual.

The estimate of a for Drosophila was obtained by first taking the observed frequency, 0.18 percent, with which "recessive" fully lethal mutations (those that invariably kill homozygous individuals) usually arise in the X chromosome per germ cell per generation when no mutagenic treatment is used (Muller 1946a, 1946b, unpublished data). This figure was then multiplied by 6, the ratio of recessive lethals in all the chromosomes to those in the X chromosome. This figure had to be obtained from experiments in which radiation was applied to spermatozoa (Berg 1937). The product, 1.08 percent, representing all lethals, was in turn multiplied by 4, the ratio which all mutations detrimental enough to have been detected by a given technique were found to bear to fully lethal mutations. This figure 4 was also based on radiation mutations (Kerkis 1935, 1938; Muller 1934; Timoféeff-Ressovsky 1934, 1935). Finally, the second product, 4.3 percent, was multiplied by 2, because each individual results from two germ cells, and the resultant percent, 8.6, was multiplied by 100,000,000, the number assumed to exist in the population.

That the application of the ratio 6, derived from radiation work, to natural mutations is legitimate has been shown by special tests. However, among natural mutations as a group, the ratio of all mutations to lethals is probably a good deal higher than 4, the ratio found among mutations produced by irradiating spermatozoa. For the radiation mutations include a greater proportion of structural changes and these are more often lethal. This is one reason why the final figure for a is very conservative. The other reason is that the methods of detection used failed to find mutations that produced less than about 10 percent risk of premature death, even if they caused considerable infertility, and such mutations may have been relatively numerous.

The figure for b is based on tests, carried out independently by two groups of investigators (Muller 1950a; Muller and Campbell, unpublished data; Stern et al. 1952; Stern and Novitski 1948) to determine how much risk of premature death is conferred by a "recessive" lethal mutation when it is heterozygous. In both cases an average figure of about 3 percent to 5 percent risk of death was obtained. This would result in only one heterozygous individual among some 25 being killed and would hence allow the average lethal a persistence of 25. That is, it would tend to be passed on to some 25 individuals, on the average, before it died out. Since, however, a considerable majority of mutations are not so detrimental as to be fully lethal when homozygous, and most of them are probably not even 50 percent lethal when in that condition, the figure of 1 in 25 (4 percent) for the risk of death when heterozygous must be considerably higher than that holding for the average mutation, and the persistence, being the reciprocal of this, would be considerably higher than 25. That is why 40 was used as a better guess for b, but the observed distribution of mortalities indicates that even it is likely to be too low.

Before we can convert our figure a for newly arising mutations in *Drosophila* into a corresponding figure a for man we must obtain some indication of the ratio of mutation frequency in *Drosophila* to that in man. As yet the only line of approach to this problem lies in a comparison of the frequencies, in the two species, of natural mutations that produce certain specific effects, and that may be inferred to occur at given highly limited positions in the chromosomes. Although the evidence of this kind is meager and imperfect, there is enough of it to show that in *Drosophila* a mutation of any one specific type, located in a specific chromosomal position (so as to give rise to what is technically known as an "allele" or "pseudoallele" of some pre-existing mutation) arises, on the average, with a natural frequency of between 1 in 100,000 and 1 in 300,000 germ cells, the most likely figure being about 1 in 200,000 (Muller et al. 1950a, 1950b). In mice there is little published data of this kind as yet but it would indicate a figure in the range between 1 in 40,000 and 1 in 400,000 or, most likely, about 1 in 140,000 (Russell 1952). In man, an estimate of between 1 in 50,000 and 1 in 100,000 has been arrived at, on the basis of a much larger amount of data than in either mice or *Drosophila*, but the uncertainties of the methods used in man are much greater (Haldane 1948, 1949; Neil and Falls 1951). These apparent differences in mutation frequency between the three species may well correspond to the different numbers of cell divisions which take place in their respective reproductive cycles, since these numbers for flies, mice, and men are related about as 1:1.5:2. At any rate, it is likely that the average frequency of mutations of any specific type in man is higher than in *Drosophila*, probably from

2 to 4 times as high. To be conservative, we will adopt the lower figure, 2.

It is however likely that the ratio of frequencies of specific mutations in man to those in the fly would not be nearly as high as the ratio of total mutation frequencies in man to those in the fly. For man, and mammals in general, give evidence of having a more complicated organization, all told, than the fly, especially when the complications of the nervous system are taken into account. Mammals may therefore be expected to have a more complex germ plasm than flies, one in which a larger number of different kinds of mutations of specific types can occur. This agrees with existence of a larger amount of the genetic substance, polymerized deoxyribonucleic acid, in mammalian than in fly chromosome sets. Therefore we are in all probability obtaining a low minimal figure for a in man if we multiply the Drosophila a by only 2.

For the value of b in man or other mammals there is as yet little basis for a decision. The existing indications point strongly to the conclusion that natural mutations in mammals in general, including man, are, as in Drosophila, prevailingly recessive, yet not completely so. Moreover, they certainly include a fairly abundant group of "recessive" lethals, but it is probable that mutations having a lesser degree of detriment are more frequent than lethals. At this preliminary stage of our knowledge of the subject, then, we have little ground for using a markedly different value of b for mammals than for Drosophila.

The figure of about 6.5 is thereby arrived at as a minimal one for the content of recessive, definitely detrimental mutations (including lethals) per individual human being. In a preliminary calculation using related methods, the figure 8 was arrived at (Muller 1950a; Muller and Campbell unpublished data). These estimates, as recently shown by Slatis (1954), can be checked in a more direct way. The method consists in observations of the frequency with which homozygous individuals, showing the more definite abnormality often associated with a homozygous mutation, appear among the offspring of marriages between close relatives. Application of this technique has led Slatis, very tentatively as yet, to the figure 8 as the most probable present approximation to the number of natural mutations of the kind in question for which a person is, on the average, heterozygous. This method now needs to be applied on a much larger scale but the present result is enough to be reassuring, in indicating that our mode of calculation is giving figures of the right order of magnitude.

It should be emphasized that in these calculations we are dealing only with those mutations which are detrimental enough to give a "sizeable" risk of genetic extinction by way of premature death; that is, one as great as about 0.5 percent in the case of the heterozygous individual, or 10 percent in the case of the homozygous one. We do not know how many mutations arise which are less harmful than this, or which cause extinction mainly by their interference with reproduction, not with life itself. However, even if there are relatively few, those few which have an average grade of detriment within the same order of magnitude as the frequency of their origination by mutation, will accumulate so as to be inordinately numerous in the population. They will provide a very considerable proportion of the superficially observable genetic variability. Moreover, the frequency of the different types of mutations of this group will differ greatly from region to region, in response to differences in the conditions of selection, as well as to random influences.

Since the frequency with which mutant genes of any given degree of detrimental effect exist in the population at any one time is the product ab, where b is inversely proportional to c, the degree of detrimental effect, it is evident that the existing mutant genes have a distribution, with respect to their harmfulness, very different from the distribution to be found on examining mutations as they arise. For, among the mutant genes as they exist in the population as compared with them at their origination, the less harmful ones are (in inverse proportion to their harmful effect) more numerous than the more harmful ones. For that very reason each slightly harmful mutation that arises tends to cause as much detriment to the population as a whole in the end as each drastically harmful or lethal mutation does, since it compensates for its relatively small degree of harm by afflicting correspondingly more individuals. In consequence, the total amount of genetic damage done to a population by mutations is much more closely proportionate to the total frequency of mutations arising per generation (a/N, where N is the number of individuals in the population) than to the frequency of mutations existing in the population (ab/N) (Haldane 1937). If a is raised or lowered, however, it may take scores of generations before its changed value becomes proportionately reflected in the altered average fitness or mutational load of the population. A similar lag occurs if b is altered, as happens when the rigor of selection is increased or decreased.

Characteristics of Point Mutations Produced by Radiation

In the plant material studied by Stadler (1941, 1954, 1948), evidence was obtained, based on the intensive study of a few types of mutations, that the great majority of apparent point mutations induced by radiation probably consisted of losses of a small section of a chromosome including more than one gene, unlike what was usually true of the natural mutations. In the animal material best studied with reference to this question, that of *Drosophila* (Muller et al. 1950b). There is evidence that such "sectional deficiencies" do comprise a good deal larger proportion of the point mutations obtained by irradiation of the mature germ cells than of the point mutations arising naturally. However, the apparent point mutations produced by irradiation of immature germ cells of *Drosophila* do not include substantially more that on further analysis prove to be demonstrable "sectional deficiencies" than are found among the natural mutations. Moreover, the characteristics of the effects produced on the individual, both in *Drosophila* and mice (Muller 1952a; Russell 1954), also indicate that a large proportion of these radiation-mutations are as truly changes within the genes as are the mutations of natural origin.

In general, then, in the animal material, the radiation-mutations strongly resemble the natural ones. Practically all types of natural point mutations that have been looked for in extensive irradiation experiments have been found to be produced by radiation also. Like natural mutations, of course, the great majority, although not quite all, of those produced by radiation, are detrimental. Moreover, the great majority have far less dominance (i.e., less expression in the heterozygous individual) than the normal genes from which they arose. Once arisen, the radiation mutations, like the natural ones, are permanent, reproducing themselves as such (Muller 1941).

Just which mutation is produced by radiation on a given occasion is of course a matter of "accident," as is true of natural mutations. However, the total frequency of the mutations produced by a given dose of radiation varies to some extent with the accompanying conditions, as in the case of natural mutations, although the conditions in question are to some extent different ones in the two cases. The conditions which influence the production of point mutations by radiation include genetic differences, differences in cell type or stage, differences in metabolic reactions, and (a category overlapping the previous one) differences caused by the application of special chemical or physical treatments.

For the most part, the same influences have been found to promote or hinder the action of radiation in causing point mutations as in causing structural changes of chromosomes. For example, chromosomes in condensed stages are more susceptible to the induction of changes of both types. Some findings of interesting differences in this respect have been reported, however. Among these are the observations that sperm cells of Drosophila several days prior to their release, and therefore perhaps in the spermatid stage, are much more susceptible than mature spermatozoa to the production by radiation of structural changes but not of point mutations (Lüning 1952).

In accordance with the view, first proposed by Rapoport (1943) on the basis of chemical work by Fricke (1934, 1935), that the mutagenic action of radiation is exerted via the production of actively oxidizing radicals or molecules, it is found that radiation mutagenesis of both major types is positively correlated with the amount of free oxygen present at irradiation. Physical or chemical influences which appear directly or indirectly to increase or decrease the abundance of oxygen available for conversion into mutagenic radicals influence correspondingly the frequency of mutations produced. There is, to be sure, evidence indicating that not all the mutagenic action of radiation takes the same pathway, and that some of it may be quite unconnected with oxidation. But, however that may be, the above and other findings, by demonstrating the conditional nature of radiation mutagenesis, constitute a disproof of the target hypothesis of such mutagenesis, at least in the simplified form in which it had sometimes been applied (Muller 1950b). Moreover, these findings are of considerable practical value in having led to the working out of treatments, (Hollaender 1955; Hollaender et al. 1952) which give hope of affording significant protection against the mutagenic action of radiation. The fact that certain treatments, even when given after irradiation, aid in such protection, is especially noteworthy, both from a theoretical and from a practical standpoint.

In material of varied kinds, but more especially in *Drosophila*, there is good evidence that over a considerable range of dose (in *Drosophila*, from some 50 r to more than 1,000 r, a more than twenty-fold range) the frequency of point mutations (like that of chromosome breaks) is directly proportional to dose (Oliver 1932; Spencer and Stern 1948; Timoféeff-Ressovsky 1937). Moreover, they are independent of the timing of the dose, over an enormous range, provided cellular conditions are held constant (Lüning et al. 1955; Patterson 1931; Ray Chaudhuri 1944; Timoféeff-Ressovsky and Zimmer 1935; Uphoff and Stern 1949). Below 25 to 50 r the mutation frequency is so low that it has hitherto been impossible to obtain sufficient data, and above 1,000 or 2,000 r the determination of frequency may be interfered with by a selective elimination (through chromosome aberrations) of the cells that happened at irradiation to be in a more susceptible state (Muller et al. 1954). Since, however, in the work with low doses and low time-rates of delivery of gamma radiation the germ cells of some series were traversed by only one electron track in a period of a half hour or more, on the average, and still showed a frequency of mutations proportional to the total dose, there is reason to infer that no dose or intensity of such radiation is without its proportionate production of point mutations. Moreover, if this is true of gamma radiation it must be at least as true of radiation producing tracks more densely crowded with ionizations.

Despite the equal mutagenic efficiency of different doses and dose rates of ionizing radiation, it is not necessary to infer that a point mutations in the chromosomes of *Drosophila* spermatozoa indirect, of a single activation or even of a single ionization. For all the ionizing radiation studied has some of its ionizations produced in clusters of minute diameter. If two or more ions commonly cooperate mutagenically, however, it might be thought that this would become evident by causing the frequency of mutations to vary as the square or some higher power of the dose. Yet this would not be true if those ions had to be as near together as the ones in a natural cluster, for such close juxtaposition as this would not be brought about with appreciable frequency by raising the dose and the dose rate within toleration limits.

That such cooperation in mutagenesis does occur is indicated by recent observations to the effect that fast neutrons appear to be approximately twice as efficient as X or gamma rays in inducing point mutations in the chromosomes of *Drosophila* spermatozoa (Ives et al. 1954; Mickey 1954; Muller 1954b, 1954c), and are probably a good deal more efficient still, relative to X or gamma rays, in inducing chromosome breaks. (Baker and Von Halle 1954; Conger 1954; Kirby-Smith and Swanson 1954; Russell et al. 1954). Presumably alpha rays likewise would be more efficient than X or gamma rays in these respects. One possible interpretation of this higher effectiveness of fast neutrons would be provided, on the Watson-Crick hypothesis of the structure of the genetic material, by the doubleness of the fibers in which the rearrangements are produced, if we suppose that the occurrence of the mutation or break is much facilitated when both fibers are simultaneously affected.

The effectiveness of fast neutrons in inducing point mutations is actually higher than it appears to be, because intensive studies of given cases of these seeming point mutations have shown that in fact a considerable proportion of them involve a double or multiple effect within a very localized chromosome region. (Muller and Valencia 1951a, 1951b; Muller 1954d). This greater clustering of effects with neutrons than with X or gamma rays is to be expected, in view of the greater concentration of the ionizations in the tracks of the ionizing particles released by neutrons, provided that the mutational effects arise in close proximity with the activations that induce them. Since this clustering of effects causes many of them to be lost to view by reason of their proximity to each other (except when special techniques of analysis are used), the mutagenic potentiality of the fast neutrons is correspondingly underrated in most experiments. So far as genetic damage to the population is concerned, however, a double or multiple effect of the given kind adds no more to the mutational load than does a single effect. Hence for present purposes fast neutrons may be regarded as no more than twice as effective as X or gamma rays in producing point mutations.

Estimation of the Total Point Mutational Damage
from a Given Amount of Radiation

It has been noted that the important quantity in the determination of the total amount of genetic damage is not the amount of harm done to the individuals who have inherited the mutations in question but only the total number of these mutations. For a mutation doing less harm to an individual will, as if in compensation, be passed down to a correspondingly larger number of descendant individuals. It has also been noted that an approach to a direct estimation of the total number of mutations arising has thus far been made only in *Drosophila,* and that this calculation has involved the use of data from radiation experiments. This work can therefore be applied to the estimation of the total damage arising from a given dose.

The principles have already been explained whereby a minimum value for the total number of mutations is obtained by getting the number of lethals in the X chromosome and then multiplying this by 6, to get the number of lethals in all the chromosomes, and again by 4, to get the total number of mutations causing at least 10 percent detriment to life, when homozygous. (A correction is made in this calculation, based on certain tests, in order to estimate the number of point mutations without including the structural changes.) When this calculation is carried out, using the results obtained at any given dose, the resulting number can then be expressed in terms of the total number of point mutations produced by a single r unit, by using the principle of proportionality of point-mutation frequency to dose. It is then found that this number turns out to be about one mutation among 2,000 germ cells per r (that is, $5 \times 10^{-4}/r$) for X or gamma rays applied in the usual way to mature spermatozoa (Muller 1951, 1954e). The more important figure, representing the result of irradiation of the more prevalent stages (gonia) of immature germ cells of adult *Drosophila*, is only a fourth to a half of this, according to the conditions. It is probable that there are even lower values for certain other immature stages of *Drosophila* germ cells, as for instance those in the embryonic polar cap (Berman 1939; Meyer unpublished data).

In order to obtain a figure for the total number of mutations produced by a given dose in mammalian material we may follow the procedure which we adopted in the calculation of natural mutations. This involved a comparison of the mutation frequencies involving particular types of mutations, located in given positions on the chromosomes, in *Drosophila* and in mammals, and then applying the ratio thus found to the figure for total mutation frequency in *Drosophila* so as to convert it into the presumed corresponding value (a minimal one) for mammals.

Fortunately, there is available for this comparison a much more reliable body of data, for both groups of organisms, than that which we had recourse to in the case of natural mutations. The average frequency of point mutations of the kind in question in *Drosophila*, based on a study of ten types (loci), was found to be about $1.4 \times 10^{-8}/r$ for any given type, when the radiation was applied to inactive immature germ cells (oogonia) (Muller 1952b). The different types seldom varied from one another in frequency by a factor of more than 2 in material abundant enough for judging this matter (that in which spermatozoa had been irradiated).

In the mammalian material, comprising irradiated spermatogonia of mice, Russell (1952) has reported an average mutation frequency of about $25 \times 10^{-8}/r$, based upon seven specific types of mutations (loci). Here the range of variation between the different types was greater than in the above *Drosophila* material, but their mean agreed well with their mode, and four of the seven types conformed fairly closely with this mean. It is clear on comparison of the two sets of results that the susceptibility of the mammalian material is at least an order of magnitude higher than that of the flies, the observed factorial difference in results being 18. To obtain a minimum estimate of the total frequency of mutation in the mice we must therefore multiply by 18 the figure arrived at for gonial cells of flies. (It is of no consequence that in the flies oogonia were studied and in the mice spermatogonia, since special comparisons [Kossiker 1937; Serebrovskeya and Shapiro 1935; Only when these two papers are taken in conjunction with one another does the equal mutagenic susceptibility of gonial cells of the two sexes become evident] have shown these two cell types to be alike in mutagenic susceptibility as they are expected to be.) Since the figure for the gonia of flies had a lower limiting value of $1.25 \times 10^{-4}/r$ the minimum value for mice becomes $2.25 \times 10^{-3}/r$. This is the frequency for a germ cell, not for an offspring derived from two such germ cells; for the offspring it would be $4.5 \times 10^{-3}/r$.

In performing this calculation we are, as in the case of the natural mutations, assuming that the hereditary material of mammals is no more compound than that of flies; i.e., that there is not a greater number of different specific types of mutations in mammals than in flies, despite their seemingly more complicated organisms and their larger amount of deoxyribonucleic acid. The total frequency of mutations per r may be a good deal higher than here calculated not only because of the inadequacy of this assumption but also because weakly detrimental mutations and those mainly affecting fertility rather than individual survival have not been included. Moreover, only the lower limiting value for the somewhat variable mutation frequency of fly oogonia was used. All this emphasizes the fact that our estimate is decidedly on the "conservative" side.

At the same time, it is true that the value is one for mice, not human beings. All that can be said to this is that, so long as we lack data on an organism still closer to man, it is necessary, provisionally, to base our judgments on this result, and that, since mice are so much closer to men than flies are in almost every other important respect, it would be strange if they were not closer in their mutagenic properties as well. Moreover, the factors which might be expected to cause a significant difference in the natural mutation frequencies of mice and men—their great discrepancies in length of life, size, and number of cell generations in the reproductive cycle—would not be expected to exert significant influences on the frequency with which mutations are produced in them by radiation.

The minimum figure of $4.5 \times 10^{-3}/r$ point mutations for the offspring of parents both of whom were exposed can be expressed in the form: "at least one induced point mutation per offspring, on the average, for each 220 r of exposure to both parents." From this it is evident that many of the children who were conceived by Hiroshima survivors at any time after their exposure must have contained one or more mutations induced by the radiation. Similarly, children conceived by parents both of whom have been exposed to the so-called "permissible dose" of 0.3 r per week (15 r per year) for as long as fifteen years would on the average contain at least one induced mutation. It is probable that the same is also true of the children of many radiologists, dermatologists, and dentists (Muller 1955a, 1955b).

The recent study of Macht and Lawrence (1955) gives direct evidence of genetic damage in such cases and is in this respect superior to the studies made in Japan. Moreover, studies of Moeller et al. (1953) show that the population in general is already receiving significant amounts of radiation from medical diagnoses. Sonnenblick (1955) finds that exposures of this kind are seldom adequately controlled.

When it is considered that practically every mutation must eventually become eliminated from the population, after having— even if imperceptibly—hampered enough descendants so as finally to be a deciding cause, in the last of the line, of his premature death or failure to reproduce, then it becomes evident that practically every mutation represents a postponed disaster. Thus the genetic damage, that to later generations, caused by a given total dose is seen to be far greater than the damage to the exposed individual himself. In view of this, measures and regulations concerned with radiation protection should be based, at least in the case of persons who may later reproduce, primarily on the risk of genetic damage or, more specifically, of point mutations in their germ cells, rather than on the risk of damage to their own bodies. This would cause such measures and regulations to be far more stringent than they are at present. (Muller 1954f).

The Induced Mutations in Relation to the Natural Load

On our conservative estimate of 16,000,000 natural mutations arising per generation in a population of 100,000,000, a frequency of 0.16, it would take only about 37 r of gamma radiation delivered to the population to produce a quantity of new mutations equal to the new natural ones, and thus to double the mutation frequency. Our conservative estimate, however, was based on the assumption of only 1×10^{-5} as the average frequency of a mutation of some specific type, involving a given chromosomal position. According to this assumption the actual data, which indicate about 2×10^{-5} as the frequency of mutations of a specific type, are misleadingly high, because of certain sources of technical error. Since, however, this is a matter by no means proved as yet it remains quite possible that the amount of radiation necessary to double the mutation frequency is 75 r or higher. This is approximately the value that we used in our earlier treatments of the subject (Muller 1954f, 1954g), in which it was assumed that the observed 2×10^{-5} frequency for mutations of a specific type was approximately correct. These considerations illustrate the considerable margins of error in any present quantitative treatments, and the need for greater exactitude of knowledge.

The present uncertainty regarding the natural mutation frequency carries with it a corresponding uncertainty regarding what proportion of the natural mutations in man are contributed by natural radiation. There is also uncertainty regarding this question based on variation in the amount of natural radiation. If we suppose that in some typical regions as much as 6 r are accumulated, on the average, in the span of one human reproductive generation (25 to 30 years), then, on the more conservative estimate that the natural mutation frequency is equal to what would be induced by 37 r, it turns out that some 16 percent of the natural mutations in man are produced by natural radiation. In the higher estimate for natural mutations, some 8 percent of them would be radiation-induced. In either case, the figure must be far higher than for short-lived organisms, such as mice or flies. On the other hand, in some human populations living at a high altitude, with its greater cosmic-ray intensity, the contribution of radiation to the natural mutation rate must be twice as high as here estimated. Still higher values must obtain for some populations living in regions where radioactive minerals are abundant.

Many persons unfamiliar with genetics have regarded the seeming normality of the children born to survivors of the Hiroshima and Nagasaki bombings as evidence against the conclusion that the amount of radiation there received produced a significant amount of genetic damage. This misunderstanding arises from their lack of realization of the following points.

1. Few mutations are sufficiently dominant to give readily perceptible effects when inherited from only one parent, as they are in the vast majority of cases.

2. Even though these effects are not perceptible they are nearly always sufficient to hamper the individual somewhat, and finally, usually in a very distant descendant, to cause the extinction of that line of descent.

3. In any heterogenously breeding population, such as is found anywhere outside of the geneticists' field and laboratories, there is already so much natural genetic variation, representing an accumulation of many generations of natural mutations, that the additional mutations caused by the radiation would become lost to view among them even if they were as abundant as those that would arise naturally in the course of a number of generations. Thus, the genetically damaged population will eventually have to pay the costs, but these will be spread out over so many small installments, and so intermingled with the greater weight of other payments, as hardly to be recognizable. All this was of course well known to geneticists before the observations on the children at Hiroshima and Nagasaki were conducted and led them to express serious doubts that any genetic effects would be demonstrable there, even though they had no doubts that they had actually been produced (Muller 1951, 1954e).

These points may be better appreciated if it is realized that in *Drosophila* also it had not been possible to demonstrate the mutagenic action of radiation by mere inspection of the individuals of the first, second, or third generations after exposure. Exact genetic methods had first to be worked out (Muller 1921, 1918, 1920, 1922, 1923, 1928) and these are of course unavailable in man. Even following an exposure of fly spermatozoa to some 5,000 r, which we today know causes each offspring, on the average, to receive at least three induced mutations, hardly one abnormal offspring is usually to be found among a hundred examined, yet the damage is there, and it will be exerted if the population is allowed to continue.

At the same time, it is true, unlike what many nongeneticists suppose, that the effects of the genetic damage are more strongly exerted in the first generation of offspring than in any subsequent generation. They very gradually subside, in the course of many generations, as the population is purged by the dying out of the unfit. Even the recessive effects, those present in individuals homozygous for the given mutations, are found most frequently in the first generation, and then less and less frequently if the population breeds naturally rather than being subjected to a geneticist's controlled inbreeding manipulations. Moreover, there is a much higher chance that a given induced mutation will become homozygous by meeting, at fertilization, a gene of the same type derived from the great accumulated store of natural mutations, than one of the type which, like itself, had been induced by the radiation.

Since the worst effects are already exerted in F_1, what the Hiroshima observations do demonstrate clearly is that the genetic damage to posterity caused by exposure to between one hundred and several hundred r is not *conspicuously* detrimental, and it is well within limits consistent with the survival and self-perpetuation of the population. This might have been reckoned as probable without the direct evidence. For, according to the conclusion that the average individual is already heterozygous for some six, eight, or even more mutations that when homozygous would be fairly conspicuous or detrimental, it does not seem likely that the addition in heterozygous condition of just one more, induced by some 200 r, would result in any very evident change in the picture. This remains true even when we take into consideration the fact that the already existing mutations have already passed, to varying extents, through the sieve of selection and are therefore not, on the average, as detrimental as the newly induced ones.

The apparent contradiction between the fact that a really serious amount of genetic damage was produced and the fact that none is evident even in the most afflicted generation (the first), is reconciled by the manner in which the damage is spread out, thinner and thinner, over a great number of generations. There is a kind of buffering or dilution of the damaging effects, by the normal genes that dominate over them and thus delay their elimination. Thus the effects are spread out in time, in inverse proportion to their dilution in any one generation, but the total damage remains just as great as if concentrated. Moreover, even though the induced mutations may be many times the number that would arise naturally in only one generation, they are nevertheless few in relation to the accumulated natural "load." Hence they can raise by only a rather small percent the number of genetic shortcomings already present in the population.

Despite these buffering influences, it would be impossible for a population to tolerate, generation after generation, an exposure which, given to only one generation, would cause no perceptible deterioration. Gradually, as elimination rose enough to balance the new mutations, an equilibrium level of accumulation would be approached, and at this new level the then existing accumulated load would be as many times greater than the original accumulated load as the then existing mutation rate was greater than the original mutation rate. Thus, if 37 r doubles the mutation rate, a population which had received this dose for many generations would at last have twice as many ills of genetic origin as we have. Yet we already have more than enough for comfort.

Not to be neglected in the picture is the other end of the balance mechanism: the rate at which elimination of mutations goes on. Under modern civilization we interfere so much with this that we are probably raising the load of accumulated mutations as fast as by applying some tens of r to every one's reproductive organs (Muller 1955a, 1955b). Under these circumstances the raising of mutation frequency at the same time, by exposure to radiation, might tend to bring us to a genetic situation that it would be difficult to cope with.

All these questions need to be not only discussed but actually investigated far more realistically than they have been in the past. Otherwise we may at last find ourselves, genetically, facing a parallel to already accomplished deforestation and erosion, on an even grander scale. This problem is not only one that is concerned with the possible aftermaths of atomic war. It must be faced equally by the proponents of peace if we are to have an atomic age, with its risk of prolonged "permissible" exposures arising from industrial uses and radioactive waste products.

For peace will, we hope, go on and on through a great series of generations. Under these circumstances, it will be the more necessary to control and limit the radiation received by the population at large in every generation. For, given enough generations, the equilibrium level of damage will be reached, at which that damage will no longer be buffered but will accurately correspond with the existing mutation frequency. Then, a relatively small number of r per generation will exert an inordinately larger effect than it seems to now. At our present juncture, before that process has more than begun, far-seeing policies should be established. These must guard us against the dangerous fallacy that what cannot be seen or felt need not be bothered with.

This subject of protection of human beings against the genetic damage produced by radiation must, until suitable policies are established, far overshadow in its importance that of the utilization of radiation in the genetic improvement, for human purposes, of organisms potentially useful to man, or in the elimination or reduction of noxious organisms. However, these constructive uses of radiation in "biological engineering" will come increasingly to the fore as the more menacing aspects of radiation are brought under control. There is already abundant evidence of the possibility of such beneficial applications on a considerable scale (Gustafsson 1952; Hollaender 1945; Muller 1951, 1954e).

At the same time, the dangerous mistake should not be made of considering man as a species who would himself undergo a long-term benefit from the application of radiation to his germ plasm. His own reproductive material is his most invaluable, irretrievable possession. It is already subject to an amount of variation which, in relation to his present reproductive practices, borders on the excessive. Under these circumstances, man's first concern in dealing with radiation must be his own protection.

References

Auerbach, C. 1952. *Cold Spring Harbor Symp. Quant. Biol.* 16:199–213.

Auerbach, C., and Robson, J. M. 1946. *Nature* 157:302.

Baker, W. K., and Von Halle, E. 1954. *Science* 119:46–49.

Berg, R. L. 1937. *Genetics* 22:225–40, 241–48.

Berman, Z. I. 1939. *Izvest. Akad. Nauk. SSSR.* Pp. 645–78.

Bird, M. J. 1952. *J. Genet.* 50:480–85.

Catsch, A.; Peter, O.; and Welt, P. 1944. *Naturwissenschaften* 32:230–31.

Conger, A. D. 1954. *Science* 119:36–42.

Demerec, M. 1954. *Proc. Amer. Phil. Soc.* 98:318–22.

Demerec, M.; Bertani, G.; Flint, J. 1951. *Amer. Natur.* 85:119–36.

Fricke, H. 1934. *J. Chem. Phys.* 2:556–57.

———. 1935. *Cold Spring Harbor Symp. Quant. Biol.* 3:55–63.

Giles, N. H. Jr. 1940. *Proc. Nat. Acad. Sci.* 26:567–75.

———. 1943. *Genetics* 28:398–418.

Glass, B. 1950. *Amer. J. Human Genet.* 2:269–78.

Gustafsson, A. 1952. *Cold Spring Harbor Symp. Quant. Biol.* 16:263–81.

Haldane, J. B. S. 1937. *Amer. Natur.* 71:337–49.

————. 1948. *Proc. 8th Int. Congr. Genet.*

————. 1949. *Hereditas* 35 (Suppl.):266–73.

Hertwig, P. 1938. *Biol. Zentr.* 58:273–301.

————. 1940. *Z. indukt. Abstammungs-u. Vererbungslehre* 79:1–27.

Hollaender, A. 1945. *Annu. Missouri Bot. Garden* 32:165–78.

————. 1955. *Science* 121:624.

Hollaender, A.; Baker, W. K.; Anderson, E. H. 1952. *Cold Spring Harbor Symp. Quant. Biol.* 16:315–26.

Ives, P. T.; Levine, R. P.; Yost, H. T. Jr. 1954. *Proc. Nat. Acad. Sci.* 40:165–71.

Jensen, K. A.; Kirk, I.; Kolmark, G.; Westergaard, M. 1952. *Cold Spring Harbor Symp. Quant. Biol.* 16:245–62.

Kerkis, J. J. 1935. *Sum. Commun. 15th Int. Physiol. Congr.* Pp. 198–200.

————. 1938. *Izvest. Akad. Nauk. SSSR.* Pp. 75–96.

Kirby-Smith, J. S., and Swanson, C. P. 1954. *Science* 119:42–44.

Koller, P. C. 1944. *Genetics* 29:247–63.

Kossikov, K. V. 1937. *Genetics* 22:213–24.

Lüning, K. G. 1952. *Acta Zool.* 33:193–207.

Lüning, K. G.; Lindell, B.; Falk, R. 1955. *Acta Radiol.* 43:89–92.

Macht, S. H., and Lawrence, P. S. 1955. *Amer. J. Roentgenology and Radium Therapy* 73:442–66.

Meyer, Helen U. Unpublished data.

Mickey, G. H. 1954. *Amer. Natur.* 88:241–55.

Moeller, D. W.; Terrill, J. G. Jr.; Ingraham, S. C. II. 1953. *Public Health Rep., U. S. Public Health Service* 68:57–65.

Muller, H. J. 1918. *Genetics* 3:422–99.

———. 1920. *J. Exp. Zool.* 31:443–73.

———. 1921. *2nd Int. Congr. Eugen., N. Y., Abstracts.* Pp. 7–8.

———. 1922. *Amer. Natur.* 56:32–50.

———. 1923. "Mutation." *Eugenics, Genetics and the Family* 1:106–12. Baltimore, Md.: Williams and Wilkins.

———. 1928. *Genetics* 13:279–357.

———. 1934. *Verh. 4 Int. Kongr. Radiol.* 2:100–102.

———. 1940. *J. Genet.* 40:1–66.

———. 1941. *Cold Spring Harbor Symp. Quant. Biol.* 9:151–65.

———. 1946a. *Yearbook Amer. Phil. Soc. for 1945.* Pp. 150–53.

———. 1946b. *Genetics* 31:225.

———. Unpublished data.

———. 1950a. *Amer. J. Human Genet.* 2:111–76.

———. 1950b. *J. Cellular Comp. Physiol.* 35 (Suppl. 1) :9–70.

———. 1951. "Radiation Damage to the Genetic Material." *Science in Progress.* Pp. 93–165, 481–93. New Haven, Conn.: Yale University Press.

———. 1952a. "Gene Mutations Caused by Radiation." *Symposium on Radiobiology.* Pp. 296–332. New York: John Wiley & Sons.

———. 1952b. *7th Annu. Rep. to Amer. Cancer Soc., Inc.* pp. 120–21.

———. 1954a. *Amer. Natur.* 88:437–59.

———. 1954b. *Rec. Genet. Soc. Amer.* 23:58.

———. 1954c. *Genetics* 39:985.

———. 1954d. "The Manner of Production of Mutations by Radiation." In *Radiation Biology,* ed. A. Hollaender 1:475–626. New York: McGraw-Hill Co.

———. 1954e. "The Nature of the Genetic Effects Produced by

Radiation." In *Radiation Biology,* ed. A. Hollaender
1:351–473. New York: McGraw-Hill Co.

――――. 1954f. *Acta Radiol.* 41:5–19.

――――. 1954g. *Amer. J. Obstet. and Gynecol.* 67:467–83.

――――. 1955a. *Bull. of the Atomic Sci.* 11:210–12, 230.

――――. 1955b. *Science* 121:837–40.

Muller, H. J.; Herskowitz, I. H.; Abrahamson, S.; and Oster, I. I.
1954. *Genetics* 39:741–49.

Muller, H. J.; Herskowitz, J. H.; Abrahamson, S.; and Oster, I. I.
Amer. 20:115–16.

――――. 1951b. *Genetics* 36:567–68.

Muller, H. J.; Valencia, J. I.; and Valencia, R. M. 1950a.
Rec. Genet. Soc. Amer. 18:105–6.

――――. 1950b. *Genetics* 35:125–26.

Neel, J. V., and Falls, H. F. 1951. *Science* 114:419–22.

Oliver, C. P. 1932. Z. indukt Abstamm. u. Vererbungslehre
61:447–88.

Oster, I. I. 1954. *8th Int. Congr. for Cell Biol.*
Excerpta Medica 8:406.

Patterson, J. T. 1931. *Biol. Bull.* 61:133–38.

Rapoport, J. A. 1943. *Zhur. Obshchei Biol.* 4:65–72.

――――. 1946a. *Compt. Rend. Acad. Sci.* URSS 54:65–67.

――――. 1946b. *Bull. Biol. Med. Exp.* URSS 23:198–201.

――――. 1948. *Compt. Rend. Acad. Sci.* URSS 61:713–15.

Ray-Chaudhuri, S. P. 1944. *Proc. Roy. Soc. Edinburgh* B62: 66–72.

Russell, W. L. 1952. *Cold Spring Harbor Symp. Quant. Biol.*
16:327–35.

――――. 1954. "Genetic Effects of Radiation in Mammals." In
Radiation Biology, ed. A. Hollaender 1:825–59. New
York: McGraw-Hill Co.

Russell, W. L.; Russell, L. B., Kimball, A. W. 1954. *Amer. Natur.* 88:269–86.

Serebrovskaya, R. I., and Shapiro, N. I. 1935. *Compt. Rend. Acad. Sci. URSS* 2:421–28.

Slatis, H. M. 1954. *Amer. J. Human Genet.* 6:412–18.

Snell, G. D. 1934. *Amer. Natur.* 68:178.

———. 1939. *Proc. Nat. Acad. Sci.* 25:11–14.

Snell, G. D., and Ames, F. B. 1939. *Amer. J. Roentgenology and Radium Therapy* 41:248–55.

Sonnenblick, B. P. 1955. *J. Newark Beth Israel Hospital* 6:31–42.

Spencer, W. P., and Stern, C. 1948. *Genetics* 33:43–74.

Stadler, L. J. 1941. *Cold Spring Harbor Symp. Quant. Biol.* 9:168–77.

———. 1952. *Science* 120:811–19.

Stadler, L. J., and Roman, H. 1948. *Genetics* 33:273–303.

Stern, C.; Carson, G.; Kinst, M.; Novitski, E.; Uphoff, D. 1952. *Genetics* 37:413–49.

Stern, C., and Novitski, E. 1948. *Science* 108:538–39.

Sturtevant, A. H. 1937. *Quart. Rev. Biol.* 12:464–67.

Timoféeff-Ressovsky, N. W. 1934. Strahlentherapie 51:658–63.

———. 1935. *Nachr. Ges. Wiss. Gottingen N. F.* 1:163–80.

———. 1937. *Experimentelle Mutationsforschung in der Vererbungslehre.* Leipzig: T. Steinkopt.

Timoféeff-Ressovsky, and Zimmer, K. G. 1935. *Strahlentherapie* 53:134–38.

Uphoff, D. E., and Stern, C. 1949. *Science* 109:609–10.

Wyss, O.; Clark, J. B.; Haas, F.; Stone, W. S. 1948. *J. Bact.* 56:51–57.

Physics in the Attack on the
Fundamental Problems of Genetics

THIS essay is virtually unknown and forgotten to geneticists and, to a less momentous extent, its burial
in the literature parallels the earlier fate of Mendel's
Experiments in Plant Hybridization. Muller was still
a Senior Geneticist in Moscow when he presented
this address to the physics section of the USSR Academy of
Sciences. Lysenkoism that year was already causing grief for geneticists; and physicists who may have been persuaded to participate in the analysis of the gene never emerged. It is also surprising
that physicists reading the Scientific Monthly, a fairly well-cir-
culated journal of scientific essays, did not respond to the X-ray
diffraction approach to gene structure which Muller urged upon
them. Ironically, an American student who had taken Muller's
course on Mutation and the Gene—J. D. Watson—(but who had
neither read this article nor heard its chief points mentioned in
class) helped to show that "the fundamental feature of the gene
structure" resided in a complementary double helix of DNA.

The evidence obtained by geneticists indicates that it is in the tiny
particles of heredity—the genes—that the chief secrets of living
matter as distinguished from lifeless are contained, that is, an
understanding of the properties of the genes would bridge the
main gap between inanimate and animate. Such a study would
be of intense interest from the point of view of physics as well as
of physical chemistry and organic chemistry, for it is already
known that these genes have properties which are most unique
from the standpoint of physics and of the sciences related to

physics. So peculiar are these properties that physicists, when first confronted with them, often deny the possibility of their existence. Yet there is really no doubt of the truth of the biologists' findings concerning the genes, so that it may well be that an elucidation of them may throw light not only on the most fundamental questions of biology but even on fundamental questions of physics as well. I am therefore making this plea to physicists in the hope that they will interest themselves more actively in these problems of such vital importance to both our fields.

To grasp the problems involved in the study of the gene it should first be explained that genes are particles of submicroscopic volume, probably of the order of about one twentieth of a micron in length, and considerably less in their other diameters, probably of protein composition (see below), and bound to one another in line, single file, so as to form solid threads ("chromonemas"). These threads are usually many microns long and thus comprise thousands of these genes, each gene in the chain usually being different in its composition and chemical function in the cell from every other gene. The nucleus of the cell contains a specific number of these gene-chains, often in more or less spirally coiled form. All these genes not only exist in the reproductive cells and constitute the ultimate particles of heredity, but they also exist in all the other cells of any living body and, as mentioned in the preceding, they probably constitute the ultimate particles of life itself. Through the varied reactions of the different kinds of genes with the various surrounding materials of the protoplasm, the basis is laid for the production of the various chemical substances and for the carrying on of the various chemical processes, and for the determination of the various morphological structures peculiar to each cell.

Now, the most spectacular property of the gene, from the standpoint of physics, is its property of *specific auto-attraction* of like with like. In explanation of this, no physicist has ever yet been able to offer any plausible hypothesis. The attraction in question has an opportunity of exerting itself, owing to the fact that in most cells there exist at least two gene-chains of each kind (one having been originally derived from the mother of the organism, the other from the father). That is, if we may represent the genes in one of the gene-chains in a cell as A, B, C, D, etc., in that order, then there is present somewhere else in that cell another gene-chain having genes of identical composition: A, B, C, D, etc., in the same order. Besides this, there are other gene-chains which we may represent as L, M, N, etc., T, U, V, etc., and of each of these long chains or chromonemas the cell contains two representatives. Now, under certain conditions, it becomes evident that each gene forms the center of a specific field of attractive force, for then gene A tends to come together with the other A, B with the other B (L with L, M with M, and so on). We know that this must be true even though the individual genes are too small for us to see, because we can see that the gene chains as a whole tend to come together in this way, like with like, so that one ABCD comes into side-by-side contact ("conjugates") with the other, one LMN with the other LMN, etc. They always do this in such a way as to be oriented in the same direction, the A end of one chain next to the A end of the partner chain, not next to the other end. Moreover, if through some prior accident one or more of the chromonemas (gene-chains) has previously become broken at any point (or even if several breaks have occurred and the fragments have then united together again in a different way than before, so as to have the genes arranged in a new order), still the corresponding segments tend to come together, like with like. Thus the attraction is in no wise a property of the chain as a whole but purely of the individual, constituent genes.

Unlike the ordinary forces of adsorption known to the physical chemists, these gene forces are of such range as to act over visible microscopic distances. In doing so, moreover, they must in some way interpenetrate one another in many directions, since the forces of attraction of many genes must be traversing the same space at the same time. And despite this interpenetration, these forces must somehow preserve their directions and their specificities. It is probable that this force of auto-attraction exists, to some extent at least, at all times, but it is sometimes prevented from expressing itself by the simultaneous existence of a non-specific repelling force of a different nature, the latter probably caused by electrical charges. It has not yet been found feasible under the conditions of biological work to make quantitative studies, after the physicist's fashion, of the nature of the force of gene attraction: studies of its variation of intensity with distance; of the effect of varying conditions upon it; of its direction; of its speed of propagation; of the possible interference with one another of the forces emanating from different genes; of its possible polarization, etc. It is probable, however, both from theoretical considerations and from the observed tendency of like strands to conjugate by twos, even when more than two are present, that the force does not issue in a radially symmetrical manner but that a certain side-surface of the gene tends to attract a specific side-surface of the other, like gene. We would like physicists to search the possibilities of their science and tell us what kind of forces these could be, and how produced, and to suggest further lines of approach in their study.

It is not unlikely that a solution of the above physical mystery would also throw much light on the nature of that property of the gene which is most peculiar and spectacular from the standpoint of the chemist. This second peculiar property is that of *auto-synthesis*. That is, each gene, reacting with the complicated surrounding material enveloping all the genes in common, exerts such a selectively organizing effect upon this material as to cause the synthesis, next to itself, of another molecular or super-molecular structure, quite identical in composition with the given gene itself. The gene is, as it were, a modeler, and forms an image, a copy of itself, next to itself, and since all the genes in the chain do likewise, a duplicate chain is produced next to each original chain, and no doubt lying in contact with a certain face of the latter. This gene-building is not mere "auto-catalysis," in the ordinary sense of the chemist, since reactions are not merely speeded up that would have happened anyway, but the gene actually initiates just such reactions as are required to form precisely another gene just like itself; it is an active arranger of material and arranges the latter after its own pattern.

The analogy to crystallization hardly carries us far enough in explanation of the above phenomenon when we remember that there are thousands of different kinds of genes, i.e., of genes having different patterns, in every cell nucleus, and that each of these genes has to reproduce its own specific pattern out of surrounding material common to them all. When, through some micro-chemical accident, or chance quantum absorption, a sudden change in the composition ("pattern") of the gene takes place, known to biologists as a "mutation," then the gene of the new type, so produced, reproduces itself according to this new type; that is, it now reproduces precisely the new pattern. This shows that the copying property depends upon some more fundamental feature of gene structure than does the specific pattern which the gene has, and that it is the effect of the former to cause a copying not only of itself but also of the latter, more variable features. It is this fact which gives the possibility of biological evolution and which has allowed living matter ultimately to become so very much more highly organized than nonliving. It is this which lies at the bottom of both growth, reproduction, and heredity. We would like the physical chemists to work on this problem of auto-synthesis for us, but it may well be that a further elucidation, by the physicists, of the property of auto-attraction of genes would greatly help in the explanation of this auto-synthesis also.

The reason that I think there may be a relation between the two properties is this: If the attracting principle of like for like, which we already know to be possessed by the gene considered as a whole, extends also to more elementary parts of the gene, to "blocks" whose differences in arrangement constitute the specific differences in gene pattern whereby one gene differs from another and which form the basis of the mutational changes, then, if we suppose that representatives of these more elementary "blocks" exist in scattered disorganized form in the space surrounding the genes, it can be seen that each gene-part or "block" would tend to attract to itself another, like part, and so a second group of parts would gather next to the original gene in the same pattern as in the latter, in much the same way as, on a still grosser scale, each chromonema as a whole builds up a second chromonema, having its individual genes identical with and arranged in the same order as in the first one. If, then, the auto-attraction holds not merely for genes as a whole but also for gene-parts, the auto-synthesis of a gene as a whole would be largely explained in terms of this auto-attraction. (Of course we should in this case still be left with the problem of the synthesis of the gene-parts, but this might be simpler as they might be of relatively limited number). It is tempting to think that this suggestion is true, in view of the great uniqueness both of the property of auto-attraction and of auto-synthesis, and in view of the possession by both of certain common, striking features: namely, auto-specificity, and the property of retaining this auto-specificity in spite of the changes called mutations. For it is to be noted that in the case of the auto-attraction also, we must suppose that when one of those rare changes called a mutation occurs, the new gene has a changed kind of attraction, such that it now attracts preferentially another gene having a pattern like that of its new self, not one with a pattern like that of its old self. Thus, the auto-attraction of the gene, just like its auto-synthesis, must depend upon some fundamental features of the gene structure, which persists despite the secondary changes in pattern (mutations). And this fundamental feature must be instrumental not only in producing an attractive force in general, but in determining that this attraction shall somehow express, in its specificity, both the fundamental structure itself and also those other details of pattern which vary independently of this fundamental structure. In the face of such problems, the biologists must perforce call to the physicists and the physical chemists. (Discussions of gene auto-attraction and auto-synthesis have been given by the author in his papers of 1921, 1928, 1935.)

In the solution of these problems, and of the general problems of gene composition, one possible line of approach might be through the study of X-ray diffraction patterns. Preliminary studies of this nature upon the proteins of hair have been made by Astbury and others (Astbury and Woods, 1933; Astbury and Lomax, 1935; Astbury and Sisson, 1935), at Leeds, but studies of such proteins may be a far cry from the study of the gene. But it may be possible for gene material to be used in such investigations. For there exist, in some of the cells of flies, bundles of identical chromonemas conjugated together in hundreds, and these bundles are so large that they might even furnish material for an X-ray diffraction study if we had people of sufficient physical training, combined with biological interest, to tackle such a job. Of course, there may be much material extraneous to the genes themselves, contained in such a bundle of chromonemas, but they are at least more nearly the material we are seeking than is any other morphologically separable constituent of the cell. It might also be objected that every gene is different from every other, along the length of the chain, and that therefore we would be studying, at best, a great mixture of gene materials. Nevertheless, as stated above, there must be much in common to the structure of all genes and these common features might give results in such a study. Needless to say, it would also be desirable to have parallel studies on such material carried out by the methods of the chemists.

In the past year the opportunity has also arisen of obtaining from another source material which may serve our present purpose. This possibility arises out of the discovery by Stanley and Loring (Stanley 1935; Stanley and Loring 1936), that the substance (or "organism") causing the so-called mosaic disease of tobacco, and likewise that of tomato (and doubtless of various other higher organisms), may be obtained in crystalline form, apparently as a pure protein. We judge that this material has the properties of a gene, inasmuch as it can reproduce itself, i.e., it can undergo auto-synthesis when present in a cell and it is probably mutable, since different "species" of it are known. We may provisionally assume, then, that it represents a certain kind of gene. The weight of its giant molecule is of the order of several million, and this agrees as well as could be expected with the very approximate estimates of size hitherto made for the genes of flies. As this substance can be obtained in some bulk and in apparently pure form, it will be very important to carry on an active investigation of it not only from a purely chemical standpoint, but also from a physical standpoint, with special reference to the problems above raised. Among other things, X-ray diffraction studies of it should be attempted by competent specialists in this field of physics.

I have tried to lay emphasis on the most outstanding problems of physical and physico-chemical science which the geneticist has found himself confronted with, and which he is practically unable to attack by means of the methods familiar to him. I have omitted a discussion of the very important problem of the way in which changes in genes—mutations—occur. Although this is a matter in which the aid of physicists is invaluable to us, the methods of genetics and physics combined—investigations of the frequency and character of mutations under varying conditions and with varying doses of irradiation—have already given valuable results. They have shown, for example, that the mutations produced by high-frequency irradiation are the results of single ionizations, and that the whole process from ionization to mutation must be rather sharply circumscribed in space. Through such studies we may be able to learn more about the nature of these variable features of the gene pattern, which determine the specific properties of one gene as distinguished from another one, and which are in a sense independent of those fundamental features of its composition which give it its properties of auto-attraction and auto-synthesis. It is in this field of mutation that the physicist is today most actively and fruitfully helping the geneticist.

There are also many other physical questions before the geneticist, such as that of the nature of the nonspecific repulsive force which exists between chromonemas, especially at certain periods and in certain portions of them; the nature of the coiling and uncoiling of these threads and of all the various motions and physical and physico-chemical changes which they undergo in their complicated life history. There is the question of what holds the genes together end to end, in single rows; how these chains may become broken and the pieces stuck together again, etc. There is the question of the manner in which they produce their effects upon other substances in the cell—probably by a kind of enzyme action—so as to act as the determiners of the properties of the cell and of the organism as a whole. And there is the problem of the so-called "position effect," that is, the fact that the arrangement of the genes in the chromonema with respect to each other has an important influence upon the kind of effects which these genes exert upon the surrounding substances. Possibly this "position effect," too, is related to the property of gene attraction. All these questions, however, important though they be, nevertheless seem secondary in comparison with the problems of auto-attraction and of auto-synthesis themselves, and of the structure giving rise to them, and with the related problem of the nature of those changes (mutations) which the gene undergoes, which do not disturb these two properties. It is becoming recognized nowadays that the gene is the basis of life. These two properties, including the fact of their undisturbability by mutation, lie at the basis of the gene. The geneticist himself is helpless to analyze these properties further. Here the physicist as well as the chemist must step in. Who will volunteer to do so?

References

Astbury, W. T. and Lomax, R. 1935. *J. Chem. Soc.,* June 1935.

Astbury, W. T. and Sisson, W. A. 1935. *Proc. Roy. Soc. London* 150:533–51.

Astbury, W. T. and Woods, H. J. 1933. *Philo. Trans. Roy. Soc. London* 232:333–94.

Muller, H. J. 1921. *Amer. Natur.* 56: 32–50.

————. 1928. "The Enigma of the Gene and of its Mutation." Address at Franklin Institute, Philadelphia, Pa.

————. 1929. *Proc. Int. Congr. Plant. Sci.* 1:897–921.

————. 1935. *Amer. Natur.* 69:405–12.

Stanley, W. M. 1935. *Science* 81, 2113:644–45.

Stanley, W. M. and Loring, H. S. 1936. *Science* 83, 2143:85.

The Gene

THE gene concept endured a tortuous history of controversies as it emerged from its original status as an undefined unit. Muller's analysis of the gene from the perspectives of microbial and higher organisms shows how many new advances in virology, developmental biology, physiology, cytology, and evolution could be attributed to studies of the individual gene and to mutations and chromosome changes induced in a wide range of organisms.

Startling in its originality was Muller's recognition that bacterial transformation, a phenomenon linking genes to DNA, might arise by a process similar to pairing and crossing-over of the introduced bacterial DNA with a sequence similar to it in the live host cell.

General Evidence of a Genetic Material

The gene has sometimes been described as a purely idealistic concept, divorced from real things, and again it has been denounced as wishful thinking on the part of those too mechanically minded. And some critics go so far as to assert that there is not even such a thing as genetic material at all, as distinct from other constituents of living matter.

However, a defensible case for the existence of separable genetic material might have been made out on very general considerations alone. Despite the bafflingly complex and seemingly erratic character of biological things, and their change at the touch of analysis—characteristics which have made them such a happy hunting ground for obscurantists—it is obvious that the whole congeries of variable processes of each kind of organism tends to go in a succession of great cycles, or generations, or even alternations of generations, with the generations in turn made up of smaller or cell cycles, and that at the end of every greatest cycle something very like the starting-point is reached again. Now the finding of the starting-point in a complex course, were it observed in any other field, would be taken to imply the existence of some guide or guides, some elements that are themselves relatively invariable and that serve as a frame of reference in relation to which the passing phases of other features are adjusted. Such constants in other fields are, for instance, the fixed mass-energy relations in the motions of a pendulum, or in the recurrent track of a comet, the steady radio beam or the map in the journey of an airplane to its destination and back, and the stable nuclear structure amidst the changing electron patterns of an atom, as it finds its state of least energy once more. So, too, in the organism it would be inferred that there exists a relatively stable controlling structure, to which the rest is attached, and about which it in a sense revolves.

In the organism, however, there is the cardinal difference from other cyclic objects that the return to the starting-point finds all structures doubled in a cell cycle, or still further multiplied as a result of the succession of cell doublings comprised in a complete generation, or alternation of generations. And this in turn requires that the material furnishing the frame of reference, whatever it is, itself underwent such doubling or reproduction, and that this too must have taken place under its own guidance. It is for this reason that it may be called the *genetic* material. And it is important to note that, unlike the controlling factors in the other cases, it is not merely statically stable, but dynamically so, in that it usually succeeds in so affecting the heterogeneous other material with which it is supplied as to impress upon it precisely its own image.

That this ability to duplicate itself is based in unique properties of some relatively stable genetic material, rather than in the multitude of diverse substances and processes that engage in the cycles, may, curiously enough, be inferred more especially from the behavior of the real exceptions to the principle of inner stability. These all-important exceptions are the comparatively rare cases in which, even in a "pure line," sudden permanent deviations of type, or "mutations," take place. Although of the most varied kinds, as judged by their unlike effects on the organism, it is characteristic of the great majority of these changes that in succeeding multiplications they become regularly incorporated, that is, they now take their place as part of the again stable, self-multiplying pattern. It is scarcely conceivable that, if the reproduction of every part of the organism were due primarily to the marvelous concatenation of a host of individual processes of the cycle, these could have been so arranged that, when disturbed in any one of innumerable ways, they would still be able to work effectively in reproduction, yet in a manner so *correspondingly* adjusted as now to effect a repetition of just the given alteration. Rather must it be inferred that the essential process of reproduction consists in the autosynthesis of a controlling genetic material, and that this occurs through some sort of laying down of the raw material after the model of the genetic material already present, no matter what—within certain very wide limits—the pattern of that genetic material happens to be to begin with. The building up of the nongenetic parts of the system would then take place, conversely, by a series of essentially heterosynthetic processes, that were ultimately controlled by the genetic material. It may be granted that this autosynthesis of variations of the genetic material would in itself be difficult enough to understand—it is, in fact, to be considered as the basic problem of living matter. Yet it does not lead to such an incomprehensible enigma as would the so-called "organism-as-a-whole" view of the phenomenon which has, implicitly or explicitly, been adopted by some physiologists and others who would deny the existence of a special genetic material.

If the above argument is followed to its logical conclusion, all other material in the organism is made subsidiary to the genetic material, and the origin of life is identified with the origin of this material by chance chemical combination (Minchin 1916; Troland 1914, 1916, 1917; Muller 1922, 1926; Alexander and Bridges 1929). Owing to its unique ability to duplicate its variations, this material will thereafter, in the course of protracted periods of time, be subject to the Darwinian principle of natural selection— that is, to the differential multiplication and accumulation, in series, of particular variants—those that happened to have properties conducive of their own survival and further multiplication. This will carry the multiplying material step by step into further and further differentiations and complications.

Among the more successful forms will be those in which the genetic material has become organized into aggregates that pro- duce, heterosynthetically, a system of companion substances— "protoplasm"—of such nature as to aid in multiplication of the genetic aggregate itself. With increasing serviceability of this protoplasm, in some lines of descent, an ever-increasing range of substances will be made available for the raw material of the sys- tem, through the development of processes of conversion and utilization, as food, of material chemically further and further re- moved from itself,[1] as well as through the development, in some lines, of powers of capturing its food and avoidance of becoming used as food itself or otherwise destroyed. Thus it would happen that even the simplest body deserving of being called a "cell" has so out-distanced in complexity the most intricate product of inanimate nature as to make the "living" world appear as a dis- tinct category of nature. And it would explain the amazing fact that in any object of this living world the whole great system of materials and processes, unlike those in any natural inanimate system, is organized *adaptively,* that is, in such wise that all pro- cesses are focused, as if by forethought, towards just one end (a

1. Horowitz (1945) has recently given convincing chemical illustrations of how the extension of synthetic activity "backward" for utilization of ever- simpler substances, must have come about by mutations. This idea itself is not a new one but has long formed a necessary part of the theory that the gene constitutes the basis of life. So, too, has the idea, ably expounded in detail in recent years by Oparin (1938), that there must have been an extended accumulation of ever more complex organic combinations, per- mitted by the absence of living organisms that would break them down, before genetic material could accidentally arise from them and be suitably provided with the components needed for its own reproduction.

sometimes distant one), namely, the multiplication of the system itself—an end that in its turn constitutes another beginning, in the endless succession of cycles.

The Linear Differentiation of the Chromosomal Nucleoprotein into Self-Reproducing Parts

Of course the establishment of the modern genetic theory of the basis of life did not historically depend, in the main, upon such very general considerations concerning cyclic behavior and the mutability of the cycles. As is now so well known, an enormous mass of observational and experimental evidence combined in establishing the fact that the material of heredity is to be found, in the main at least, in the chromosomes. It may be recalled that the chromosomes are not really the lumpish bodies that they superficially appear to be at the time of cell division but are extremely delicate, relatively very long threads that are not readily discernible in their ordinary more extended condition, but that take on the more conspicuous lumpish aspect by becoming compactly coiled into a helical spiral, or spiral of spirals. This constitutes a form of packing for their transportation at cell division. Arranged in fixed linear order in each long thread is a multitude of distinctive parts, each with its characteristic chemical effect in the cell. In preparation for each cell doubling, there is an exact duplication of each distinguishable part of each chromosome, so that two identical daughter threads are formed, not really by splitting as the process is often miscalled, but by the synthesis of new material.

It may also be recalled that, at the time of the preparation of the mature germ cells, or meiosis, the chromosome threads, then in relatively extended form, undergo the remarkable phenomenon of synapsis, that is, a side by side juxtaposition, by twos, of like parts of corresponding threads, and that this involves, as its most important consequence, crossing-over. In crossing-over there is a breaking of pairs of synapsed threads at one or more points, identical in the two members, just at or just after the time when each had doubled again, as if—as Darlington (1935) has suggested

—the strain of reassociation into twos of the suddenly fourfold groups were at some points too much for two of them. Following or attendant upon the breakage is a reattachment between the broken ends of pieces not originally together, resulting in an exchange of corresponding segments. And finally (if other significant features are omitted) the segregtion of the parts into different germ cells is carried out in such wise as to give rise to the known principles of Mendelian segregation and recombination, and of crossing-over as genetically observed.

The methods need not be recalled by which, through breeding tests, the relative positions of many of the parts in the chromosome threads, first, of the fruit fly *Drosophila melanogaster,* and later of various other species, have been mapped, or how direct verification of this mapping was obtained, through cytological observation of cases in which, through abnormalities of inheritance, given changes in chromosome number or structure were predicted, as well as through some cases in which the sequence of the testing was the reverse of this. Such work, in *Drosophila,* has been greatly aided by the discovery some twelve years ago, by Painter (1933) and by Heitz and Bauer (1933), that the relatively enormous cable-like bodies in the cells of the salivary glands of fly larvae are really chromosome formations. As Koltzoff (1934) first suggested, each cable is derived from one original pair of ordinary extended ("resting stage") chromosome threads that have undergone repeated duplication but remain lying in parallel. Thus the appearance is given of a relatively extended chromosome that is greatly magnified in its transverse direction; so much so as to be able to show, along its length, characteristic variations in "density" of nucleic acid (really caused, if H. Ris's interpretation is correct (Ris and Crouse 1945), by differences in degree of spiralization); thereby, the different parts of the chromosomes can be recognized.

That the material of the chromosomes is of a specific type, chemically, being composed in predominant measure of nucleoprotein, a compound of protein with nucleic acid, was shown in analyses of sperm chromosomes by Miescher (1897) before the turn of the century, though only recently has it become reasonably certain—through the analogous finding in viruses—that it is really this major component rather than some elusive accompaniment of it which constitutes the genetic material itself. As protein is so potent, labile, and versatile chemically and has such possibilities for different permutations and combinations of its amino-acids and, as is now known, for the intricate folding of the chains and for their interconnection into larger complexes, by all of which processes its properties can become radically altered, and as, on the other hand, the basic structure, at least, of nucleic acid is everywhere much the same, it has usually been assumed that the differences between genes reside in the protein component of the chromosomes. However, it should be noted that the nucleic acid also exists in highly polymerized form, and, as will be seen later, this reservation may be a very significant one.

The main point of all the above familiar work, for our present purposes, is that it has given incontrovertible evidence of the existence of definite genetic material, of a particulate nature, which certainly has, in each part, the property of self-determination in its own duplication. For, if any given part has somehow been removed, the same deficiency will be evident in succeeding generations. If, on the contrary, an extra part has been added, this too will be found to have become reproduced later. And if, instead of mere removal or addition, there was any cytologically visible rearrangement of chromosome parts, or even a change too small for this and only detectable through its effects on the organism and placeable on the chromosome diagram purely by breeding tests, this alteration, too, will be found to have undergone multiplication. This then, shows that it is the chromosome material itself that is already present, and not other material, which determines the type of chromosome material that is again to be produced, in duplication, and that is what is meant by saying that this material is "self-duplicating," "self-reproducing," "autosynthetic," or "genetic" material. Most other materials in the cell are certainly not genetic in this sense. It is clear, secondly, that this self-duplication is not, primarily, a resultant of the action of even the genetic material as a whole but of each part of it separately. That is, the material is potentially particulate, and each separable part, which determines the duplication of just its own material, may be called a *gene*.

Before considering further the properties of individual genes, as judged by results of their passage through generations, it should be emphasized that, though particulate in their self-reproduction, their products in the cell interact in the most complicated ways, both with one another and with the products of environmental conditions, in determining the characters of organisms, contrary to what many early Mendelians had assumed. Their integration, however, is essentially one of gene *effects* only, since in the immediate process of their autosynthesis they remain substantially independent. Very complicated integration occurs to be sure in the preparation of material for this final gene synthesis, but these processes, too, are properly to be considered as more remote gene effects, of a heterosynthetic nature.

The Independence and Stability of the Genes in their Self-Reproduction

Now consider some of the results of studies on the stability and mutability of genes. It has long been evident that in its mutation, just as in its self-duplication, the genetic material acts particulately. Early observation showed that the conspicuous, visible mutations, at least, usually affect only one kind of gene at a time. And after a given mutation has arisen, there seems to be no tendency for the cause of it to go on producing other obvious mutations,[2] and even the gene that has just become changed does not, ordinarily, show any heightened tendency to change again; that is, it appears to reproduce its new self in about as stable a manner as its predecessor had reproduced the original type. Any individual type of conspicuous mutation arose with such extraordinary low frequency that, with the older genetic techniques at least, there was no thought of obtaining any quantitative estimate of it. The incidence of the mutation was quite unpredictable, and, even when all readily observable mutations were considered at once, they

2. Since this was written, exceptions to this principle have been found by Auerbach (personal communication) in cases of mutations produced by mustard gas; in these cases, given genes, and their descendant genes, are found to be unstable for some time after treatment.

still appeared to arise quite randomly, and no relation was observable between the environmental or physiological condition of an organism and the kind of effect produced by the gene mutations that might arise in it.

It was a long time, however, before these results could be shown to be applicable to gene mutations in general. For there are many genes whose mutations may produce minor effects, of degree, confusable with the effects of changes in environment and in other genes, and such mutations cannot so easily be studied. Moreover, it was important to know whether the principles in question hold for these genes not merely when they are in "pure lines," as in Johannsen's work, but also under those conditions of cross-breeding which give rise to wide variations of an apparently continuous nature.

For tests of these less clear-cut cases, the development of elaborate techniques of breeding was necessary, in which certain known genes with conspicuous visible effects were utilized as so-called "identifying factors" or "markers," to enable the distribution of the "minor" genes (i.e., genes with minor differences in effect), present in the same chromosome with them, to be ascertained among a group of the descendants produced in cross-breeding. Thus descendants known to have received any given combination of the original minor as well as major genes could be distinguished and subjected to quantitative tests for the determination of whether the minor genes had undergone change in the meantime. In work on the fruit fly, *Drosophila,* especially, there were a number of cases that had been put aside as "skeletons in the closet," in which it looked as though the genes themselves were undergoing continuous quantitative variation. But application of these methods showed in every case that this appearance had been deceptive. It was due, first, to temporary effects of environmental differences on the visible characters, not on the genes themselves, effects which were not inherited; secondly, that many minor genes were simultaneously undergoing segregation and forming new combinations; thirdly, that the so-called "pure" or homozygous combinations formed were in these cases often unable to live or to breed effectively, so that most of the individuals that did breed continued to give rise to diverse types. At the same time the individual genes themselves, despite this superficial appearance of continuous variation, gave evidence of being highly stable, not subject to contamination by opposite types even on long-continued crossing with them and subject to rare definite mutations only. It appears that so-called "multiple factor" inheritance of this kind is typical for the great majority of characters in natural cross-breeding populations. For these are heterogeneous with regard to many minor as well as major mutations that have occurred within them and have accumulated through hundreds of generations. But this in no wise indicated a real instability of their individual genes.

It should be mentioned in this connection that the same quantitative tests were adapted to disclosing inheritable variation of any kind whatever in the given characters, even if it were not due to mutation or recombination of chromosomal genes at all. Since the characters studied were unusually sensitive indicators of changes of all kinds, they were especially suitable for such a study. However, no such other kind of variation was to be found in them. Thus it became evident that other forms of genetic differences within the species must, if they exist, be exceedingly rare at best in this *Drosophila* material. Since then, essentially similar results have been obtained in other species of animals and plants, with certain important qualifications to be mentioned later. A series of analyses of the differences between species also have been carried out, by various investigators. These indicate, in a number of ways, that the vast majority at least (subject to the same qualifications) of the differences between species are of this same stable, particulate chromosomal nature. All this confirms us in the conclusion that most of evolution must have been built up of mutations of the individual chromosomal genes.

So rare are mutations of any given type under natural breeding of any kind that, before enough mutations could be collected under controlled, "normal" conditions to put their study on a quantitative basis comparable to that of the older fields of segregation and crossing-over, a new set of genetic methods, again employing the principle of conspicuous "marker" genes for given chromosomes as a whole, had to be developed. At the same time, special technical devices had to be introduced that allowed the scale of the experiments to be increased by several orders of magnitude. Such work has now been carried on for nearly three decades. Its results are on the whole consistent and have agreed in demonstrating a number of principles concerning gene mutation and gene stability. Only some of these can be considered here.

One of the first questions of interest concerns itself with the degree of stability of the gene. Here one is hampered by the fact that no one has discovered how many mutations are below threshold in their effects, or so drastic as to kill an individual before it can be observed, or in directions other than those subject to observation. There are, however, ways of making allowance for these, as by noting the effect on the data of extending the range of observation, and by taking especial note of genes in which large changes are seen to occur oftener than small ones that would also be readily detectable. Making such allowances, it appears probable that in *Drosophila* the overall frequency of mutations, under ordinary conditions, is such that something between one in ten and one in thirty germ cells carries in some one of its many genes a new mutation that arose in a cell of the parent. This figure does not make mutation in general appear so rare. But in terms of the individual gene, and the single cell cycle, it means that there is an average chance of less than one in a million of any given gene undergoing a mutation in any given cell cycle.

Stating the same result from another point of view, it may be said that the gene makes no mistake whatever in building its daughter gene, the daughter gene in building its own daughter, etc., throughout something like a million copyings carried on in series, so accurate is the duplication process. This makes the half-life of the individual self-duplicating gene in *Drosophila,* traced through one descendant gene taken at random at each doubling, until a 50 percent chance for its mutation has accumulated, over a thousand years and possibly longer than ten thousand. For different mutations, and different genes, there is, to be sure, a great range. And yet, for some widely different types of higher organisms, the present meagre evidence indicates that the given average figure in terms of cell cycles holds very roughly true, in general. On the other hand, where the cell cycles are of much longer duration, as in a man as compared with a fly, preliminary figures, such as those of Haldane (1935) and others, indicate a correspondingly greater stability per unit of time, with a half-life, for the few genes studied, that approaches the order of a million years.

The Blindness and Molar Indeterminacy of Gene Changes

If the primary cause of the adaptiveness of life processes lies in the natural selection of random mutations, then the individual mutations would not be expected to be adaptive, except as a result of a rare accident; in fact, the more elaborate a working organization already is, the more unusual would be a chance alteration that happened to improve it further. And in accordance with this it is found that the vast majority of the mutations that occur naturally are actually deleterious, and the larger the change involved the more harmful does it tend to be (Muller 1918, 1921b). This again confirms the inference that natural selection has been the indispensable guiding agency in biological evolution, and it indicates that most of the evolution has come about through the prolonged selective accumulation of a multitude of individually small mutations, chosen to form a system of gene products ever better integrated, internally, for taking advantage of conditions that would originally have been inhospitable. Thus, as Huxley (1942) has pointed out, the range of conditions open to the collection of species as a whole has widened, and also the range open to certain particular kinds of species, that may legitimately be called the progressive ones.

That the determining causes of the ordinary individual mutations lie in the realm of essentially uncontrollable submicroscopic events (rather than in the gross conditions thought of by earlier generations of biologists as the causes of inherited variations) is more particularly indicated by the revealing fact (gained as a result of the application of specialized methods) that when a particular gene undergoes a mutation, not only do the genes of other kinds in the same cell remain unchanged, but even its partner gene of identical type (originally derived from the opposite parent but now usually lying but a fraction of a micron away from it) also stays undisturbed. This proves that the disturbing process has an ultramicroscopic degree of localization, just as in the case of changes of individual molecules by thermal agitation. Some evidence that the individual events of thermal agitation are themselves responsible for mutation was gained from the finding, since confirmed by others, that, within the range of temperatures normal to the organism, a rise of 10°C causes a several-fold rise in the general gene-mutation frequency (Muller and Altenburg 1919; Muller 1928). In fact, as Delbrück (1935; see also Timoféeff-Ressovsky, Zimmer and Delbrück 1935) has since pointed out, the rise is of just about the amount to be expected on the basis of the absolute frequency at a given temperature, if the cause were thermal agitation.

But if any activations obtainable by thermal means at ordinary room temperatures can succeed in producing mutations, then surely the activations or ionizations of much higher energy content, produced by bombardment with X or gamma rays or by particles of similar energy, and perhaps even by ultraviolet, ought to produce correspondingly greater results. All this has proved to be decidely the case. Thus, it can be calculated from the results that the application of a half hour's treatment of 5000 r units of X rays to *Drosophila* spermatozoa at, say, 17°C causes a rise in the mutation frequency of about 50,000 fold, over what it would have been in the same period without the treatment. This effect of the X or gamma rays is produced by the activations or ionizations, or tiny ultimate clusters of ionizations, *acting individually*, since the frequency of the gene mutations induced is simply and directly proportional to the frequency of the induced ionizations, regardless, within very wide limits, of the size of the dose, the hardness of the rays, and their manner of distribution in time. As these individual "hits" must certainly be random, it is important to observe that the gene mutations produced by them in the flies are as a group indistinguishable from those occurring "spontaneously" and have a sensibly similar distribution of qualitatively different effects. This similarity then confirms our inference as to the essential randomness of the natural mutations also. However, it can be calculated that these could not, except for a few, have been produced by the sparse radiation present in nature but must rather have been produced by some form or forms of thermal agitation.

Mutational Evidence on Gene Structure and Size

A major purpose of our first radiation experiment had been to obtain evidence concerning the degree of inner particulateness of the gene, that is, to what extent it is compounded, like most macroscopic bodies, of several or many substantially identical, interchangeable components, such as molecules, all of them self-reproducing, as had often been assumed. It may in the first place be pointed out that such an assumption of compoundness seems opposed by evolutionary considerations. For if the gene were originally compound, in this sense, then by the separate mutation of any one of the parts, which should occur as a result of the individual impacts (unless one supposes a very specialized mechanism that always spreads such effects completely), a nonhomogeneity would be introduced into the compound gene. If this nonhomogeneity were to persist, then by successive mutations of one after another of the parts in different directions, accompanied by the selective survival of the more highly adaptive gene systems having greater complication, the genes of today would have become internally heterogeneous in regard to practically all their components and would no longer be merely compound, their compoundness having been replaced by complexity. Analogous to this is the evolutionary process whereby, within the chromosome as a whole, the genes themselves, originally alike, have differentiated from one another, as considerable evidence has shown.

But such nonhomogeneity within the individual gene could thus survive repeated gene duplication only if the inner parts of the gene, like the genes as a whole within the chromosome, are in entirely fixed positions with regard to one another, and if even in duplication they may not ordinarily substitute for one another (Muller 1926, 1927). If, on the other hand, following the mutation of a given component, one daughter gene may sometimes receive the two representatives of this component while the other does not receive either of them, but receives normal components instead, then, by a continuation of this process of inexact apportionment, some descendant cells would finally come to receive nothing but the mutated type of component within the gene in question, and others nothing but the original type. In this case then each gene would become again truly compound. Because it is a matter of chance to which pole of a dividing cell a given daughter gene is pulled, there would come about in consequence an irregular distribution of the cells of all-mutant type among those of mixed and of all-original type, as in an old fashioned crazy quilt. Further division must therefore result in whole batches of mutant cells interspersed among batches of nonmutant ones. Special attention was therefore paid to the distribution of mutant tissue with respect to normal tissue in cases in which mutations had been freshly induced, by irradiation, in a cell ancestral to the tissues studied. However, no crazy-quilt effects attributable to such an interchangeability of gene parts was found, among many cases in which it should have been found had it occurred.[3] It was therefore to be concluded that the parts of the gene, whatever they are, do have fixed positions and consequently are differentiated from one another, forming together one organized system. Either they constitute, together, just one molecule or megamolecule or, even if some of the parts are held together only by residual or van der Waals's forces, these parts are not merely repetitions of one another as in macroscopic bodies. Instead, the internal structure of the gene itself must be nonrepetitive, or, to use a term recently applied by Schrödinger (1945) to the succession of genes in the whole chromosome, aperiodic.

3. However, since the above was written, Auerbach has reported (personal communication) effects which might be interpreted in this way, obtained by the chemical treatment mentioned in the next section. It will be important to attempt to devise criteria here which might distinguish between the putative shuffling about of gene parts above considered and the origination of a mutant gene which was unstable for some chemical reason. The latter seems more probable in view of the X-ray results. One possible criterion would be the obtaining of evidence for or against the affected gene passing through different grades of instability as the cells containing it proliferate.

The fact that both intra- and intergenic relations turn out to be aperiodic makes more acute the question, raised by other considerations as well, as to how the limits of an individual gene may be defined. While the ultimate answer must be a chemical one, beyond present knowledge, it might meanwhile be held, theoretically, that one gene should designate an amount of genetic material so small that it cannot be further divided without loss of the property of self-duplication by at least one of the fragments. Substantially this definition, without use of the word "gene," was in fact given by Wilson in 1896 but there is no empirical test to establish the limits of the gene on these grounds and it is even possible that, so defined, the genes might be found to be overlapping.

There are at present, however, a number of empirical means for defining small bits of genetic material that remain capable of self-duplication as such, when detached from their original genetic neighbors and attached to others. In certain studies carried out for this purpose, there was evidence of a limit of size when X rays were the agents used to cause the breakage (Muller and Prokofyeva 1934; Muller 1935a). In these studies, some dozen breaks in a minutely delimited region of a chromosome were found to fall into just four definite positions, so far as these positions might be judged by the admittedly imperfect criterion of expecting effects to be produced on the characters of the organism by removal of the genetic material lying between two different positions of breakage. By measuring the proportion of the dark region of the salivary chromosome corresponding to the total length of the three breakage segments thus constituted, and then estimating the volume that this portion would occupy in the small mitotic chromosome, it was found that the individual segment, or "gene," i.e., that part included between any two most nearly adjacent positions of breakage, would occupy a space smaller than one-twentieth of a micron in diameter, if it were considered as compressed into a cubical form. How much smaller than this it may really be there is no means of knowing by this method. For, in the first place, there might have been interstitial genes that escaped us because their removal caused no lethal or other detected effect. Secondly, one does not know how much of the cytologically visible chromosome is occupied by the gene material itself, even in a mitotic chromosome. And, thirdly, the ultimate possible division of the genetic material may not have been attained by this method.

The above qualifications show, however, that the given value is certainly a maximum one for the size of a gene as thus defined. And this maximum value proves to be that of an object too small to be visible by ordinary microscopic methods. Moreover, even if a gene of this size were padded in its transverse directions with adventitious material, its length in the salivary chromosome turns out to be too small for it to be optically resolvable there. This maximal gene might be termed an X-ray breakage gene, without commitment as to whether or not its limits would eventually be found to coincide with those determined by some future more refined method. It happens, however, that this estimate agrees in a very rough way with others of the maximum possible gene size, based on calculations dealing primarily with gene number.

It is evident that if one had a minimum value for the number of genes and divided it into the total possible volume which they could occupy (represented by the mitotic chromosome volume), a maximum size can be converted into a minimum for gene number. Minimum number values were first derived from data on the frequencies of crossing-over between given genes (Muller 1916), in comparison with overall crossing-over frequencies, and later they were derived, in several different ways, from data on the frequencies of mutation of given genes (Muller and Altenburg 1919; Muller 1926), in comparison with overall gene-mutation frequencies. These various methods (including the above method based on breakage) was agreed sufficiently to show that, in the fruit fly at least, the number of genes is well over a thousand, perhaps as high as ten thousand. And there is always the possibility that, by some special means, the division might be pushed still higher. However, even taking the highest probable number of genes, the complexity and the degree of refinement in the determination of the organisms dependent upon them is so extreme as to require of the individual genes present in them today a very high degree of inner intricacy indeed, perhaps even greater than that which would be expected of the ordinary protein molecule.

Chemical and Physiological Influences
on the Mutation Process

It has sometimes been supposed that gene size can be taken as equal to the average number of atoms in the volume that includes one hit (one ultimate ion cluster) when a given mutation is produced, but this is probably an oversimplification. For one thing, the effective hit probably need not always strike the gene itself, for in the case of chromosome breaks at least it has been shown that two nearby breaks are sometimes caused simultaneously by a hit too small to have impinged upon both spots. In such a case, localized chemical changes must have been induced that spread a short distance beyond their point of origin and so, indirectly, caused the genetic change.[4] Thus, it is not only the amount of energy but its quality and form that count. This being the case, it is also unlikely that each hit on any part of the potentially "sensitive volume" at any time would always be effective in causing a mutation.

That this second stricture is correct is shown by the fact that certain states of the cells or chromosomes are much more vulnerable than others to the mutational effects of radiation. For these reasons, it is not surprising that species appear to differ significantly in the vulnerability of their genes to radiation mutations (though this is also open to other interpretations), and that, even within the same species, genetically different stocks sometimes differ greatly in their so-called "spontaneous" mutation frequency—a situation which by the way shows that the mutation frequency is itself subject to regulation through natural selection.

In view of all this, it is also to be expected that the so-called "spontaneous" mutations would tend to occur more often in some physiological conditions, regions of the body, or stages of

4. The criticism that the effects might have resulted from different hits in the course of one electron path appears invalidated by quantitative considerations and by the fact that with γ-rays, which produce hits much farther apart, the results seem substantially similar.

development, than others, and this might be important in its bearing on evolutionary potentialities. Till recently no certain and substantiated evidence of such effects on normal genes had been obtained, and even the highly pathological conditions that attend nearly fatal doses of various chemicals have not seemed conducive to mutation. It is true that some slightly positive results have in the past been reported from chemical treatments, but because of technical doubts these have not been widely accepted. In addition, rather mild effects have also been produced by "temperature shocks" in some apparently reliable experiments, yet in others even this agent has seemed ineffective. In the absence of more decisively positive and consistent effects, then, some authors have tended to treat mutations as the result of an inexorable statistical process, dependent purely on thermal agitation per se, together with such radiation as may be present, and therefore bound to accumulate at a practically constant time-rate at any given temperature, under ordinary conditions of natural radiation.

During the past two years, however, we have been conducting large-scale experiments on "spontaneous" mutations in *Drosophila* in which the frequencies from young individuals and those aged in various ways have been compared, and these show definitely, in harmony with certain earlier results of Russian and Indian workers (Sacharov 1939; Olenov 1941; Zuitin and Pavlovetz 1938; Singh 1940), that there are decided differences in the mutation frequencies of different stages. These may in fact explain the apparent effects of some of the tests of chemical and heat-shock treatments previously referred to, if the time and conditions of breeding were not well controlled in these cases. A more precise analysis of the physiological factors at work in our ageing experiments is much to be desired, but meanwhile a sort of net result already reached is the conclusion that, in *Drosophila* at least, the germ cells of older adults are no more, and in some cases not as much, contaminated by mutations as those of very young ones. This may involve a mechanism which has helped to make it possible for species like man, whose individuals live to be so much older than those of lower organisms, to escape the genetically damaging effects of too high a mutation frequency. And further, the practical breeding problem arises, whether reproduction by older or younger parents is genetically more desirable. If the situation in man is like that in flies, then, in view of the relaxation of selection obtaining in civilized man, the answer would be that it is genetically preferable to have reproduction by the older people, for this would actually delay the accumulation of mutations in the population.

Attacking the problems of chemical effects on mutation from another direction have been the very remarkable studies of Auerbach & Robson (1944) carried on in Edinburgh during the war years, beginning in 1941. In these it has been possible to show for the first time that there are whole groups of known substances, the application of which results in diverse gene mutations, as well as chromosome breaks, with frequencies comparable with those produced by considerable doses of high-energy radiation.[5] Among the other very interesting features of their results are evidences of delayed action in the production of some of the mutations. I have no right, however, to speak for these investigators in more detail, as most of their publication has been delayed by war conditions. In a paper just sent to press by Ernst Hadorn, another substance, phenol, is reported to be moderately effective in *Drosophila*, the technique of dipping the larval gonad in a solution of it being employed. And last year Emerson (1944) announced the obtaining of varied mutations in the fungus *Neurospora* by treatment with rabbit serum. The rabbits used had been immunized against the fungus, although it is not yet known whether this had anything to do with the effect. These three series of experiments constitute the first decided break in the impasse that had developed in studies directed towards the chemistry of the mutation process. The leads provided by them appear far reaching in their promise.

Evolutionary Indeterminacy?

Despite the success of these attacks it should be emphasized that in none of the cases has there been evidence of just specific muta-

5. Since the lecture was given, it has become permissible to reveal that mustard gas was the substance primarily dealt with in this work (see Gilman and Philips 1946).

tions being induced. The chemical processes have affected the frequency of gene mutation in general, but each individual mutation remains a chance and uncontrollable event, from the macroscopic standpoint, and is no doubt the result of a quantum exchange caused by the impact of a suitable form of thermal agitation or radiation, as the case may be. For such macroscopically indeterminate events to become expressed in those changes in the characteristics of the whole individual which can be seen directly there has to be an amplification, on each occasion, of the order of 10^{21} times, when considering the size of the gene in relation to that of, say a whole mammal. This amplification is, of course, attained by virtue of the gene's power of duplication during the growth of the individual, combined with its ability to affect catalytically the body of protoplasm far larger than itself which surround it in each cell. In reality, the amplification may be almost unlimitedly greater than this, since, if the mutation has been one of the beneficial ones, the organism containing it will tend to multiply many-fold during an unlimited succession of generations and so will serve as the basis for further mutations. Thus the quanta of physics become the quanta of evolution (Muller 1935b), and the ultramicroscopic events, with all the possibilities born of their statistical randomness and even of their ulterior physical indeterminacy, become translated into macroscopic ones with a magnification vastly surpassing that of such an instrument as the Gieger counter, and almost approaching, if not possibly some day exceeding that of the primordial cosmogenic quanta proposed by Haldane.

I do not wish to deny that in special cases mutations may occur predictably, but all the above evidence agrees in indicating that this must ordinarily be so rare as to have played comparatively little part in evolution. It would be of interest to show that, nevertheless, because of the orderliness of selection working on these random mutations, combined with the statistically great amount of mutational material which it has to work on, the direction of evolution is in large measure stable and determinate, up to a given point. It seems likely, however, that at certain special crises and turning points, where unusual changes or combinations of changes become important, evolution itself may sometimes become indeterminate, at least in a molar sense.

Nonchromosomal Genes

Evidence concerning the nature of the gene is to be gained not only from the genes in the chromosomes. Despite what has been said concerning the preponderantly chromosomal nature of species differences, it has been known since the work of Carl Correns over forty years ago that plastids of plant cells are self-duplicating bodies in the same sense as chromosomes. They differ very significantly from the chromosomes in their transmission, however, in that: (a) they do not have their two daughter plastids regularly allotted to different daughter cells at cell division, (b) they are included to only a very limited degree or, in some species, not at all, in the male germ cells, and (c) they do not undergo synapsis and orderly segregation in germ-cell formation. But, like the chromosomal genes, they are capable of undergoing rare, sudden, definite mutations, of diverse kinds, that are transmitted to the daughter plastid in duplication. Under special cellular conditions, the mutations of some plastids at any rate become more frequent, and so become themselves subject to some extent to gene control. Owing to their inexact distribution in cell division the plastids undergo a chance process of sorting out, after any mutation, until all the plastids in a cell are again alike. Because of this, together with the limited opportunity for formation of whole-plastid recombinations in sexual reproduction, the lack of crossing-over, and the relatively small quantity of genetic material each single plastid contains, the amount of evolution due to plastid mutations must be very small as compared with that based on chromosomes, and this is confirmed by analysis of species differences in plants. Animals get along without them. They are most plausibly conceived as having had a common ancestry with the chromosomal genes, dating back to the period before the latter had become organized into typical nuclear chromosomes.

Only recently have most geneticists awakened to the fact that there is still other genetic material, self-reproducing and probably mutable, in the cytoplasm of some plant cells at least, in the form of much smaller, perhaps ultramicroscopic particles, called by Darlington (1944) "plasmagenes." Again there seems to be no mechanism for their exact apportionment or effective recombination. This limitation, as with the "plastogenes," would provide explanation enough of the great rarity of cases of inherited differences due to this cause, as compared with cases of chromosomally inherited differences. It is not known to what extent the multiplication of different materials of this kind is subject to a unitary regulation, whether the amounts of each or of all present tend to reach stable equilibria, or whether they compete with one another in their multiplication, as some viruses do (Delbrück 1942), and so become mutually exclusive. At any rate, some of them are more vulnerable and subject to loss as a result of special conditions than are the chromosomal genes.

Cases of cytoplasmic inheritance in yeast found by Winge & Lausten (1940) were postulated by them to have their seat in mitochondria, particles which are not supposed to be derived, in any direct manner at least, from the chromosomes but are by some investigators classed with plastids. Yet in Lindegren's (1945) and Spiegelman's (1945) recent important work on cytoplasmic enzyme of yeast that seemed to play a part in its own production, clear evidence was obtained that the "cytogene," as they called it, is in the first place derived from, or at least dependent for its origination on, a particular chromosomal gene. Being liable to loss when its substrate is absent, it is necessary to have it renewable, in this way, from a more dependable genic source, even though it may be self-reproducing. It would seem highly significant for gene theory that the material in this case is itself an enzyme and, hence, is also presumably of protein nature. However, certain links of the evidence for proving that it is directly self-reproducing in the same sense as a gene, rather than of indirect aid for synthetic processes in general through its function in carbohydrate utilization, have yet to be made clear.

Until Sonneborn's (1943a,b,c; 1945a,b) remarkable findings in certain varieties of the peculiar one-celled animal *Paramecium*, no instances of self-reproducing substances in the cytoplasm of *animals* have been known, apart from some which, by reason of infectivity or curability or visible structure, have rightly or wrongly been attributed to minute parasites or symbionts. The so-called "kappa substances" in the *Paramecium* cytoplasm appear to be less fully self-reproducing than chromosomal genes, in that they require for their continued synthesis the simultaneous presence not only of themselves but also of specific chromosomal genes. Sonneborn believes that they are in fact parts or derivatives of these chromosomal genes, which have become detached for special reasons—reasons connected with the prior detachment and differentiation of a peculiar form of nucleus, the macronucleus, from a germinal or micronucleus. This work, like that on yeast, opens a new chapter in genetics and appears to afford a new angle of attack on gene problems in general. In common with the yeast work, it is at present in such a formative period that no attempt can be made to do it justice here. It should, however, be pointed out that, according to the theory proposed, the phenomena which may be studied in the cytoplasm are largely reflections of those which, in ordinary organisms, and even in other existing varieties of *Paramecia*, more primitive in this respect, are proper to the genes in the chromosomes. But, in the chromosomes, they are not isolable, and therefore escape detection as such.[6]

There remains room for the speculation, put forward by several authors, that in the cytoplasm of the body cells even of higher animals there may be plasmagenes, or "kappa substances," causing differences between tissues, and perhaps capable of mutating unfavorably so as to give rise to virus-like bodies, such as those of some cancers. Darlington (1944) has postulated that such genes and viruses might arise by the metamorphosis of ordinary cell proteins, and their combination with the cytoplasmic nucleic acid. There are additional possibilities, not necessarily exclusive of this or of one another, which require investigation. For example, Alten-

6. As proof of this article is returned to the press, Sonneborn has, in an address in the *Cold Spring Harbor Symposium on Heredity and Variation in Micro-organisms* (12 July 1946), undertaken a revision of the interpretation of these phenomena. He now regards the cytoplasmic substances in question as plasmagenes, not necessarily of nuclear origin though, like other known plasmagenes, capable of survival only in a given protoplasmic environment, in part conditioned by the nuclear genes.

burg (1946; personal communication early in 1945) has suggested that viruses which originally entered as invaders may in the course of evolution have become symbiotic or even necessary "viroids" that thereby take their place as part of the normal cytoplasimc equipment, subject, however, to mutations that may give abnormal effects.

But despite all present uncertainties regarding these crucial questions, the mass of evidence concurs in pointing to the exceeding rarity, at best, of effective genes in the cytoplasm of the *germ cells* of multicellular animals. Certainly this not because genes in the cytoplasm are impossible, but rather, as Darlington has pointed out, because they lack those potentialities for persistence and for evolution, dependent on fixed linear arrangement, that the genes which are tied together into chromosomes have developed. For this fixed linear arrangement has been a prerequisite in allowing, for the chromosomal genes, controlled duplication and apportionment, instead of competition or sorting out, for their progressive increase in number of types and differentiation from one another (see below), and for the effective means they have of forming new combinations.

Increase in the Number of Kinds of Chromosomal Genes

So far as the chromosomal genes themselves are concerned, there is every reason to infer that, being the product of an extended evolution, they cannot arise de novo by any sudden change from extra-chromosomal substances. True, it is known that the number of genes in the chromosomal germplasm can increase in evolution, but in these cases there is evidence that each chromosomal gene arises from a preexisting one. Occasionally this happens by a mere doubling of a whole chromosome or set of chromosomes, followed by their failure of separation into two daughter cells, but in cases that become permanently established it happens more often by the misplacement of a small piece of a chromosome, which becomes broken out and then inserted somewhere else into the line of a set of chromosomes that already contains the duplicate of this piece in its older position as well. Such an increase in gene number does not forever remain merely a change in the quantity or proportionate number of these genes. For in the course of geological time different mutations are bound to accumulate in the inserted group of genes from those that become established in the group that occupies the original position. Thus the germplasm becomes not merely more compound but more complex and, other things being equal, the possibility of organizational complexity for the body in general should rise also.[7]

On the Nature of the Self-duplication Process

All the above-mentioned studies and numerous others, many of them of a cytological nature, have helped to furnish a biological setting that should be of use in the coming *chemical* attack on the nature of the gene, on the mechanism of its self-duplication, its mutation, its behavior in meiosis, and its action on the organism. On the chemical side, it has become clear that the gene is really of nucleoprotein nature, since the work of Stanley and Knight (see their review, 1941), of Bawden and Pirie (see Pirie 1945) and of others has shown that even the virus particles infecting some plants, which fulfill the definition of genes in being self-determining in their reproduction and capable of transmitting their mutations, are composed of nucleoprotein, in fact, of *nothing but* nucleoprotein. This at the same time lends encouragement to the conception, though it does not by itself actually prove it, that the most primitive forms of life consisted of nothing else than a gene: that is, a bit of substance of specific chemical composition, nucleoprotein or proto-nucleo-protein in composition (possibly much simpler than the present-day material—see Muller 1926), which was capable of duplicating not merely itself but even its mutations, and which lost this ability on being divided further. Other work

7. These conclusions were reached at substantially the same time in the author's genetic analyses of the normal "scute" region in *Drosophila* and of the minute rearrangements to which it was found to be subject (Muller 1935c) and in the observations of Bridges (1935) on normal salivary gland chromosomes, in which "repeat" regions were microscopically evident.

has shown that nucleoprotein is also contained in viruses infecting animals and bacteria, and that it is contained in plastids, although in these cases there is other material present as well. However, the problems concerning how the nucleoprotein works in gene duplication and in other gene activities remain as yet almost an unworked field, so far as experimental evidence is concerned.

It has been misleading and unhelpful to refer to the self-duplication of the gene as "autocatalytic," and Troland's otherwise brilliant papers (1914, 1916, 1917) are marred by his insistence on this. For the term is a blanket one, referring merely to the end result, that more material of a given kind is produced if some of that material is present to begin with than if it is not. There are many totally diverse mechanisms by which such a result is brought about, and an understanding of one of them seldom helps with another. For example, the formation of pepsin from pepsinogen by the action of pepsin itself, which, as Herriott (1938, 1939; Heriott, Bartz & Northrup 1938) has shown, digests away in nonspecific fashion a certain part of the pepsinogen molecule, thus freeing the pepsin component, can have no relation to gene synthesis. Most autocatalytic reactions are mere accelerations of those which would otherwise take place anyway, but more slowly; this, too, is untrue of gene duplication. The example most commonly cited, crystallization, fails in several essential respects to be analogous to gene duplication. The most distinctive features of the latter, not found in the former, are that complicated chemical changes are induced by the self-duplicating agent that would not take place otherwise, and that from a heterogeneous medium which may be alike for many different agents and in this sense nonspecific, the given agent selects the components necessary for itself and arranges and combines them into a form modeled on its own. Accordingly, given a change (mutation) in the agent, a corresponding change is wrought in the identical product. It is this modifiability, leading to improvability, of the reaction, that allows it, unlike other so-called autocatalytic reactions, to form the basis of biological evolution and so of life itself. If, as Troland for instance thought, this were a common property of matter, all matter would be potentially living.

In an ingenious attempt to account for the nature of this autosynthetic reaction, Delbrück (1941), elaborating upon a suggestion by the Russian Frank-Kamenetzky (1939), has recently given a detailed but admittedly hypothetical picture of how amino-acids might conceivably be strung together in the same pattern as that in a preexisting gene model. On this scheme, peptide-precursors from the medium, having unfinished peptide links, become attached to the amino-acid residues corresponding to them in the polypeptide model, by means of a resonance occurring at the sites of the peptide links; this is followed by a finishing up of the peptide connections, and associated undoing of the resonance attachments between the old and the newly formed polypeptides. Although this scheme deserves serious consideration, it is not yet known that gene synthesis really involves the making of peptide links. For it is conceivable that the chains were ready made so far as the gene itself is concerned, and that the specific synthesis consists rather in the making of other connections, as between "R groups" of different parts of one or more chains, resulting in a special kind of folding and superstructure. It can be calculated, at any rate, that gene specificity can hardly reside merely in the linear arrangement of amino-acids in protamines like those which form the bulk of the material isolated from some fish sperm, since their paucity of kinds and regularity of order in the molecules investigated seems to be such as to allow less than a thousand possible combinations (author's calculation, unpublished). Such an objection would not necessarily apply, however, to protamines in a more polymerized condition (as they might be in the living material), or to other proteins of higher type (such as those reported by Stedman and Stedman 1943). However, it may be that an analogous mechanism of resonance could as well be used to explain the making of other connections than peptide groups, in imitation of those in a preexisting gene model.

In this as in previous proposals for explaining gene duplication, starting with Troland's, in 1914, the raw materials in the medium are supposed to become attached to like parts of the preexisting gene and so to arrive at the some arrangements as it has. As I pointed out in 1921, there is a known parallel for this in the phenomenon of synapsis, whereby like chromosome parts, that is, like individual genes, become attached to one another in twos, and one has only to suppose that this phenomenon may extend even to the parts of the gene as they are put together during the process of its duplication, to get an explanation of duplication in terms of this remarkable synaptic force. Delbrück and others also have adopted this view that the same principle is acting in gene synthesis and synapsis. Thus any knowledge of basic principles of synapsis, such as the fact that it appears to consist primarily of an attraction in twos, even when more than two like members are available, which would indicate a face-to-face attraction, may be expected to help, eventually, in the explanation of gene duplication also.

But whereas in Delbrück's and some other interpretations the like particles are in the first place brought into atomic distances of one another in the correct position purely by the accidents of thermal agitation—an agent the exactitude of which for the purpose is dubious—cytologists have long considered their observations to indicate that the attraction of like chromosome parts for like extends over microscopically visible distances. That the union is not merely due to a chance coming together of likes at some single point, followed by a zipper effect, is indicated, among other things, by some new observations of McClintock (1945). These show that in the meiosis of the fungus *Neurospora* the chromosomes regularly come into side-by-side contact while still in a condensed, closely coiled condition and only later become extended. But there is the apparently insuperable difficulty in attraction at a distance, pointed out by various physicists, that no spatial pattern of attractive forces could retain its specificity over a distance many times its own diameter, for the lines of force from different parts would become too dispersed and mixed with one another. It would therefore seem necessary, for explaining a self-specific pattern capable of operating at a distance, to postulate that it is expressed in the form of a temporal fluctuation, that is, a vibrational effect of some sort, varying with each gene. This would not be subject to the same limitation of distance as a spatial pattern, for its special characteristics and direction would to a considerable extent withstand both distance and intermixture with other patterns, just as is true of simultaneous musical notes. And although two such mutually attracting bodies would have to be in the right phases with respect to one another they would automatically tend to impress each other into such phases, as their state of least energy. I will not go into the further possibilities of this proposal, which have been put forward independently by Jordan (1938, 1939), myself (1941), and Faberge (1942), in rather different forms, following Lamb's (1908) proposal of such a scheme for centrosomes. It is true that objections have been raised to these ideas (Pauling & Delbrück 1940). In any case the effect would, if it exists, have to be derived from a peculiar dynamic condition within the gene, of a kind not hitherto touched upon by chemists.[8] Such an effect would demand detailed explanation, for it might well hold the secret of the uniqueness of the processes of both gene duplication and gene synapsis.

In most discussions of these phenomena it has been assumed that they are of a direct nature, involving the immediate union, or building, of like by like. But as Friedrich-Freksa (1940) pointed out, what *may* happen is the union of each part with an opposite or complementary part, which, serving as an intermediary, becomes in its turn attached to another component opposite or complementary to itself, and therefore like the first component. On this scheme, one of the two components is the protein of the gene, electrically negative because of its basic arginine, while the component complementary to this is a structure of nucleic acids, with its positive charges so arranged as to match the negative ones of the protein. The nucleic acid is then pictured as tending to hold a like protein on each side of it. By ordering the placement of heterogeneously arranged parts into proper pattern next to the original gene this two-step process was supposed to serve not only in the synapsis but also in the synthesis of the genes. Generalizing further, the author observes:

8. Since the presentation of the above passage, J. D. Bernal has stated (in a private communication) that he has inferred the existence of a vibrational attraction between viruses. In a paper by Bernal and Fankuchen (1941) evidence was given for long range attractions between viruses, caused by their ionic atmospheres according to the principles of Pieter Debye; granting these, it is only necessary to postulate regular periods for the size and shape of these atmospheres (cf. variable stars) to obtain temporally specified attractions.

Die hier entwickelte Vorstellung von der identischen Verdoppelung von Nucleinproteinen lässt sich vergleichen mit den Vorgängen, die wir von technischen Vervielfältigungsverfahren gewohnt sind. Die Reproduktion geht nie unmittelbahr, sondern immer nir auf dem Umweg über etwas Gegensätzliches vor sich. Die Gegensätze erhoben und tief, hell und dunkel, Bild und Spiegelbild, positive und negative Ladungen, Können zur Formwiederholung führen.

(The models of the identical duplication explained here can be compared with the processes with which we are familiar from mechanical duplication. The reproduction never takes place immediately, but always through some roundabout complementary way. Complementarity [high and low, light and dark, picture and mirror image, positive and negative charges] can lead to a structural reproduction.—Ed.)

It may be noted that this scheme does not seem to be capable, in the way Friedrich-Freksa thought, of explaining, by itself, specific attractions extending over microscopic distances. However, it might conceivably be modified to do so, by having the charges go through periodical changes, with complementary temporal patterns characteristic of the individual parts. In another respect also the scheme is incomplete, as in the protein the positions of only the arginine (or of the hexone bases in general) are accounted for by the nucleotide arrangements. Possibly other extensions of the hypothesis could be devised to alleviate this deficiency.

Another scheme using complementary unions had been proposed, for synapsis, by Lindegren & Bridges in 1938. They treated the gene as an antigen, against which an antibody became formed, that joined on to it, and this antibody in turn then tended to join on to the other gene of the same kind as well, thus bringing the two like genes together indirectly. Again, the process does not give long-range attractions. Emerson (1945), supported by Sturtevant (1944), has proposed essentially the same complementary mechanism for gene duplication. In this case, separate parts are not supposed to be collected from the medium since, following Pauling's idea, antibody formation involves only an appropriate folding of an already existing protein, to bring its parts into a relation complementary to the original in regard to surface shape and surface position of reactive groups. This corresponds most nearly to Friedrich-Freksa's category of *erhoben und tief* ("high and low"). Here, then, by the molding of a second antibody to the first antibody, the type of surface characteristic of the original antigen is supposed to be regained and the gene duplication is thus completed. It happens, however, that the "anti-antibodies" hitherto examined in serology do not fulfill this condition, as they involve different parts of the surface from those participating in the original antigen/antibody reaction, and are probably too imperfect anyway. Moreover, antibodies against proteins native to cells have not hitherto been found to be produced by them at all. But here, as before, it is hardly fair to require of a preliminary suggestion, lacking any experimental evidence, a complete solution, and various accessory hypotheses could doubtless be proposed for taking care of these difficulties.

On Possible Roles of the Nucleic Acid

Finally, however, some remarkable experimental evidence having a further bearing on gene chemistry has appeared, and from an unexpected quarter, namely, in investigations on the bacteria of pneumonia. Griffith (1928), in England, had shown in 1927 that under certain conditions pneumococci of one variety become somehow transformed into another by growing them in the presence of killed bacteria of that other variety. Avery, MacCleod, and McCarty (1944) have gone further, and have given evidence which they believe points to the conclusion that the effective substance in this treatment is the nucleic acid itself, of the variety to be imitated, in practically protein-free condition, and in fact that nucleic acid in its naturally polymerized form. If this conclusion is accepted, their finding is revolutionary, no matter whether, with these authors, one adopts the radical interpretation that a transformation of the genetic material in the treated organisms has been induced, converting it into material like that used in the treatment (cf., "Kappa substances?"), or whether it is supposed that genetic material of the donor strain actually becomes implanted within the treated strain and multiplies there, or whether the material used in the treatment is regarded as merely exerting a selective action so as to favor the survival of such exceedingly rare spontaneous mutants as happen by accident to agree with the other variety.[9] There are certain obvious tests for distinguishing between these very different possibilities. But, in any case, it would be proved that the substance used for treatment is able to assume highly individualized forms, capable of influencing cell metabolism in far-reaching and specific ways. And so, if this substance really is composed solely of nucleic acid, it would follow that the tetranucleotides, despite their relative uniformity, have richly varied and specific forms of polymerization that give them very diverse and distinctive properties.

9. Since the above was written, and just as this paper was about to be sent in, Delbrück, speaking at the Mutation Conference in New York City on 26 January 1946, reported an instance of apparent transformation of one strain of bacteriophage by another, though in respect of a portion only of its properties. In this case, the rate of change is so high as to exclude the hypothesis of spontaneous mutation and selection. In my opinion, the most probable interpretation of these virus and *Pneumococcus* results then becomes that of actual entrance of the foreign genetic material already there, by a process essentially of the type of crossing-over, though on a more minute scale. At the same conference, on 28 January, A. E. Mirsky gave reasons for inferring that in the *Pneumococcus* case the extracted "transforming agent" may really have had its genetic proteins still tightly bound to the polymerized nucleic acid; that is, there were, in effect, still viable bacterial "chromosomes" or parts of chromosomes floating free in the medium used. These might, in my opinion, have penetrated the capsuleless bacteria and in part at least taken root there, perhaps after having undergone a kind of crossing-over with the chromosomes of the host. In view of the transfer of only a part of the genetic material at a time, at least in the viruses, a method appears to be provided whereby the gene constitution of these forms can be analysed, much as in the cross-breeding test on higher organisms. However, unlike what has so far been possible in higher organisms, viable chromosome threads could also be obtained from these lower forms for in vitro observation, chemical analysis, and determination of the genetic effects of treatment.

The question thus becomes acute whether it is really the nucleic acid or, as has commonly been thought, the protein, which is primary in determining the differences between genes, or whether, as a third possibility, the two are of comparable value and, perhaps, complementary in some sense as Friedrich-Freksa proposed. The hope of further analysis of gene structure through extensions of this method rises high. It may perhaps provide us at the same time with the first instance of that Eldorado of geneticists, directed mutation, although the geneticist characteristically insists on being driven to this conclusion before accepting it.

Recently, until this *Pneumococcus* work, what has increasingly seemed to be the most plausible chemical role for the nucleic acid in the gene has lain in its possible contribution to the energetics of gene reactions, and it is very likely, even now, that this too will somehow fit into the picture. As the beautiful work of a considerable group of biochemists has been showing, some of the nucleotide fractions of nucleic acid, or close derivatives of them, are fundamental in those varied processes of the cell where it is necessary to effect a transfer of energy from a substance or group of substances relatively rich in energy to one relatively poor, with resulting synthesis, mechanical work, secretion against osmotic pressure, or other form of potential energy storage. Often, an energy-rich phosphate bond is used by the nucleotide for the transfer. Even amino-acids may be strung into polypeptides by such a mechanism, if a hypothesis of Lipmann (1941) is correct. Thus it may be that nucleic acid in polymerized form provides a way of directing such a flow of energy into specific complex patterns for gene building or for gene reactions upon the cell.[10] But to what extent the given specificity depends on the nucleic acid polymer itself, rather than upon the protein with which it is ordinarily bound, must as yet be regarded as an open question.

10. Since the presentation of the above passage (which is unchanged from that of the original lecture) Spiegelman, at the Mutation Conference in New York in January 1946, independently proposed the same view for the role of the nucleic acid of the gene and presented supporting evidence for it, derived from his experiments on yeast.

On the Nature of Gene Effects

Concerning the nature of the primary reactions of the gene, in producing its effects upon the cell, there is as yet almost as much ignorance, so far as real experimental evidence goes, as there is concerning gene duplication. It has usually been assumed, perhaps gratuitously, that the gene acts here through its protein component. De Vries (1899) long ago suggested that the primary product is much like the gene itself and produced by a process akin to its duplication, and he thought that this product then migrates into the cytoplasm to do its work. Since Driesch (1894), also in the last century, suggested that the hereditary determiners act as "ferments," that is, enzymes, it has been easy to conceive of the different genes, or these supposed products that represent them, as carrying out all sorts of catalytic reactions by means of their surface structure, and since Troland's (1914, 1916, 1917) able advocacy of this idea, which he called the "Enzyme Theory of Life," it has been especially popular. On different variants of this view, the original gene itself, in situ in its chromosome, thus acts as a heterocatalytic enzyme, or products like itself and still surrounding it in the chromosome do this work, or products like it that migrate out. The apparently self-reproducing melibiozymase reported by Lindegren (1945) and Spiegelman (1945) in the cytoplasm of yeast, derived originally from a chromosomal gene, would seem to be an example of the last-mentioned type.

It is at least evident that if the primary gene products are *not* like (or complementary to) the gene itself, and so are not produced by a process akin to gene duplication, then the gene must certainly act as an enzyme in producing them, whatever they are, otherwise it itself would get used up. Since different enzymes can initiate or accelerate the most varied types of reactions, the primary products of gene activity would in that case be correspondingly varied and would belong to no one category of substances. If, on the other hand, the primary gene action is to produce more molecules similar in composition (or complementary) to itself, or to a part of itself (but perhaps unable to reproduce themselves further), it would be taking too much for granted to assume that the process of their production was an enzymatic one in the usual sense. For, as has been seen, gene duplication probably involves a very special kind of mechanism that it would be misleading casually to lump with that of heterocatalytic enzymes, at least until more is known about it. And the gene products themselves, in case they were produced by such an essentially autosynthetic process, would not necessarily have to act as enzymes either: that is, they might actually become used up in the reactions which they in turn take part in, inasmuch as the original gene would presumably be able to replace them by the same autosynthetic process as before. This is not to deny, however, that they *could* act as enzymes, in some cases at least, particularly if they represented the protein component of the gene.

Hence, despite the appeal of simplicity presented by the view in question, it seems too early to conclude that either the gene or its primary products do always, or usually, acts as enzymes. One should be even more cautious in assuming, conversely, that most enzymes represent primary gene products. It has long been known, to be sure, that various identified enzymes in the cytoplasm are gene-determined, like everything else in it. And this method may be used, as in the remarkable studies of George Beadle and his coworkers on *Neurospora,* to analyse in great detail, by the comparative chemistry of different mutants, how various complicated nets of chemical processes in the cytoplasm are carried out. For each step at least one enzyme usually seems to be required. However, the fact that an enzyme has been found to be lost, incapacitated, or changed as a result of the mutation of a given gene by no means proves that it has been directly derived from that gene, and further work may show that in some or most of these cases mutations in various other genes can affect the given enzyme as much.

Somewhat similar considerations apply concerning the relations between genes and proteins in general, including protein antigens. Only if the primary products of genes were autosynthetically produced would it seem probable that they were always proteins (if one overlooks the possibility of their representing only the polymerized nucleic acid component instead). And while any higher protein may serve as an antigen, such an autosynthetic relation would still be far from a proof of the converse proposition, that all (or most) protein antigens are primary gene products. The modifiability of the antigenic properties of proteins is in fact against this view. It is, of course, true that if a class of substances were found, such that each member of the class was never dependent for its production on more than one gene, these substances would in all probability be primary gene products. It has been thought that such evidence existed in the case of the antigens dealt with in intra- and interspecific blood and tissue transfusions and transplantations. However, the relatively few cases where one of these antigens has been found to arise only in the presence of a given combination of two or more different genes are enough to cast serious doubt on this conclusion. For the gene differences dealt with in any given test are usually but a small sample of all the genes in the genotype. And if, even in this small sample, two are found which interact in the production of an antigen, it can be calculated that, if the whole genotype could be considered, the number of antigens found to be produced by interaction would probably be far higher than the maximum number produced singly. It would accordingly seem necessary to have an enormous body of data of such a kind before it could be proved by this method that any given class of isolable substances usually constitute primary, unmodified gene products. And it may well be that new methods will be needed before the primary gene products can be identified as being such.

Whatever the primary or remote gene products, it seems likely on general considerations that there is a limited number of possible types of building blocks in the gene, and that genes differ only in the arrangements and numbers of these. Under differences in arrangement may here be included not only changes in the linear sequence of amino-acids in the polypeptide chains but also changes in shape, involving folding of the chains, and attachments between R groups, whereby their active surfaces would acquire very different chemical properties. In this way radically diverse organic compounds may be pictured as being formed under the influence of different genes in the cell.

Most of the mutations leading to the different compounds of a relatively simple type as compared with proteins (so-called "extractives" and prosthetic groups, vitamins, the common monosaccharides, lipoids, etc.) seem to have occurred in the lengthy evolution that must have intervened between the early virus and the bacterial stage. For bacterial protoplasm is, fundamentally, surprisingly like ours in innumerable complicated details. A large part of the evolution beyond the unicellular stage, on the other hand, has involved changes in the time and space patterning of materials which themselves were much like those already present in one-celled organisms. Included here were alterations in the sizes and proportions of parts, relative rates of growth, placing and timing of ingrowths and outgrowths, of contractile or supporting fibres, etc. Moreover, most of these changes can be seen to have derived their selective advantage from the effects of these redistributions themselves, rather than from the chemical changes behind the latter. It is true that even the redistributions must have had a chemical basis, but it seems unlikely that most of them are due to the formation of new prosthetic groups or of other substances which, as compared with proteins, are relatively simple. Rather does it seem likely that largely the same stock outfit of these substances became modified in their rate, place, and time of action by more subtle changes in the proteins, including the enzymes, with which the simpler substances interact, and which undoubtedly interact also with one another in the determination of such effects. The quantitatively variable character of protein-with-protein reactions renders them especially suitable for such adjustments in degree, rate, and time-and-space pattern of effects.

It must of course be the future task of biochemistry, combined with genetics, to unravel the whole complicated web of protoplasmic and bodily interactions, from the primary gene products to the last phenotypic effects. In this work, as I stated in an earlier paper (1933), the production of a change in any individual gene provides us with what is, "in effect, a scapel or injecting needle of ultramicroscopic nicety," for "experiments in which the finest, most fundamental elements of the body fabric are separately attacked." Such studies as those on pigment production in flowers and in insect eyes, on the synthesis of amino-acids and vitamins in *Neurospora*, and on the trains of effects following given mutations in mice and in poultry, illustrate the progress which this general method is capable of making. It can, of course, be vastly extended, as when, for example, not only the substances that naturally diffuse out of cells but also those obtainable by extraction are employed in the tests of the effect of one strain on another, and when in addition to the processes known as "autotrophic" the large number that have to do with higher conversions and utilizations are brought into the picture, as by analogous cross-tests of mutations that prove lethal even in the presence of media adequate for ordinary saprophytes. The tracing of the courses of reaction of the substances in question will need even more refined biochemical methods but, proceeding from step to step, and with the aid also of the tracer isotopes now becoming more available, it should provide a field which for a long time will be ever more fertile in results. Most difficult of all, it may be anticipated, will be the working out of the details of protein structure and reactions (and perhaps that of nucleic acid polymers). At present, such work with proteins themselves is in its earliest stages, and adequate methods have still to be worked out, but one can at least see that the field is there.

"Position Effect"

In considering the way in which genes exert their effects, some evidence from genetics may be mentioned which indicates that even the same gene nucleoprotein may react very differently in the presence of unlike physical influences from other nucleo-proteins nearby. Reference is made here to the peculiar finding that in *Drosophila* genes may be induced to undergo changes in their effects even without intrinsically conditioned gene mutations, merely by shifting their position in the chromosome and so giving them different gene neighbors. If many generations later replaced in their original positions, they resume their previous mode of action. It is conceivable that these "position effects" are due to localized chemical reactions between the products of nearby genes. But it seems more likely that they are caused by changes in shape of the gene, which give it a different amount or even direction of effectiveness (Muller 1935d). As the degree of change in the effect would necessarily depend also upon other cellular conditions, varying with the region of the body, it is not strange that positionally induced changes have been observed in the patterning of an effect as well as in its general quality or intensity.

Such positional changes in gene shape might conceivably arise directly from the synaptic forces exerted by the neighbor genes. For the same force which, when applied to like genes, causes a uniform attraction of all parts, might affect the parts of different genes unevenly, so as to warp them. Or, as Ephrussi and Sutton (1944) have plausibly suggested, and as some recent evidence tends to favor, the cause of the shape changes might in some cases lie in the degree or type of coiling of the chromosome thread, a condition which in its turn is influenced by synaptic forces. Considering the matter more broadly, the result further suggests that many actual gene mutations also may owe their effects to changes in the gene shape, but that, in those cases, the changes are permanent, inwardly conditioned ones.

If the extraordinary results reported by Noujdin (1936, 1938, 1944) are taken at their face value, results studied further by Prokofyeva-Belgovskaya (1945), there is in addition an inter-mediate class between permanent gene mutations and immediate position effects, involving semipermanent changes of the gene inducible by a special type of positional influence, and capable of being repeated in gene duplication long after the influence has been withdrawn, but gradually subsiding. These cases, more especially, seem to be best understood as due to differences in coiling, if one takes into consideration in this connection the work not only of Noujdin, and of Prokofyeva-Belgovskaya, but also of Ephrussi and Sutton (1944), and of Ris and Crouse (1945). At any rate, the changes lie in the degree of "heterochromatiza-tion," whatever this may finally turn out to mean. A peculiar case of semipermanent change reported by Sonneborn (1943c) may lie in a different category.

The Recombining of Genes

There are grounds for the inference that higher organisms repre-sent the accumulation of millions of separate mutational steps.

Each one of these was an exceedingly rare event, probably occurring, on the average, in considerably less than one in a million germ cells. Moreover, each such event had to be followed by a long process of selective multiplication of the mutated gene, extensive enough to overcome the original excessive majority against it. A second favorable mutation does not get a foothold in an asexually reproducing line until, on the average, as many individuals bearing the first mutation have already been produced as may be expected to include a favorable mutation again. Owing to the small selective advantage usually possessed even by a successful mutation, this will probably take thousands of generations. That may not be so bad for bacteria and forms below them, as they reproduce so rapidly and present so inordinately many individuals for the selective process. In addition, they benefit by not having so many directions in which change must be almost simultaneously coordinated before it can become decidely advantageous. But for higher forms, where the opposite of all these conditions obtain, geological time would have been insufficient to bring their evolution to anything like its present state, had not a great innovation been instituted, namely, sexual reproduction.

Sexuality really opened the door of the germplasm not merely to one other individual, but through it to a congress of the population as a whole. After the establishment of sexual reproduction, mutations no longer had to wait their turn in line, but those occurring anywhere throughout a species could become multiplied simultaneously and could meanwhile become combined with one another. Moreover, multitudinous combinations could thus be tested out as combinations. This was a great cooperative genetic undertaking, in which the contributions of all were pooled for the common benefit, a circumstance which multiplied their mutational resources and the speed of their evolution over what it would otherwise have been.

For the sexual process to succeed in giving this genetic advantage in organisms with a complex genotype, not only some sort of fertilization process but also the essentials of the mechanism of meiosis, including some sort of synapsis, segregation, and whatever else is necessary for orderly recombination of genes, had to operate, for it is the final recombination that counts. And in this recombination it can be calculated that crossing-over must usually make a much larger contribution to the potential speed of evolutionary change than does the random assortment of genes lying in different chromosomes, contrary to some current opinion.

Crossing-over thus turns out to be the key process in sexual reproduction. The basis which made it possible for the chromosomal genes to have developed crossing-over lies not only in their linear attachment to one another but also in certain of their other fundamental properties. Among these are to be noted especially their specific autoattraction, the essentially "by twos" nature of this attraction, the ability of the chains of genes to develop tensions in spiralization, and the capacity of broken ends to reunite. And all of these properties, by the way, have come to light chiefly as a result of studies of crossing-over.[11]

One reason why it has been necessary for organisms to take so many mutational steps as to require crossing-over for their accumulation is because so many of the successful steps must be very minute. Their minuteness is indicated by the exceeding delicacy of adjustment of quantitative characters which often obtains, a degree of precision which must have been attained through many small whittlings, so to speak. The phenomenon of dominance of normal genes over most of the more frequently appearing mutants provides one line of evidence for a long and as it were invisible selective process, as Fisher (1928, 1930) first pointed out, and as has been accepted either in the original or a modified form by most geneticists. Analysis of species differences also shows that numerous small steps have usually been involved. Striking evidence of the meticulousness of selection is further given by the phenomenon in *Drosophila* called "dosage compensation" (Muller 1932). This is too complicated to be explained here, but the conclusion to be drawn from it should nevertheless be stated. That is, that the degree of development of the visible characters studied has commonly been determined

11. If these are in fact very fundamental properties of linearly attached genes, it would not be so surprising that a process of crossing-over should occur even in bacteria and viruses, as suggested in a preceding footnote.

through the action of past selection to a nicety considerably exceeding human powers of optical discrimination.

For the almost continuous range of genetic variation which this implies, the changes possible in proteins seem especially suited. It will, however, be realized that, as a result of any given character having been determined through such a multitude of variations, especially if these are mainly protein in the basis of their action, the analysis of the biochemical details involved in the production of just this one character becomes a task requiring an army of investigators, even at a stage of scientific development in which adequate methods for protein study have become available.

The Survival of Mutated Genes

The process of gene mutation which made the attainment of our present stupendously complicated, integrated organizations possible, is still going on. In itself mutation is really a disrupting, disintegrating tendency, like the thermal agitation which seems mainly to cause it. For the overwhelming majority of mutations are bad, and it is only the Maxwell demon of selection inherent in gene duplication, that is, the differential multiplication of the mutations, which brings order out of mutation's chaos despite itself. Let the previous course of selection be relaxed through natural or artificial means, and the tendency to disorder and degeneration gains and lowers the level. That is, not merely evolution of a species to its present state, but even its maintenance requires a continuance of selection, for the gene population is always in a dynamic equilibrium between mutation and selection, not statically fixed. Any cross-breeding population always contains many harmful genes, most of them recessive and seldom manifesting themselves, inherited from tens and hundreds of generations back. But they are ordinarily not increasing in number because an equilibrium has been reached at which they die off, through the death or failure to reproduce of some of the individuals that do manifest them, at a rate as fast as new ones appear through mutation, as Fisher (1930), Wright (1931), and Haldane (1927), more especially, have pointed out.

From some imperfect human data one may calculate (unpublished) that probably the great majority of persons possess at least one recessive gene, or group of genes, which, had it been inherited from both parents, would have caused the death of the given person between birth and maturity. (And this does not include those which kill off just prenatal stages.) That such genes are not still more abundant is only due to the fact that, in the past, the individuals getting the genes from both parents did die. If one could and would let them live and breed without limit, their number would creep up until finally it would be a case of treating everyone for everything—for thousands of things besides those ailments now known—and thus, in fact, making completely artificial men.

I am not arguing here against medicine and better conditions and against compensating for hereditary lacks by environmental benefits, otherwise I should be arguing against myself and my children and against all other persons and their children. Only one must recognize and somehow make the best of the inexorable rule that practically every mutation, even a "small" and nonlethal one, with the rarest of exceptions, requires finally a genetic death, that is, a failure to live or to breed, somewhere along the line of its descent, if the population would remain genetically at par. For each mutation, then, a genetic death—except in so far as, by judicious choosing, several mutations may be picked off in the same victim. If new mutations occurred in one germ cell in ten, as perhaps in flies, then this (with the reservation just mentioned) would be the proportion of genetic deaths of individuals eventually required. If, as could easily happen, by reason of the prevalence of injudicious X-ray treatment, exposure to artificial radioactivity or to special chemicals, or unwise average age of parenthood, the mutation frequency became doubled or tripled, so as to be increased to one in five, or one in three, then the proportion of genetic deaths, and of those manifesting the mutant characters, would finally rise correspondingly, before attaining its equilibrium value.

It would, however, be many centuries before these effects were fully manifest, and it might be that before that time a way would have been discovered of identifying mutants in the germ-cell stage and selecting them out then, or of reducing the frequency of mutation, or even of directing mutations. Moreover, the most constructive task is not that of merely keeping undesirable mutant genes down to a reasonably low level, but of fostering that timy minority of possible types having biologically progressive effects, in which lie all the genetic hope of the future. All this seems very utopian now, and quite out of harmony with the recent pronouncement of a most eminent and influential American scientist who has stated that the aim of "biological engineering," as he calls it, is the provision of "better food and clothing" (perhaps for Americans?). It is also out of harmony with the strong negative correlation between education or I.Q. rating and rate of reproduction, found in modern civilized communities generally, including the U.S.A. and even the USSR (see Price 1939). But does it not seem proper to think in utopian terms in a year which has marked the greatest revolution of all time in man's powers over his physical environment and in which at the same time, as by a double miracle, the interrelations of man with man also are being consciously reorganized on a grand scale (though just now preeminently on this island as a model), in such a way as may yet be fitting to control for our common benefit these and other physical powers that transcend the rights of individual manipulation?

But before any kind of conscious guidance over our own genetic processes would be attempted, it is to be hoped that education would lead us gradually to desire it, so that it became an entirely voluntary concern of all, and that increasing understanding and a better developed social consciousness would help us in revising our judgments as to what was really important and what was really desirable. As a part of all this there would be required a growth in our appreciation of the importance of the factors of the physical and especially of the social environment in the determination of human traits, since, in regard to his most salient characteristics, his psychological ones, man is by far the most plastic, somatically, of all organisms. So much is this the case that, in the realm of the psychological, most of the differences commonly regarded as due to genes are usually only characteristics that have been superimposed by training or by largely unwitting conditioning. The costly lesson taught us by the terrible Nazi perversion of genetics should help to make these facts better realized.

Surely, however, it will not be our desire, after understanding the manner of origin of the organization we have inherited, to remain forever content with merely maintaining or even making the most of that inheritance which we already have, without adding to it. For mankind is cursed or blessed with what has been called "the divine discontent," which drives him even further everywhere. With knowledge comes power, and as the use of power cannot forever be denied it will behoove us in the biological as in the physical field to develop also wisdom, including that social attitude which is a part of wisdom. With power so used, indeed, the wisdom could be further increased, self-multiplied, by genetics in combination with other methods, to a degree which would seem to be unlimited. Thus the self-reproduction of the gene and the self-reproduction of intelligence would reinforce one another in an ascending curve.

The day seems far off for so using our knowledge of the gene, but in these times of rapid movement in the physical and social realms, we might as well recognize this even more distant star to which our biological wagon is hitched. Meanwhile, for today, we must remove our gloves, and be content to work with our fingers in the protoplasmic mud, to get the heavy wheels of our science turning. And in this work, if we can cause even a little movement forward, that should be sufficient adventure for our own little lives.

References

Alexander, J; and Bridges, C. B. 1929. Some physiochemical aspects of life, mutation and evolution. *Colloid Chem.* 1:9–58.

Altenburg, E. 1946. The viroid theory in relation to plasmagenes, viruses, cancer, and plastids. *Amer. Natur.* (in the Press).

Auerbach, C., and Robson, J. M. 1944. The production of mutations by allyl isothiocyanate. Nature, 154, 81.

Avery, O. T.; MacCleod, C. M.; and McCarty, M. 1944. Studies on the chemical nature of the substance inducing transformation of Pneumococcus types. J. Exp. Med. 79:137–58.

Bernal, J. D., and Frankuchen, I. 1941. X-ray and crystallographic studies of plant virus preparations. J. General Physiol. 5:111–65.

Bridges, C. B. 1935. Salivary chromosome maps. With a key to the banding of the chromosomes of Drosophila melanogaster, J. Hered. 26: 60–64.

Darlington, C. D. 1935. The time, place and action of crossing-over. J. Genet. 31:185–212.

Darlington, C. D. 1944. Heredity, development, and infection. Nature, 154:164–169.

Delbrück, M. 1935. Uber die Natur der Genmutation und der Genstruktur. Dritter Teil: Atmosphysikalisches Modell der Genmutation. Nachr. Ges. Wiss. Gottingen, Math.-phys. Kl., Biol., N.F., 1:223–34.

Delbrück, M. 1941. A theory of autocatalytic synthesis of polypeptides and its application of the problem of chromosome reproduction. Cold Spring Harbor Symp. Quant. Biol. 9:122–26.

Delbrück, M. 1942. Bacterial viruses. Advance Enzymol. 2:1–32.

Emerson, S. 1944. The induction of mutation by antibodies. Proc. Nat. Acad. Sci., Wash., 30:179–83.

Emerson, S. 1945. Genetics as a tool for studying gene structure. Ann. Missouri Bot. Garden 32: 243–49.

Ephrussi, B., and Sutton, E. 1944. A reconsideration of the mechanism of position effect. Proc. Nat. Acad. Sci., Wash., 30: 183–97.

Fabergé, A. C. 1942. Homologous chromosome pairing: the physical problem. J. Genet. 43: 121–144.

Fisher, R. A. 1928. The possibe modification of the response of the wild type to recurrent mutations. Amer. Natur. 62: 115–26.

Fisher, R. A. 1930. *The genetical theory of natural selection.* Oxford: Clarendon Press.

Frank-Kamenetzky, D. A. 1939. Resonance theory of autocatalysis. *C. R. Acad. Sci. U.R.S.S.,* N. S., 25: 669–70.

Friedrich-Freksa, H. 1940. Bei der Chromosomenkonjugation wiksame Krafte und ihre Bedeutung fur die identische Verdopplung von Nuceloproteinen. *Naturwissenschaften,* 28: 376–79.

Gilman, A., and Philips, F. S. 1946. The biological action and therapeutic application of the B-chloroethyl amines and sulfides. *Science* 103: 409–15, 436.

Griffith, F. 1928. The significance of pneumococcal types. *J. Hyg. Camb.,* 27: 113–59.

Haldane, J. B. S. 1927. A mathematical theory of natural and artificial selection. *Proc. Camb. Phil. Soc.* 23: 834–44.

———. 1935. The rate of spontaneous mutation of a human gene. *J. Genet.* 31: 317–26.

Heitz, E., and Bauer, H. 1933. Bewise fur die Chromosomennatur der Kernschleifen in den Knauelkernen von *Bibio hortulanus* L. (Cytologische Untersuchungen an Dipteren, I). *Z. Zellforsch.* 17: 67–82.

Herriott, R. M. 1938. Isolation, crystallization, and properties of swine pepsinogen. *J. General Physiol.* 21: 501–40.

———. 1939. Kinetics of the formation of pepsin from swine pepsinogen and identification of an intermediate compound. *J. General Physiol.* 22: 65–78.

Herriott, R. M., Bartz, Q. R.; and Northrup, J. H. 1938. Transformation of swine pepsinogen into swine pepsin by chicken pepsin. *J. General Physiol.* 21: 575–82.

Horowitz, N. H. 1945. On the evolution of biochemical synthesis. *Proc. Nat. Acad. Sci., Wash.,* 31: 153–57.

Huxley, J. 1942. *Evolution: The Modern Synthesis.* New York: Harper and Bros.

Jordan, P. 1938. Zur Frage einer spezifischen Anziehung zwischen Genmolekulen. *Phys. Z.* 39: 711–14.

Jordan, P. 1939. Zur Quanten-Biologie. *Biol. Zbl.* 59: 1–39.

Koltzoff, N. K. 1934. The structure of the chromosomes in the salivary glands of *Drosophila*. *Science* 80: 312–13.

Lamb, A. B. 1908. A new explanation of the mechanism of mitosis. *J. Exp. Zool.* 5: 27–33.

Lindegren, C. C. 1945. Mendelian and cytoplasmic inheritance in yeast, *Ann. Missouri Bot. Garden* 32: 107–23.

Lindegren, C. C., and Bridges, C. B. 1938. Is agglutination an explanation for the occurence and for the chromomere-to-chromomere specificity of synapsis? *Science* 87: 510–11.

Lipmann, F. 1941. Metabolic generation and utilization of phosphate bond energy. *Advance Enzymol.* 1: 99–162.

McClintock, B. 1945. *Neurospora* I. Preliminary observations of the chromosomes of *Neurospora crassa*. *Amer. J. Bot.* 32: 671–77.

Miescher, F. 1897. *Die histochemischen und physiologischen Arbeiten*. 2 Leipzig: Vogel.

Minchin, E. A. 1916. The evolution of the cell. *Amer. Natur.* 50: 5–39, 106–19.

Muller, H. J. 1916. The mechanism of crossing-over. *Amer. Natur.* 50: 193–221, 284–305, 350–66, 421–34.

————. 1918. Genetic variability, twin hybrids, and constant hybrids, in a case of balanced lethal factors. *Genetics* 3: 422–99.

————. 1921. Mutation. Read before Int. Eugenics Congr., New York. Publ. 1923 in *Eugenics, Genetics, and the Family* 1: 106–12.

————. 1922. Variations due to change in the individual gene. *Amer. Natur.* 56: 32–50. Read before Amer. Soc. Natur. Toronto, 29 Dec. 1922.

———. 1926. The gene as the basis of life. *Proc. 4th Int. Congr. Plant Sci. (Ithaca)*, 1: 879–921 (publ. 1929).

———. 1927. The problem of genic modification. *Ver. V. int. Congr. Verebungswiss. Z. indukt. Abstamm.-u. VererbLehre,* Suppl. 1: 234–60 (publ. 1928).

———. 1928. The measurement of gene mutation rate in *Drosophila,* its high variability, and its dependence upon temperature. *Genetics* 13: 279–357.

———. 1932. Further studies on the nature and causes of gene mutations. *Proc. 6th int. Congr. Genet. (Ithaca)* 1: 213–55.

———. 1933. The effects of Roentgen rays upon the hereditary material. *The Science of radiology,* pp. 305–18. Springfield, Ill.: Charles C. Thomas.

———. 1935a. On the dimensions of chromosomes and genes in Dipteran salivary glands. *Amer. Natur.* 69: 405–11.

———. 1935b. The status of the mutation theory in 1935. Read at de Vries Memorial Meeting, Leningrad, Nov. 1935. Publ. in *Pravda,* no. 6 pp. 40–50. (1936), and under title "The present status of the mutation theory," in *Curr. Sci.* Special no., March, pp. 4–15 (1938).

———. 1935c. The origination of chromatin deficiencies as minute deletions subject to insertion elsewhere. *Genetica.* 17: 237–52.

———. 1935d. The position effect as evidence of the localization of the immediate products of gene activity. *Summ. Commun. 15th Int. Physiol. Congr.* (Leningr.-Mosc.), 286–89; and *Proc. 15th Int. Physiol. Congr.* (Leningr.-Mosc.), pp. 587–589 (1938).

———. 1941. Resumé and perspectives of the symposium on genes and chromosomes. *Cold Spring Harbor Symp. Quant. Biol.* 9: 290–308.

Muller, H. J., and Altenburg, E. 1919. The rate of change of hereditary factors in *Drosophila. Proc. Soc. Exp. Biol., N. Y.,* 17: 10–14.

Muller, H. J., and Prokofyeva, A. A. 1934. Continuity and discontinuity of the hereditary material. *C. R. Acad. Sci. URSS,* N. S. 4:74–83. (Reprinted in revised form, 1935, under title, "The individual gene in relation to the chromomere and the chromosome," *Proc. Nat. Acad. Sci., Wash.* 21: 16–26).

Noujdin, N. I. 1936. Influence of the Y-chromosome and of the homologous region of the X on mosaicism in *Drosophila* 137: 319–20.

———. 1938. A study of mosaicism of the eversporting displacement type in *Drosophila melanogaster. Bull. Biol. Med. Exp. URSS* 5: 548–51.

———. 1944. The regularities of the heterochromatin influence on mosaicism. (Russ. with Eng. sum.) *J. Gen. Biol.* (U.S.S.R.) 5, no. 6: 357–89.

Olenov, J. M. 1941. The mutational process in *Drosophila melanogaster* under avitaminous B_2 conditions. *Amer. Natur.* 75: 580–95.

Oparin, A. I. 1938. *The origin of life.* New York: The Macmillan Co.

Painter, T. S. 1933. A new method for the study of chromosome rearrangements and the plotting of chromosome maps. *Science* 78: 585–86.

Pauling, L. and Delbrück, M. 1940. The nature of the intermolecular forces operative in biological processes. *Science* 92: 77–79.

Pirie, N. W. 1945. Physical and chemical properties of tomato bushy stunt virus and the strains of tobacco mosaic virus. *Advance. Enzymol.* 5: 1–30.

Price, B. 1939. An interpretation of differential birth-rate statistics. *Proc. 7th Int. Congr. Genet:* 241–42.

Prokofyeva-Belgovskaya, A. A. 1945. Heterochromatization as a change in the chromosome cycle. (Russ. with Eng. sum.) *J. Gen. Biol. (USSR)* 6, no. 2: 93–124.

Ris, H., and Crouse, H. 1945. Structure of the salivary gland chromosomes of Diptera. *Proc. Nat. Acad. Sci., Wash.* 31: 321–27.

Sacharov, W. W. 1939. The mutation process in ageing sperm of *Drosophila melanogaster* and the problem of the specificity of the action of the factors of mutation. (Submitted to 7th Int. Genet. Congr. 1939) mim. 1941, *Dros. Inf. Serv.* 15: 37–38.

Schrödinger, E. 1945. *What is life?* New York: Cambridge University Press.

Singh, R. B. 1940. The influence of age and prolongation of larval life on the occurence of spontaneous mutations in *Drosophila.* (Ph.D. diss., University of Edinburgh).

Sonneborn, T. M. 1943a. Gene and cytoplasm. I. The determination and inheritance of the killer character in variety 4 of *Paramecium aurelia. Proc. Nat. Acad. Sci., Wash.* 29: 329–38.

———. 1943b. Gene and cytoplasm. II. The bearing of determination and inheritance of characters in *Paramecium aurelia* on the problems of cytoplasmic inheritance, *Pneumococcus* transformation, mutation and development. *Proc. Nat. Acad. Sci., Wash.* 29: 338–43.

———. 1943c. Acquired immunity to a specific antibody and its inheritance in *Paramecium aurelia. Proc. Ind. Acad. Sci.* 52: 190–91.

———. 1945a. Gene action in *Paramecium. Annals Missouri Bot. Garden.* 32: 213–21.

———. 1945b. The dependence of the physiological action of a gene on a primer and the relation of primer to gene. *Amer. Natur.* 79: 318–39.

Spiegelman, S. 1945. The physiology and genetic significance of enzymatic adaptation. *Annals Missouri Bot. Garden* 32: 139–63.

Stanley, W. M., and Knight, C. A. 1941. The chemical composition of strains of tobacco mosaic virus. *Cold Spring Harbor Symp. Quant. Biol.* 9: 255–62.

Stedman, E., and Stedman E. 1943. Distribution of nucleic acid in the cell. *Nature,* 152: 503–4.

Sturtevant, A. H. 1944. Can specific mutations be induced by serological methods? *Proc. Nat. Acad. Sci., Wash.* 30: 176–78.

Timoféeff-Ressovsky, N. W., Zimmer, K. G., and Delbrück, M. 1935. Über die Natur der Genmutation und der Genstrucktur. Vierter Teil: Theorie der Genmutation und der Genstruktur. *Nachr. Ges. Wiss. Gottingen* (Math.-phys. Kl., Biol.), N. F. 1:234–41.

Troland, L. T. 1914. The chemical origin and regulation of life. *Monist* 22: 92–134.

———. 1916. The enzyme theory of life. *Cleveland Med. J.* 15: 377–87.

———. 1917. Biological enigmas and the theory of enzyme action. *Amer. Natur.* 51: 321–50.

de Vries, H. 1899. *Intracellulare Pangenesis.* Jena.

Wilson, E. B. 1896. *The cell in development and inheritance.* New York: Columbia University Press.

Winge, O., and Laustsen, O. 1940. On a cytoplasmic effect of inbreeding in homozygous yeast. *C. R. Ser. Physiol.* 23: 17–39.

Wright, S. 1931. Evolution in Mendelian populations. *Genetics* 16: 97–159.

Zuitin, A. I., and Pavlovetz, M. T. 1938. Age differences in spontaneous mutation in males of *Drosophila melanogaster* of different origin. *C. R. Acad. Sci. URSS* N. S. 21: 50–52.

Bibliography of Other Relevant Literature

Altenburg, E. 1930. The effect of ultra-violet radiation of mutation. *Anat. Rec.* 47: 383.

Altenburg, E., and Muller, H. J. 1920. The genetic basis of truncate wing—an inconstant and modifiable character in *Drosophila*. *Genetics* 5: 1–59.

Bernal, J. D. 1940. Structural units in cellular physiology. *The Cell and Protoplasm* Pp. 199–205. New York: Science Press.

Bjerknes, F. V. 1900–1902. *Vorlesungen uber hydrodynamische Fernkrafte nach C. A. Bjerknes' Theorie*, 2 vols. Leipzig.

Blackwood, O. 1931. X-ray evidence as to the size of a gene. *Phys. Rev.* 37: 1698.

Caspersson, T. 1939. On the role of the nucleic acids in the cell. *Proc. 7th Inter. Genet. Congr.* Pp 85–86.

Darlington, C. D. 1932. *Recent advances in cytology*. London: J. and A. Churchill Ltd. (2nd ed. 1937).

———. 1937. The biology of crossing-over. *Nature* 140: 759–61.

———. 1939. *The evolution of genetic systems*. New York: Cambridge University Press.

———. 1942. Chromosome chemistry and gene action. *Nature* 149: 66–68.

———. 1945. The chemical basis of heredity and development. *Discovery* (March: 79–86).

Darlington, C. D., and La Cour, L. F. 1945. Chromosome breakage and the nucleic acid cycle. *J. Genet.* 46: 180–267.

Delbrück, M. 1944. Problems of modern biology in relation to atomic physics. Lectures at Vanderbilt University School of Medicine (Mimeographed.)

Demerec, M. 1933.. What is a gene? *J. Hered.* 24: 369–78.

———. 1935. Role of genes in evolution. *Amer. Natur.* 69: 125–38.

———. 1938. Eighteen years of research on the gene. *Publ. Carnegie Inst.* no. 501: 295–314.

Driesch, H. 1894. *Analytische Theorie der organischen Entwicklung*. Leipzig. Ellenhorn, J.; Prokofyeva, A. A.; and Muller,

H. J. 1935. The optical dissociation of *Drosophila* chromomeres by means of ultraviolet light. *C. R. Acad. Sci. URSS,* N. S. 1:234, 242.

Engelhardt, W. A., and Ljubimova, M. D. 1939. Myosin and adenosinetriphosphates. *Nature* 144: 668–69.

Greenstein, J. P. 1944. Nucleoproteins. *Advance. Prot. Chem.* 1: 209–87.

Greenstein, J. P., and Henrette, W. V. 1941. Physical changes in thymonucleic acid induced by salts, tissue extracts, and ultraviolet irradiation. *Cold Spring Harbor Symp. Quant. Biol.* 9: 236–54.

Gulick, A. 1938. What are the genes? I. The genetic and evolutionary picture. *Quart. Rev. Biol.* 13: 1–18.

————. 1938. What are the genes? II. The physio-chemical picture; conclusions. *Quart. Rev. Biol.* 13: 140–68.

————. 1941. The chemistry of the chromosome. *Bot. Rev.* 7: 433–457.

————. 1944. The chemical formulation of gene structure and gene action. *Advance Enzymol.* 4: 1–39.

Haldane, J. B. S. 1932. *The causes of evolution.* London: Harper and Bros.

Hollander, A. 1939. Wave-length dependence of the production of mutations in fungus spores by monochromatic ultra-violet radiation. *Proc. 7th Int. Congr. Genet.* Pp. 153–54.

Horowitz, N. H.; Bonner, D.; Mitchell, H. K.; Tatum, E. L.; and Beadle, G. W. 1945. Genic control of biochemical reactions in Neurospora. *Amer. Natur.* 79: 304–17.

Knapp, E., and Schreiber, H. 1939. Quantitative Analyser der mutationsauslosenden Wirkung monchromatischen U.-V.-Lichtes in Spermatozoiden von *Sphaerocarpus. Proc. 7th. Int. Congr. Genet.* Pp. 175–76.

Lea, D. E. 1940. A radiation method for determining the number of genes in the X-chromosome of *Drosophila*. *J. Genet.* 39: 181–88.

Luria, S. E., and Delbrück, M. 1943. Mutations of bacteria from virus sensitivity to virus resistance. *Genetics* 28: 491–511.

Marshall, W. W., and Muller, H. J. 1917. The effect of long continued heterozygosis on a variable character in *Drosophila*. *J. Exp. Zool.* 22: 457–70.

Mirsky, A. E. 1943. Chromosomes and nucleoproteins. Advance. *Enzymol.* 3: 1–34.

Moglich, F., and Schon, M. 1938. Zur Frage der Energiewanderung in Kristallen und Molekulkomplexen. *Naturwissenschaften* 26: 199–200.

Morgan, T. H. 1926. *The theory of the gene*. New Haven Conn.: Yale Univ. Press.

Morgan, T. H., and Bridges, C. B. 1919. The inheritance of a fluctuating character. *J. Gen. Physiol.* 1: 639–43.

Morgan, T. H.; Sturtevant, A. H.; Muller, H. J., and Bridges, C. B. 1915. *The mechanism of Mendelian heredity*. New York: Henry Holt and Co. (Rev. ed. 1923).

Muller, H. J. 1929. The method of evolution. *Sci. Mon.* 29: 481–505.

———. 1932. Some genetic aspects of sex. *Amer. Natur.* 66: 118–38.

———. 1934. Radiation genetics. (Abstr.) *Verh. 4 int. Kongr. Radiol.* (Zurich) 2: 100–2.

———. 1936. The need of physics in the attack on the fundamental problems of genetics. *Sci. Mon., N. Y.* 44: 210–14.

———. 1946. Age in relation to the frequency of spontaneous mutations in *Drosophila*. *Yearb. Amer. Phil. Soc.* 1945: 150–53.

Oliver, C. P. 1930. The effect of varying the duration of X-ray treatment upon the frequency of mutation. *Science* 71: 44–46.

Painter, T. S. 1934. A new method for the study of chromosome aberrations and the plotting of chromosome maps in *Drosophila melanogaster. Genetics* 19: 175–88.

Pauling, L.; Campbell, D. H.; and Pressman, D. 1934. The nature of the forces between antigen and antibody and of the precipitation reaction. *Physiol. Rev.* 23: 203–19.

Plough, H. H. 1941. Spontaneous mutability in Drosophila. *Cold Springs Harbor Symp. Quant. Biol.* 9: 127–36.

Schultz, J. 1943. Physiological aspects of genetics. *Annu. Rev. Physiol.* 5: 35–62.

Schultz, J. 1944. The gene as a chemical unit. *Colloid chemistry; theoretical and applied.* 1, 819–850, ed. by J. Alexander. New York: Reinhold.

Stadler, L. J. 1932. On the genetic nature of induced mutations in plants. *Proc. 6th Int. Congr. Genet.* 1: 274–94.

Stadler, L. J. 1939. Genetic studies with ultra-violet radiation. *Proc. 7th Int. Congr. Genet.* Pp. 269–76.

Sturtevant, A. H. 1917. An analysis of the effect of selection. *Pub. Carneg. Inst.* no. 264.

Tatum, E. L., and Beadle, G. W. 1945. Biochemical genetics of *Neurospora. Annals Missouri Bot. Garden.* 32: 125–29.

Timoféeff-Ressovsky, N. W. 1934. The experimental production of mutations. *Biol. Rev.* 9: 411–57.

————. 1935. Uber die Natur der Genmutation und der Genstruktur. Erster Teil. Einige Tatsachen der Mutationsforschung. *Nachr. Ges. Wiss. Gottingen,* Math.-phys. Kl., Biol. N. F. 1: 190–217.

————. 1937. Experimentelle Mutationsforschung in der Verebungslehre. Beeinflussing der Erbanlagen durch Strahlung und andere Faktoren. *Wiss. Forsch. Ber. Naturw. Reihe,* 42. Dresden and Leipzig: Theodore Steinkopff.

Waddington, C. H. 1939. The physiochemical nature of the chromosome and the gene. *Amer. Natur.* 73: 300–314.

————. 1939. *An introduction to modern genetics.* London: Allen and Unwin.

Wright, S. 1941. The physiology of the gene. *Physiol. Rev.* 21: 487–527.

————. 1945. Genes as physiological agents: general considerations. *Amer. Natur.* 79: 298–303.

Zimmer, K. G. 1935. Uber die Natur der Genmutation und der Genstruktur. Zweiter Teil: Die Treffertheorie und ihre Beziehung zur Mutationsauslosing. *Nachr. Ges. Wiss. Gottingen.* Math.-phys. Kl., Biol. 1:217–23.

The Darwinian and Modern
Conceptions of Natural Selection

MULLER's claim that Darwin's theory of evolution "was undoubtedly the most revolutionary theory of all time" requires a thorough philosophic analysis of evolution and its implications. This Muller tries to provide. He seeks out the real meaning today of "natural selection" and explores the false conflicts between continuous and discontinuous evolution, between stability and change, between blind chance and apparent long-term trends. Muller also challenges many naive interpretations of evolution: that species benefit from "a large reserve of hidden recessives" in the event of a sudden change in environment; that the dominance of genes is nearly complete; that species must be geographically isolated to generate new species. Most important to Muller was Darwin's integrity in rejecting the internal driving and perfecting forces that have repeatedly been used to nullify the most revolutionary attribute of evolution and man's arrival on earth, "the only possible scientific interpretation, that of the natural selection of essentially blind variations."

Darwin's theory of evolution through natural selection was undoubtedly the most revolutionary theory of all time. It surpassed even the astonomical revolution ushered in by Copernicus in the significance of its implications for our understanding of the nature of the universe and of our place and role in it. Surely, the most miraculous seeming phenomena in existence are the superlatively intricate organizations of plants and animals (including ourselves), with their manifold complications all directed, as if by design, towards an end—that of perpetuating their own kind.

Even the general idea of evolution, shared by not a few before Darwin, did not help, fundamentally, to explain how this result had been attained. For, so long as evolution was thought to be guided chiefly by an internal perfecting principle, or by the direct action of external conditions, or by the inheritance of adaptive effects of use, principles all of which were advocated by Jean Baptiste Lamarck, men were no nearer a real solution of what caused the changes to form a working system that was for the organism's benefit. In lieu of an explanation, in fact, they started out by assuming the prior existence of the main thing to be explained, namely, design, but they assumed its existence in a generalized and insubstantial form that was even more miraculous than the specific forms in which, on this view, it finally crystallized. Thus it remained for Darwin—and independently although in lesser degree Alfred R. Wallace—to provide the only possible scientific interpretation, that of the natural selection of essentially blind variations. Moreover, Darwin's masterly marshalling of the evidence for this, and his keen-sighted development of many of its myriad facets, remain to this day an intellectual monument that is unsurpassed in the history of human thought.

It is true that Darwin did defer to past views enough to accept to some extent the ideas of directive change of heredity by "definite" environmental "effects on the reproductive system," as he termed them, and by the inheritance of effects of use and disuse. But he pointed out that these supposed processes would be insufficient by themselves to explain the origin of adaptations in general. And he showed that, in many kinds of cases, as in neuter insects and in numerous ecological adaptations, natural selection by itself must have achieved the whole of the remarkable organization found. It is also true that a few others before Darwin and Wallace, going back at least as far as Empedocles and Aristotle, had occasionally had glimpses of the idea of natural selection. So did, in a much more cogent and modern way, Dr. W. C. Wells, originally of Charleston, S.C., in 1813.[1] But all these fore-

1. See Shryock, R. H. 1946. The strange case of Wells' theory of natural selection, in *Studies and essays in the history of science and learning in*

runners had only applied this notion in a very limited manner, or to a limited group of organisms, and had missed the chance of elaborating upon how it served as the grand clue to the whole system of developments.

The word Darwinism then, should rightly connote *the* distinctive contribution of Darwin and Wallace—natural selection as the key to evolution in general. This contribution stands not merely unimpaired today but corroborated and implemented in innumerable ways. It is curious however that, on the official and compulsory Soviet view, Darwinism means everything except this: that is, it means everything that Darwin had grudgingly borrowed from pre-Darwinian times. Natural selection, in so far as it means the supplanting of one kind of individual by another of the same species—and in this intraspecific competition Darwin as well as modern students of the subject see its chief means of operation—is explicitly denied on this anachronistic version of Lamarckism, which uses Darwin's name.

It is unfortunate that Herbert Spencer proposed the expression "survival of the fittest" for Darwin's very apt term "natural selection," and that Spencer's expression was accepted even by Darwin himself, as well as by many others, as equivalent to Darwin's own. For the word "fittest" in Spencer's phrase can only be properly defined as meaning "having such a character as better to survive." Thus his expression, taken literally, must be translated as reading: "the survival of those that survive." This tautological form has led people into philosophical muddles and has caused them even to question the validity of the entire concept. However, the underlying idea is of course not "the survival of the survivors," nor in fact, mere survival in itself. It is the principle that there is, in the first place, *heritable* variation in *different directions,* and that this is followed by *differential* survival and *multiplication* of the variants. We might abridge it all more accurately by terming this "the differential multiplication of diverse variations," but "natural selection" is terser. Moreover, Darwin's own term is the more explana-

---

honor of George Sarton; also Zirkle, C. 1941. Natural selection before the origin of species, *Proc. Amer. Philos. Soc.* 84:71–123; and Kofoid, C. A. 1943. An American pioneer in science, *Sci. Mo.* 57: 77–80.

tory, because it calls to mind the analogous and more familiar process of artificial selection. In both the terms natural and artificial selection, after the tacit assumption has been made that the variants can be multiplied *as such,* the emphasis is on a wide range of choice for this multiplication process. For without this diversity of material the term "selection" would be meaningless. The adaptiveness of the products of evolution follows this, as a necessary consequence of this wide range of natural choice, and so the process as a whole is quite appropriately called "natural selection."

Of course all matter, inanimate as well as animate, is to some extent subject to variations of diverse kinds, some more conducive to survival than others. But what makes living matter so uniquely subject to indefinitely accumulated evolutionary accretions is the fact that its variations are, as we say, heritable, which really means that they can be multiplied. They have to be multiplied differentially because, as Malthus and following him Darwin pointed out, there is obviously far too little room and means of subsistence for all descendants, i.e., there is a "struggle for existence." But if there were infinite room and means of subsistence, and if all descendants could somehow be kept alive, still the very fact of the multiplication of diverse variations, without its being differential, would eventually result in the stepwise origination of all the forms of life we have today.[2] However, in that case the forms corresponding to our living ones, though in absolute numbers as great as today, would be so vanishingly few, relatively to the total, as to be lost in it. For that total, including all the conceivable "misfits," would be so stupendous as not to be containable in a universe of universes.

An indefinitely continued and quite unrestricted multiplication of variations, then, would in the end, through the sheer numbers attained, give opportunity for the most improbable of all arrangements, namely, complexly working adaptive organizations like ourselves, to come into existence without design. They represent

---

2. We neglect here the selective influence of elimination in restricting the process of intercrossing, and in this leading to a concentration of different adaptive variations within particular lines of descent.

however the almost infinitely rare, the most select, combinations of chances. *Differential* multiplication, with its struggle for existence, allows these to be generated practically in this imperfect world, despite its physical limitation of room, and in fact as if there were infinite room for them, by eliminating those others which would stand in their way and simply giving reign to their own natural powers of multiplication and further variation. If those who found it inconceivable that such complicated organizations could arise by a succession of "chance events" would take the trouble to reckon what an infinitesimal proportion of the total number of trials made in an unrestricted multiplication process these successes represent, they would arrive at a figure so staggeringly minute as to be quite commensurate with their quality, as I have pointed out on a previous occasion.[3]

The one great requisite for all this is the possession by living matter of the property of multiplying its variations. It is just this that, in our view, most fundamentally distinguishes living matter from nonliving. And it is this that distingiushes what we now recognize as the gene, whether it lies in the chromosome or elsewhere, from the rest of living matter. This makes the gene prior and basic and makes the rest of living matter only a complex resultant, which arose as a series of by-products of the gene's variations that happened to be useful in furthering the multiplication of these genes, and hence of the organisms containing them.[4]

In view of this evolutionary mechanism it is semantically confus-

3. The argument in this and the preceding paragraph was set forth in greater detail in the author's 1929 paper, The method of evolution, *Sci. Mo.* 29: 481–505. There it was also pointed out that even multiplication is not, theoretically, necessary for the result, if the number of individuals finally reached by multiplication had somehow been provided from the beginning, and if all had simply been kept in existence and allowed to vary in diverse directions with the same frequency and permanency as if they had multiplied. But again, the total number required would be great far beyond all bounds of possibility, and the adaptively organized product would form but an infinitesimal part of this total.
4. This was pointed out in the author's 1922 paper, Variation due to change in the individual gene, *Amer. Natur.* 56:32–50. Timoféef-Ressovsky has termed this process "convariant reproduction."

ing to dispute as to whether natural selection is "creative," for the answer depends only on our definition of that word. We have just seen that if selection could be somehow dispensed with, so that all variants survived and multiplied, the higher forms would nevertheless have arisen. This shows that the *vis a tergo* here is not selection but diverse variation and the multiplication of variations. Yet in actuality this situation is impossible, and so it is selective elimination which gives the conditions under which the "fitter," and they alone, can really assume their shapes. This process is far more "creative" than the pruning of a tree, to which it has sometimes been compared, and more creative even than the whittling of wood from a block to form an image which, among an infinite number of other potential images, had, in a sense, lain latent within the block. If this is not actual creation, then no sculptor creates his statues, and no poet, in selecting his particular words out of an almost infinite number of possible combinations, creates his verses.

As for providing the diverse range of material needed for natural selection, Darwin laid emphasis upon what he called "individual variations," which he regarded as being produced by the "indefinite effects," as he put it, of external conditions acting "upon the reproductive system" in no directive way. He regarded the production of these variations, unlike that of the supposed "definite effects" previously referred to, as governed by the operation of "chance" factors, which at bottom, however, were subject to natural law. These indefinite effects, according to him, embraced most of the differences, of varying size but usually small, distinguishing individuals of the same population. Darwin also recognized noninheritable differences but said that he was not concerned with them. That most of the inheritable individual differences were not directively induced by given conditions of the general environment he considered evidenced by the fact that the same kinds so often occurred under different kinds of environment, and by the converse fact that different kinds occurred under the same kind of environment.

As previously stated, however, Darwin believed that there were also directed, or as he called them "definite" heritable variations, caused by particular types of changes in conditions. These variations on his view tended to make the population as a whole vary in a given direction, but he ascribed to them a minor role. Not presenting a wide range of choice, they could not solve the general problem of adaptation. Along with such definite variations we might here include also characters acquired by use and disuse if, as Darwin thought, they might be inherited.

Modern genetics has substantiated and intensified Darwin's main conclusion concerning the variations that furnish material for evolution. Studies of spontaneous and induced gene mutations have shown the practical independence of the types that occur from the kinds of environmental conditions prevailing, even in bacteria. This is certainly true so far as any directive effect of environment on evolution is concerned. There is also evidence that, under any known conditions, the adaptive mutations form an exceedingly small minority of them all, as would be expected on a chance relationship of adaptive effect to type of condition. The manner of variation of their total frequency with the amount of thermal agitation and of radiation present, and the relative indiscriminancy with which the different genes are affected by such chemical agents as are known to be mutagenic, are telling facts in this connection. They demonstrate that mutations, in general, have their basis in ultramicroscopic accidents occurring on a molecular and submolecular level, and that the amount and form of energy required for the different gene mutations are very similar. Thus Darwin's so-called "indefinite" effects of environment on individual variation are not only proved to exist but made in a general way understandable, in terms of our modern knowledge of the finer structure and behavior of matter. It thus becomes clear that the nature of the gross environmental conditions, such as climate, food, or opportunity for exercise of this or that type, is of little or no practical importance, in the origination of the so-called "indefinite" variations.

At the same time careful study has shown, in all cases well analyzed, the nonexistence of the "definite" or the directive type of inheritable change in the individual gene. We need except here only some cases of abnormal, so-called "mutable genes," but these are now suspected of involving atypical chromosome breakage and union of pieces, and they are in no sense to be considered as adaptive to the special conditions that produce them. Moreover, unlike what Darwin thought, even a *change* of a given kind in environmental conditions is found not to be in itself a cause of the putative variations of "definite" types, i.e., of variations in a prevailing direction, different from the direction otherwise found. In believing that this phenomenon does exist, Darwin had been misled by the increased number of deviant individuals or varieties of particular kinds found under changed conditions, although he himself had warned of the difficulty of distinguishing between the effect of selection, in giving such results, and effects due to differences in the process of variation itself.

As for the inheritance, from one generation of multicellular individuals to another, of characters acquired by the somatic tissues, this group of readers need not be told that, with the passing decades, more and more evidence has accumulated against the existence of any such process in nature. This generalization is not threatened by the occasional cases of transmission, through the germ cells, of microorganisms, viruses, or other gene-containing bodies or genes, that can be acquired by some sort of infection. For no general mechanism for the inheritance of adaptive somatic modifications is thereby provided. The same stricture applies for the "plasmagene" and "plastogene" types of inheritance that have been found in some microorganisms and throughout the plant kingdom.

There used to be much argumentation as to whether the main material for natural selection was furnished by so-called "continuous variations," or by "discontinuous" ones, and for a time the latter were identified with the "mutations" of de Vries. Darwin actually made no sharp distinction here but realized that there are all degrees of change, with the larger steps, especially those giving distinct abnormalities, the rarer. And he held that the very large steps were much less likely to be advantageous, and so to furnish favorable material for natural selection. In this matter we now stand much closer to the view of Darwin than to that of de Vries. This despite the fact that our modern knowledge of the small steps of individual variation proves them to be mixtures, individually almost unravelable, of small mutational differences with the continuous, noninheritable somatic modifications.

We have evidence that, in general, mutations giving small phenotypic changes arise more frequently than those giving large ones. It is also clear that the large changes are on the average correspondingly more disadvantageous. Moreover, crosses between varieties or species show that tiny steps, occurring in multiple factor systems, usually form the basis of the observed differences between the groups, especially where these differences themselves are relatively large.

With Darwin we believe that the greater disadvantageousness of a larger change, in cases in which the main feature of such a change is advantageous in its direction and even in its magnitude, if considered by itself, is due to the correlation of other characters with the primary one. This works out in two ways. First, a mutation causing a more drastic change in one character is apt to entail, at the same time, larger and on the whole more harmful changes in other characters as well. Second, the large change in the primary character, even if it would, when able to function adequately, be more advantageous than a smaller one, meets with the difficulty of finding itself with a system of coexisting characters that have not yet been brought up to its level, so to speak. An example of the latter relation would be a case in which larger size appeared without the disproportionately larger muscle and bone cross section, and the more pillar-like leg structure, required to support and move the increased mass. For the above two reasons, then, most selected steps will be small. And the taking of many small steps in the same direction by a given character will be deferred, to allow the correlatively necessary steps in other features to be taken, virtually *pari passu*. As for the relatively few large mutational steps allowed to gain a foothold, these will have to become elaborately "buffered," as Julian Huxley terms it, by small "modifying" mutations that take care of their disadvantages, before evolution can proceed again in the same direction. Thus evolution is caused to move slowly and for a long time in a given direction, as Darwin pointed out. And the effect was seen by him to be one of selection—or as it has recently been termed, "orthoselection"—rather than of "orthogenesis" in any of its older meanings.

Of course, as he also saw, there is often a further reason for such continued change in one direction, lying in the fact that the environmental conditions to which the organism is adjusting may themselves continue to change in a given direction. This is especially true when some character or group of characters of other organisms, which are undergoing their own evolution, constitute the key environmental condition for the organism primarily in question. Sometimes indeed this relation is mutual, the changes in the "primary" organisms giving by reaction changes in the others which then react back upon the first organism and so, step by counterstep, through ecological channels, result in a long drawn out evolutionary chase. An example of this is seen in the parallel increases in the wearability of mammalian teeth and in the silica content of vegetation; another is seen in cases of mimicry in which the mimicked type tends to become selected away from the mimicking while the latter follows after. None of this gradual evolution is opposed to modern mutation theory but, on the contrary, it is to be expected of it.

In line with this emphasis on small steps it is increasingly found that, as Darwin had thought, even small differences are of importance in survival. So much is this the case that, as modern genetics has discovered, selection has brought into being morphogenetic and physiological systems that give a high stability of development to the characters of organisms in the face of varying outer conditions which would, but for these special regulating mechanisms, cause much more considerable fluctuations in them. In part, this stabilization has been accomplished by increasing the potencies of the genes more primarily concerned with a given character to a near-saturation level, while keeping their final effects down to the optimal through groups of "modifying genes." Pertinent evidence for this conclusion has been obtained by studies on the effects of changes in gene dosage and on the peculiar dosage-compensation mechanisms possessed by sex-linked genes. The high grade of dominance exhibited by most normal genes over their mutant alleles appears to be merely a by-product of this more general stability. Moreover, as the dosage-compensation work more especially shows, the degree of stabilization thus achieved is often such as to prevent deviations of development far smaller than could be detected by our unaided eyes. This result shows that even changes which to us seem subliminal are nevertheless important for survival and furnish material for the operation of natural selection.

Darwin thought that high stability, both with regard to varietal and specific characters, resulted in some automatic way from long continued selection for a given grade of character. He also thought that, in other cases, characters of no particular use served as good systematic marks merely because of a low intrinsic variability. Geneticists today would look with skepticism upon both of these views. Instead, they would interpret the greater stability of given characters as being usually due to an actual selection of such genes as produce somatic reactions especially resistant to disturbing influences, and even reactions of a self-regulatory ("cybernetic") type. It is here implied that all these characters, including the systematic ones, are in some manner useful. Of course characters that have been longer selected for are correspondingly better guarded in these ways, both from the effects of varying environment and of mutant genes. Conversely, there is a relatively high variability on the part of newly established characters, and more especially of mutant characters not yet established at all. At the same time, we also recognize that intrinsic variability itself is subject to modification by selection. This occurs, on a piecemeal scale, by the replacement of more mutable genes by stabler alleles. Much more important, however, are the effects produced by the natural selection of genes, and genetic systems, that favor a lower or a higher general mutability (as the case may be), in adaptation to the needs of the species.

Now while the stable development of a character in relation to most environmental disturbances is on the whole a great advantage, there are innumerable special cases in which it is more useful to have a character change in a given way in the presence of a particular kind of alteration of the surroundings. In many of these cases, particularly if the environmental change in question is a frequently occurring one, adaptive developmental or physiological reactions have been evolved by selection, providing the appropriate response, as is to be expected. In fact, the whole fabric of a living thing, with its "adjustment of internal to external conditions," in such a manner as to favor perpetuation and multiplication, is a system of just such reactions. This has often fooled the Lamarckian by confronting him with adaptive morphogenetic processes, such as the growth of a muscle accompanying its use, which, being *results* of evolution, he has mistaken for its causes. There can be little doubt that many of the laws of heterogonic growth, such as those determining the shapes of ant castes, or the overgrowth observed in some of the bony and horny structures of larger reptiles and mammals, as well as such principles as Gloger's rule, belong in this category. In line with this, as Darwin recognized, the rules of correlative development are not themselves immutable but can be modified or even overcome by variation and selection. In fact, plenty of examples of the breaking of the rules are known.

We would, however, go beyond Darwin in applying the above principles and maintain that few if any widespread, long-lasting characters of the adult are to be explained away, in the manner proposed by him, as secondary effects of a selection that had really acted only on certain more important characters, with which the ones in question had merely been correlated in their developmental mechanism. For the evidence concerning the importance for survival of even apparently minor differences indicates that they would not ordinarily be carried along passively in the evolutionary current. Their developmental correlation, unless giving a beneficial result in the given instance, would in most cases be compensated for by appropriate mutations affecting them separately, if enough time were allowed. On the other hand relatively newly established characters and, still more, mutations that are not established, must often entail developmental correlations that are not advantageous, or that are distinctly disadvantageous. So also must unusual environmental conditions, for which the species has been insufficiently or not at all selected. Included in the latter category are conditions created by a more efficiently evolving competing organism, such as a parasite whose genes have evolved so as to produce in the host a gall adapted to itself but damaging to the host.

It would take us too far afield here to consider in detail the factors affecting evolutionary speed or direction. Modern students of evolution agree with Darwin that selection must work to alter the species more rapidly when conditions of importance for the organism have changed, and that among the most influential of such changes are those in other species, in relation to which the organism becomes adjusted. The opening up of new ecological niches for the organism, as well as its immigration into other territory, is usually associated with significant alterations in the physical and organic conditions of its existence. As before noted, however, we do not follow Darwin in believing also that outer changes tend, per se, to increase, to an extent significant for evolution, the genetic variability, nor is this necessary for the result.

Sometimes following in consequence of the outer changes which alter the course of selection, but also capable, theoretically, of occurring without them, is the evolutionary origination, within the organism, of "innovations" that alter its mode of life, either qualitatively or in a radical quantitative manner. These inner changes themselves can in turn react to alter the course and speed of the further selection. As Darwin reiterates, while variations are common, innovations are rare. The distinction between the two categories remains a valid one, even though there is no sharp line between them, and although we must follow Darwin in inferring that the innovations themselves have usually arisen by slow degrees, through the cumulation of minor variations that are not, individually, to be regarded as innovations. However, in some cases, especially in those involving change in function, to which Darwin calls attention, the inwardly conditioned change in some important aspect of living may have been a relatively sharp one. Now the innovation, whether sudden or gradual in its onset, will tend to usher in a period of rapid change by selection, as it becomes improved and other characters become altered to suit it. Occasionally, broad new avenues to survival and multiplication are opened up thereby, and in such cases opportunities are apt to arise in a number of different directions, all new for the organism. Thus in addition to the "spurt," or acceleration in evolutionary speed, there may be a kind of "burst" of diversification or, as H. F. Osborn called it, "adaptive radiation." Gradually, however, new limits, temporary or permanent, are approached, and the evolutionary movement becomes slowed down again in both its length and breadth.

On this view, there is no cogent reason for regarding those great groups which have long ceased undergoing important evolutionary changes as being intrinsically less variable than the others. We might however grant that a selection of genes which reduced the mutation frequency would be favored in them, provided even short-range changes in conditions, of a sort that rendered temporary genetic alterations useful, had largely ceased to exist for these organisms. Such a contingency would seem rare, however. And, in any case, their stasis would primarily, have been caused by the fact that they had reached a blind end of selection, an "optimum" for any mode of life presently attainable to them.[5] This would be because of limitations in the advantages of further developments in their own characteristic structures, taken in relation with the fact that they were hemmed into their own niches by other organisms, which hopelessly outdistanced them for other possible fields of conquest. Thus, although changes in them could

5. The "optimum" is of course only relative to the possibilities more immediately around it. It presents an analogy to the relatively stable state reached in chemical combinations that have a lower "potential energy" level (higher entropy) than those from which and into which they can readily be transformed. Such structures therefore tend to remain as they are despite the fact that other combinations of their parts, with still lower energy level, are possible. To jump the surrounding energy wall and attain another low level, an unusually large amount of energy must first be supplied. Similarly, for the organism to escape from its selective dead end, the radical jolt in its mode of living brought about by a significant outer change or inner innovation becomes necessary. There are of course all degrees of this phenomenon. Wright has graphically described the same phenomenon by analogy with troughs, peaks, and other changes in the contour of a surface over which an object may move. In this case also the analogy is to energy levels. It is important to remember, however, that in the evolutionary situation we are not dealing with differences in actual energy, in the physicists' sense. For the steps in our case are steps of differential multiplication of such a kind as to result in increasing organization, and no more transfer of energy need be involved when the multiplication is differential in this way than when it is differential in some other way or not differential at all.

still occur, there would be virtually no important ones that presented long-term advantages.

But even though organisms may have reached a virtual stopping point in evolution, the mere maintenance of their present structure requires, as we realize today, the persistent operation of natural selection. Darwin, to be sure, stated that a relaxation of selection leads to an increased accumulation of individual variants. But in his time the knowledge was apparently lacking that the relaxation of selection with regard to any character would lead to decay down to the level at which selection does operate, and that an actual cessation of selection for a character would in time lead to its complete disappearance. In fact, the entire organization would deteriorate similarly, if selection in all directions were relaxed. Before the advent of modern mutation study, it was not known that genetic changes in the downhill direction are in general far more frequent than those which increase or intensify an organ or character. True, Darwin was so astute as to point out that such a principle, if true, would be of great service in explaining the reason for the decline, and more especially for the total disappearance, of features which had lost their usefulness, like the eyes and the pigmentation of cave forms. Today however this principle is accepted by geneticists. And it gives a new importance to natural selection, as a process which not only leads, sometimes, to further adaptations but which is everywhere actively at work in maintaining all things biological that merely continue in existence.

As to the forms which natural selection can take, we can enter into no adequate discussion here. Sexual selection is of course only one kind—in fact, it includes several kinds—of natural selection, and modern geneticists are not inclined to share that doubt of it which actuated many biologists of the older generation. They might, rather, raise the question more actively as to how that more basic natural selection had worked which established and maintained the particular characters through which the given sexual selection itself operated.

It is to be noted that there are usually more or less conflicting kinds and currents of selection at work together. Most characters of a complex organism, living in complex surroundings, are advan-

tageous under some circumstances or in some of their relationships and to some extent disadvantageous under others. Moreover,
we may distinguish between advantages of longer or shorter duration, and correspondingly, between longer- and shorter-term selection. Related to these problems are those of intragroup and
intergroup selection, processes which often are opposed in their
direction. The final outcome then must be a resultant of the combined action of the various selective tendencies.

Sometimes, however, instead of a compromise, an enduring
dimorphism or polymorphism is attained, as in the establishment
of separate sexes, of neuters, and of other specialized divisions of
the species. It would be interesting to examine the evolutionary
mechanisms involved in such cases, in the light of modern genetics, had we the time. Suffice it here to say only that in each case
in which the different individuals are able to breed independently
of one another (as in polymorphic butterflies), a stable equilibrium is necessarily involved. This is so constituted that a diminu-
tion of numbers of a given type puts a higher premium on just
that type while, conversely, a rise in its frequency above the
equilibrium level leads to its lowered survival, so that in either
case the balance is again restored.

Darwin, unlike many of his followers, recognized that the
resultant of selection is not always for the ultimate profit of a
species. In particular, he drew attention to the problem of characters which benefit the group without being of greater advantage
(and sometimes being of actually lesser advantage) to the individual himself and his own descendants than to the rest of the
group. Such characters are, for instance, the sting of the bee, which
causes its own death, and (under some circumstances at least)
breadth of sympathy in a man, which may handicap his own and
his children's struggle for existence. Characters which are useful
only to the group as a whole cannot be selected for except by
means of an intergroup biological competition between numerous
small groups which fail to interbreed freely. The converse of these
social characters are those which are actively selected for in
intragroup competition but which work to the whole group's
detriment. The counteracting of the latter process, in nature, also
requires intergroup selection. As Darwin realized, such intergroup

selection is now much diminished, if not absent or even reversed in its direction, in civilized man. So also is that intragroup biological competition which tended to lead to the survival of those who were physically and mentally strongest. And although Darwin did not realize that a mere absence of selection above any given level would inevitably lead to biological degeneration all the way down to that level, he did call attention to the danger, in civilized mankind, of reversed selection. In his day, however, scientific techniques of control over reproduction had not yet been devised, and so he saw little hope of mitigating an evolutionary decline except the admittedly unlikely one of voluntary restriction of marriages.

Our discussion is intentionally concerned mainly with those topics regarding natural selection which were taken up by Darwin, in order that we may assess the extent to which we still agree or disagree with his conclusions. At the same time, it should be realized that our modern knowledge of the genetic mechanism in its varied forms, of mutation rates, gene flux, chromosome changes, breeding systems, population dynamics, etc., allows us to go far beyond Darwin in our understanding of the details of the evolutionary process, and of the qualitative as well as quantitative interrelations of the factors concerned. But Wright's magnificent quantitative treatment must be left to Wright himself, nor can we do more than mention the names of Fisher, Haldane, and Lancelot Hogben, which are likewise classical in this connection. All of them, however, as I think they would agree, serve to make far more definite, and to implement, the fundamentals of that theory of natural selection which Darwin and Wallace conceived, as it were, at a distance.

What has made all this possible is, first of all, the proof of the particulate or (in the older sense of the term) the "atomic" character of the hereditary material; second, of the precise rules of transmission of these particles; third, the information concerning their phenotypic interrelations, as in dominance, pleiotropy, and multiple-factor cases; and fourth, the evidence as to the quantum character of their changes, together with some data on the frequency of changes of different types. Thus evolution study from the standpoint of genetics has risen to a higher level or, more correctly speaking, has bored down to a deeper level of analysis, and in consequence is also able to make more far-reaching and reliable deductions and integrations.

At the same time, it is worth noting that Darwin's general conclusions regarding selection do not stand or fall according to this or that genetic mechanism, if only we admit the existence of heritable change in numerous directions, or, in other words, the differential multiplication of diverse variations. So, for example, even if inheritance were perfectly blending, the selected individual variations would not in time become completely swamped out as some have maintained and as even Darwin seemed to suspect. Their increment, established by one generation of natural selection, would not be lost but would be duly added to the species, in each succeeding generation to be reinforced by the additional selection. Thus the mean would progress as rapidly as with selection of a dominant gene which goes in full strength to half the progeny. Of course, the variance due to freshly arisen inheritable variations would on this view have to be much greater than that supplied by new mutations in the genetic scheme recognized today, but it would by no means be as great as the observed variance and, more important, it would not be necessary to postulate that quantitative variation in a favorable direction exceeded or even equalled that in the opposite direction. But the rate of establishment of rare, qualitatively peculiar variations would be very slow.

Another claim—in the present writer's view fallacious—that is sometimes made for the superior evolutionary worth of the genetic mechanism known to us, has to do with the supposed advantage for evolution conferred by the recessiveness of most mutant genes. For this, it is said, leads the species to accumulate a large reserve of hidden recessives, which may be drawn upon in case of need arising from a change of conditions, and which can then enter into varied combinations. The thing that is forgotten here is that the frequency with which a completely recessive gene shows itself at any given time is, on the average, only equal to the frequency of mutation, per generation, to the given gene, multiplied by the average number of generations during which it is allowed to express itself before it is eliminated by selection. And the number of individuals showing it would be just the same, for a gene having a given frequency of origination and a given survival value, no matter whether this gene expressed itself fully and immediately in every individual carrying it, as it would in a haploid species, or whether it expressed itself as a recessive in a diploid species. In fact, be it noted, the rate of increase of individuals expressing a recessive (or on the whole recessive) gene is actually slowed very considerably in an ordinary diploid species as compared with a haploid, when selection acts in the gene's favor. This is because of the circumstance that so small a portion of the recessive genes are expressed in the diploid individuals which contain them and that selection is therefore greatly restricted in the force of its operation on them. This lag in selection may sometimes be of real value, however, not for the mistaken reason sometimes given that a short-term selection is aided by the phenomenon of recessivity, but rather for the opposite reason, namely, that it acts as a damper to prevent a merely temporary selection from altering the population too hastily and so doing long-term damage greater than the short-term good.

Another fact in regard to recessivity and dominance which will call for revision of some modern treatments is the assumption so often made of the usual completeness of dominance. There are a number of lines of evidence, not well enough known, derived from dosage and dosage-compensation studies as well as from direct tests, which indicate that most so-called recessive genes do have some degree of expression in the heterozygote, and that although this is usually below the threshold for our ordinary observation, nevertheless the effect is after all significant for survival.[6] This being the case, many of our calculations concern-

6. For further treatment of this matter see the following papers by the present author: Evidence of the precision of genetic adaptation, in the volume of *Harvey Lectures* for 1948, pp. 165–229 (publ. 1950); Some present problems in the genetic effects of radiation, Oak Ridge Symposium on Radiation Cytogenetics, Apr., 1948, *Jour. Cell & Comp. Physiol.*, supp. vol.; H. J. Muller and S. L. Campbell, 1950. Further evidence that most "recessive" genes exert their main action as dominants, (unpublished). Direct evidence on the matter was furnished by C. Stern and E. Novitski in their 1948 paper. The viability of individuals heterozygous for recessive

ing selection should take much more account than they do of heterozygous individuals. When they do this, they will assume a form which is in some respects a good deal simpler than now, for selection is thereby made more direct, and nearer to the kind of process envisioned by Darwin.

On the other hand, the genetic knowledge of Darwin's day was too primitive to allow him to have a good comprehension of the role of sexual reproduction in relation to evolution, although Galton had noted that recombination types can be formed in subsequent generations and had based a mosaic conception of heredity upon it, and Weismann's ideas of panmixia and of chromosomal inheritance approached somewhat nearer still to the truth as we now see it. Today we recognize that the basic function of sexual reproduction is an out-and-out evolutionary one, pure and simple: namely, that of allowing, through the processes of crossing-over and of random assortment of chromosomes, the simultaneous differential multiplication of diverse independently occurring variations which otherwise would have to compete. They are thus allowed to form combinations, even though they had usually originated in different lines of ascent, and the process of their accumulation by selection is inordinately speeded beyond what it would be if, as in asexual forms, the different selected mutations which it was advantageous to have in combination had to wait until they arose successively within the same reproductively isolated line. This advantage is further heightened by the fact that the genes entering into some of these favorable combinations are useful only, or mainly, when in that combination, for these would have had still less chance to gain a foothold by the procedure of single-file origination and selection.

We have not yet touched upon the topics of the influence of population size and population division upon selection. It does not seem to be widely realized that these are themes which Darwin by no means neglected, and that, in fact, he came remarkably near to some of our most important modern conclusions concerning them. For one thing, he recognized that large popula-

---

lethals, *Science*, 108: 538–39; this paper had, however, not come to the present author's attention when the above was written.

tions, by providing a greater absolute number of rare variants of diverse types, afford richer material for selection than small ones. However, he could not know how important the infrequent accidental processes are which enter into the obtaining of a foothold for advantageous rare variants, or variant combinations, especially if they be recessives, and so he could hardly grasp the force of this point as well as we do. For the rarer an accident is the more are large numbers necessary to achieve its realization. Moreover, in just this kind of case the nonswamping of the rare variations, caused by the noncontamination of alleles by each other, assumes especial importance in giving them value, as previously mentioned in our discussion of swamping effects, and this too is a property of them that was unknown to Darwin.

Secondly, Darwin recognized that the dispersal of a population over a wide area, by bringing it into contact with diverse conditions of selection and so leading it to form local varieties or races, was an aid in evolution. He saw these varieties often competing with one another later, and so—again by offering more diversified material for selection, but this time on the varietal level—achieving a success for the species as a whole which surpassed that of a completely panmictic population of equal size. The species small in numbers or limited in range, on the other hand, he saw to be more subject to accidental vicissitudes which were likely to exterminate it, and unable in the long run to keep abreast of its larger, more versatile and better insured competitor-species.

Today, thanks especially to the work of Wright, utilizing the facts of modern genetics, these conclusions have been greatly extended and refined upon. The principle of gene "drift," applying more strongly to small populations, increases the divergence of the local groups of the large species. And, through both drift and special local, often temporary, types of selection, some of these semiisolated groups are carried through the stage of genetic combinations which in the species as a whole would be disadvantageous—situations called "troughs" by Wright. These, however, sometimes serve as stepping stones to unusually advantageous genetic combinations that could not be attained by a large species subject only to a steady generalized selection. Thus prize local products are formed which may then spread, in more or less fair competition, throughout much or all of the species. Turning now to the small species, we find that it suffers not only from the disadvantages listed by Darwin, but also, if small enough, from the fact that in it there is a considerable drift, which in the great majority of cases will be disadvantageous, and may drag it down despite selection.

In the further evolution of the large widely spread species, Darwin saw it tending to split into ever more different types in different places, until they finally ranked as separate species. Like some or most of the geneticists and systematists concerned with evolution today, he thought of the splitting as occurring between groups inhabiting different areas, although sometimes contiguous ones, rather than as occurring in the same area, sympatrically. Related species now inhabiting the same area he regarded as having usually invaded one another's territories since their differentiation, a view for which Ernst Mayr has recently presented cogent arguments. However, since Darwin was not aware of the rules of genetic recombination which, as we see the matter, form the chief block to sympatric speciation, his conclusion had to rest on a less secure theoretical (as well as observational) basis than that of today.

It is interesting to note that Darwin regarded the evolutionary acquirement of what is called physiological or genetic isolation— the inability to cross effectively, in the sense of allowing an interflow of hereditary material between populations—as a mere byproduct of an evolutionary divergence that was caused primarily by the selection for other features. To this there must now be added the factor of drift. With this addition, this is the view of the matter which the present author at least has taken so far as the production of inviable or sterile offspring on intercrossing is concerned. Some geneticists however have thought this property to have been acquired by selection, by virtue of the protection against contamination by the other population which such a barrier to mixing affords. In regard to this question, Darwin himself had taken the trouble to point out that the very individuals which possessed this advantageous feature of cross-incompatibility could hardly benefit their descendants thereby and so undergo a selective multiplication. For if they actually tried the crossing, even though it failed to lead to mixture, they would tend in consequence to be checked in their own multiplication. For this reason there could be no effective intragroup selection for this characteristic in itself. While this argument does not appear entirely valid so far as concerns the inability to cross-inseminate or to cross-fertilize, it would seem to hold for the inability to form fertile or viable hybrids. And since, as a matter of fact, this is the kind of block to interchange of hereditary material which often or usually appears first, the conclusion would still stand, for many or most cases, that the physiological isolation was only a by-product of other changes, and not a product of selection for this property itself.

It was long ago asserted by Bateson (1921) that genetics had thrown no light on the problem of how the property of genetic isolation which prevents species from mixing had originated, and this statement has often been repeated by others, mainly by nongeneticists. However, in the intervening years there have been many excellent genetic studies of differences which cause considerable genetic isolation between subspecies or species. The groups concerned are nearly enough related to allow some genetic recombination and analysis, when special means are employed, yet far enough apart, either physiologically, ecologically, or geographically, to be practically isolated when in a state of nature. The studies on multicellular animals have agreed in showing that chromosomal genes are responsible for the incompatibilities, and that they give their characteristic isolating effect not singly, but only as a result of differences invoked by given combinations of them. There is no reason to doubt that these genes originated by the same kind of mutation process as the others.

As for plants, much evidence of the same sort has been obtained (chiefly through the findings on sterile hybrids that give fertile tetraploids). In plants and some microorganisms, however, owing to the existence of plastogenes and plasmagenes in addition to those located in the chromosomes, it is found, as is to be expected, that the former sometimes (though by no means always) participate in the causation of the genetic isolation. Nevertheless, the story even in them remains the same in regard to this funda-

mental feature: that more than one genetic difference exists between any two genetically isolated groups of such a nature that,
to produce the isolation, a minimum of two mutational steps
(one of them sometimes in genes located in the cytoplasm) must
have taken place. So, for example, in two species of algae of the
genus *Acetabularia* studied by J. Hämmerling, the plastids from
one of the species give an inviable combination when present
with nuclear genes from the other species. This situation could
have arisen only if at least one plastogene mutation and at least
one chromosomal gene mutation (though probably more) had occurred—either one in each line or two in one line—since these
two species had diverged from their common ancestor.

For the establishment of the differentiating genes which in their
given combinations serve as the genetic isolators of their respective populations, it must be inferred that, in the first place, an outwardly enforced physical isolation, essentially of the type of
geographical isolation, was necessary. For if the two populations
had been allowed to mix during the genesis of their differentiation,
then, whichever of the two (or more) differentiating mutations had
arisen first, this would have become exchanged, in part, for its
allele in the other stock. In that case, the complementary mutation
(or mutations) that was necessary for the production of the in-
compability could not have become established, since the lethal
or sterilizing action which it had in the cross-combination would
have worked against it even in the stock of its origin. If we attempt to avoid this objection by postulating that the genetic isolation depended upon just one gene mutation instead of two or
more complementary ones we meet with still greater difficulties.
For in that case the one isolating mutation is even sooner wiped
out in the stock in which it arises through the killing or sterilizing
action which it has when it tries to cross with the individuals of
the original type. For these theoretical reasons, then, as well as
because of the evidence derived from the genetic study of species
differences, it seems necessary to conclude that the genes causing genetic isolation are effective only in combinations, and that,
because of this, they usually arise in populations which are
separated from one another by outer circumstances, i.e., by geographical or at any rate topographical isolation, as Darwin thought.

Moreover, this being the case, it becomes necessary to conclude that the isolating genes were not established by a process of selection which derived its original advantage from the achievement of the isolating effect itself but were established, in their original local populations at any rate, through their selective value in other respects, or through drift, as the case might be.

The above discussion has touched upon many topics in a very cursory way. This was necessary in view of the very wide yet searching analysis which Darwin made of the whole subject of selection, if we were to follow out our intention of reviewing the conclusions which he reached and of seeing them in relation to our newer concepts. It is hoped that enough has nevertheless been outlined to show that, meagre though the knowledge of heredity and variation was in Darwin's day, he succeeded in fore-shadowing in a most extraordinary way our modern view, which we base upon the solid findings of modern genetics, systematics, and paleontology. We have to be sure traveled far beyond Darwin. And there is now a world of new problems of first-rate importance open to students of the subject. But none of these are in contradiction of Darwin's fundamental theory of natural selection, especially when we divest it of the accretions derived from still earlier authors. And his individual contributions on most major points stand, in fact far better vindicated than ever before, as the basis upon which we are building ever higher.

Evolution by Mutation

HOW *improbable are we? Can blind chance through natural selection sift through sufficient combinations of mutant genes to yield protoplasm from the "protogenes," to transform protoplasm to cells, and to bring about the ultimate tour de force, cells of sufficient complexity and in abundant number to wonder, as men, whence they came? And all of this in a few billion years? Muller's essay[1] exemplifies his gift for generating unexpected and exciting insights from a few facts and principles.*

It is not possible for me to represent the high tradition of Josiah Willard Gibbs by offering you a mathematical treatment. Nevertheless, the subject of biological evolution and its mechanism must be of great interest to you, the most exemplary products of its operation. Perhaps, then, our reconnaissance flight over these biological jungles, and our attempts to measure certain aspects of them, may serve to entice some of you or, through you, some of those with whom your influence counts, into bringing your higher powered mental tools to bear in the more effective and more elegant mapping and analysis of this territory. If so, my intention to inveigle you into it will have been successfully accomplished.

To those philosophers who declare "I think, therefore I am," their own existence seems the one complete certainty. To others, it does not seem so certain that they do think, nor even that they

1. This article is Contribution No. 649 of the Department of Zoology, Indiana University.

202 Modern Concept of Nature

produce a significant imprint on reality in general. It is, however, evident that they, along with all things living, if they do exist, are utter improbabilities, far less plausible than any other phenomena that have been encountered.

Herein we shall attempt to assess how fantastically unlikely we and our fellow creatures are, and by what means such preposterous anomalies could have come about. The old-time philosopher still insists that such extravagances of organization could have arisen only by design, inasmuch as accident cannot be expected to convert itself into order. However, a dispassionate examination of the rules of this game of life should throw some light on the question of how such a massive compounding of improbabilities may have taken place.

1. *The genetic alphabet.* Studies in Mendelian heredity, supplemented by microscopic observations, gave evidence some half-century ago that at the core of our being, and of that of every living thing, there is a remarkable material, that is particulate, exceedingly constant in its parts, subject to orderly mosaic rearrangements, and in a sense self-multiplying. All this was shown by the kaleidoscopic, yet statistically predictable effects it gave on being transmitted and multiplied from generation to generation in the form of diverse combinations. The term "genes" was applied to the regularly recombining parts of this mosaic. Moreover, the fact was established on the basis of the quanitative relations which were observed in the recombinations of these genes, that they are strung together in a single-file arrangement, like the links in a chain, so as to form the microscopically visible filaments called chromosomes (Morgan et al. 1915).

It further became clear that despite the constancy of the individual genes they are separately subject to rare, sudden changes, or "mutations," from one stable state to another. This is proved by the changed effects on the descendants that inherit them after such an occurrence. For these descendants then constitute exceptions to the original predictions. They are, potentially, the seed of new, although usually only slightly new, forms of life.

The most unique characteristic of these genes has long been realized to lie in the fact that, after a mutation has occurred, the gene in its changed form, on reproducing, gives rise to daughter genes that incorporate its new feature. That is, the mechanism of the gene's self-reproduction is such as to result in the perpetuation and, if circumstances permit, the multiplication of the deviant type. As has been pointed out elsewhere (Muller 1922, 1929a, 1947), it is the possession by the gene of this faculty of self-copying, of a kind that is capable of being retained despite changes in that gene's own composition, that causes the gene to serve as the basis of evolution. And the enormous complications to which evolution may go are made possible by the fact that these changes in genes and in groups of genes can become accumulated to a virtually unlimited extent, without entailing the loss of the genes' self-copying faculty. Moreover, it has become clear that, as had been surmised, the self-copying involves an attachment, next to each characteristic component of the gene, of a particle of corresponding[2] type that had been floating about in the medium surrounding the gene. In this way there becomes pieced together next to each gene a replica of itself, that is, a structure having the same internal pattern. A mutation consists of a permutation in this pattern.

Through the brilliant recent theory of Watson and Crick (1953a, 1953b, Crick 1954), backed by strong evidence from work of Benzer, Alfred D. Hershey, Stanley, and many others, it has been virtually proved that the components in question are nucleotides, combinations of phosphoric acid, a simple sugar, and a nitrogenous base, the whole having a molecular weight of about 300. In the gene there are only four types of these nucleotides, that we may here call A, B, C, and D. The gene consists basically of these nucleotides polymerized into the form (termed DNA) of a pair of relatively long parallel but coiled chains, of which the nucleotides form the links. In any such pair of chains A is always complementary to B and C to D, in such a way that A in one chain regularly has B lying opposite to it in the other chain, and C has

2. As will be seen in what follows, however, the "corresponding" type here turns out to be a complementary one, rather than an identical one as had been first assumed. But since the gene contains pairs of complements to begin with this process works out to give a product that is identical with its producer after all.

D opposite to it. These opposite, or rather, complementary components form effective cross-unions with one another, and not with the other types of nucleotides, by means of hydrogen bonds. It is this fact that explains their selectivity in attaching to themselves only appropriate (complementary) particles derived from the medium, during the process of gene reproduction.

Now, although there are only two types of *nucleotide pairs*, these amount to four types so far as the gene is concerned. For their arrangement within the gene is different according to which of the two members of a pair of nucleotides lies in a given member of the pair of chains. Hence, unless there are additional features that we do not yet know about, we could specify the entire composition of a gene through the use of four letters, *A* to *D*, setting them down in line, as in a word, in the order in which they occur in either one of the two members of the double chain. As yet, we are far from knowing this order in any case. But there is reason to infer that a gene-word is composed of thousands, even tens of thousands, of "letters."

A mutation, on this scheme of representation, consists in the substitution, loss, or insertion, of one or more of these same letters. Benzer's work (1955) may be taken as indicating that only one letter, or nucleotide pair, is usually involved, but that at times a whole block of them may be inverted *in situ*, lost, or inserted. This same principle of what may be called point and line mutation has long been known to hold, on a far larger scale of magnitude, in the case of those greater chains, the chromosomes, the links of which are whole genes, some hundreds or thousands of them per chromosome.

2. *A measure of our own improbability.* We are now in a position to make some first estimates of the degree of improbability represented by our own genetic material. The total mass of nucleotide material, or DNA, contained in one set of human chromosomes, such as would be found in a human sperm or egg nucleus just before they united in fertilization, is approximately 4×10^{-12} of a gram. Since the mass of one pair of nucleotides is about 10^{-21} of a gram there must therefore be about 4×10^9 nucleotide pairs in the chromosome set.

It is not certain that in higher animals the gene string, as we call it, contains only *one* double chain of nucleotides, but there is morphological as well as autoradiographic evidence that this is the case in bacterial viruses, and autoradiographic evidence in some higher plant material also. Moreover, the way that mutant genes have been observed to express themselves in some higher forms after a mutation has occurred, that is, the fact that in some cases all and in some cases about half of the cells descended from the cell in which the mutation has occurred may receive a replica of the mutant gene, indicates that this gene had not been in the form of more than two parallel threads. It therefore appears highly probable that even in man the genetic material of the sperm cell is in the form of unreplicated, merely double, chains of nucleotides.

This would lead us to conclude that all human gene strings of one chromosome set taken together contain some 4×10^9 nucleotide pairs arranged in one double line. It is possible some of the nucleotides are not in this line and are nongenetic, as Levinthal's preliminary results on bacterial viruses (1956) had indicated to be the case in them. However, certain more recent findings have raised questions concerning this interpretation in the viruses, and the higher plant studies by Taylor et al. (1957) have given grounds for considering virtually all the chromosomal DNA in them to be genetic.[3] This is a matter that the application of autoradiography to higher forms should soon give definite information about. Meanwhile, it will here be assumed that the number of genetic nucleotide pairs arranged linearly in a human chromosome set is the full number, 4×10^9, present in a human sperm cell.

Inasmuch as for each nucleotide pair there is a choice of four possible forms (representable as *A, B, C* or *D*) in a given member of the double chain, it is evident that the number of possible permutations of these four forms, in a line containing four billion of them, is four to the four billionth power or approximately

3. At the time of the lecture the reports giving the most recent evidence had not yet come to hand and the conservative assumption was therefore made that in man only 40 percent of the chromosomal DNA is genetic. Thus, in the text that follows, the figures are correspondingly higher than those that were presented orally.

$10^{2,400,000,000}$. It is true that this number should be reduced by dividing it by the number of permutations that would be possible among the twenty-three chromosomes and, more importantly, among all (some 10,000 to 40,000) entire genes, on the dubious supposition that most of these permutations would leave the genes' effects substantially unchanged. Nevertheless, on making the maximum possible estimate for the magnitude of this divisor, a "mere" $10^{270,000}$ at most, we find the size of our exponent reduced by an amount that is entirely insignificant, in terms relative to its own size, and we may therefore feel justified in settling on the above approximation. Now, since any given individual chromosome set represents but one combination we may say that the "chance" of its occurrence is the reciprocal of this number, or $10^{-2,400,000,000}$.

It should be recognized that this figure may give an exaggerated impression of our uniqueness, since we do not know whether many nucleotide substitutions might be made that would have no effect, or virtually none, on the resulting organism. Moreover, many of them have such relatively slight effects as we see differentiating the persons about us. As against this consideration, however, there are grounds for inferring that losses of nucleotides, or of blocks of them, from the chain, occur as much more frequent accidents than do gains (that is, insertions) of them, so that there is a tendency for unnecessary elements to be eliminated eventually. Let us then take our approximation at its face value and try to arrive at a working idea of its magnitude by comparison with something familiar to us in everyday life. It can be estimated that a large, finely printed edition of the *Unabridged Webster's International Dictionary* contains about thirty million letters. If, then, we used only the letters *A, B, C,* and *D* to represent the four nucleotide pairs, we could represent the entire arrangement of them in a single human sperm or (prefertilization) egg nucleus by the use of about 133 volumes, each of the size and fineness of print of this dictionary.

Here, presumably, we should have the entire genetic specification for a man, at least so far as his inheritance from one of his parents was concerned, and another 133 volumes would give that from his other parent. With the know-how (as yet not in sight) of how to string nucleotides together indefinitely as desired, and to give them the right wrappings, we should then be able to insert them into an egg from which its own nucleus had previously been removed and thus, after enormous labor, helped perhaps by automation, to produce a man as much like the one who had furnished the specifications as if he were an identical twin. Or we might incorporate alterations in him to order.

If instead of representing each nucleotide pair separately by *A, B, C,* or *D,* we utilize the entire English alphabet of 26 letters, plus half a dozen distinctive Cyrillic letters to make 32, and if we then allowed the letters to be either in lower case or capitalized, either in the slanting italic or vertical roman style, and either heavy faced or fine, thus gaining 256 distinguishable characters, we could allow each character to represent a group of four nucleotide pairs instead of just one pair (since for each group of 4 there would be 256 possibilities). We could thereby reduce our 133 volumes to 33. We could also greatly condense the representation of the inheritance from the second parent by designating only those items of it that differed from the corresponding items derived from the first parent, and by inserting these modifications, with appropriate punctuation, at the points in question, in line with the specifications of the first parent's contributions. By then transferring our perhaps 34 great volumes to especially thin microfilm we should be able to get our coded *homo* into the space of one volume having the outer dimensions of a scientific handbook. However, we may recall that, by contrast, the actual nucleotide material of a human or other mammalian germ cell, when mature, would occupy only about four cubic microns of weight 4×10^{-12} grams.

3. *An alternative measure.* There is an older method of estimating our improbability (Muller 1929b) that can now be brought more nearly up to date. Both observations and general considerations make it likely that, very conservatively, not one among 100 mutational changes with a presently detectable effect on the organism is conducive to its survival or fertility and thereby favors the multiplication and establishment in the species of the given mutant type. Moreover, any accidental accumulation of smaller changes that together resulted in as much deviation from the original type

as those here in question would have a similarly small chance of being advantageous. The reason for this prevailingly detrimental character of mutations is of course the fact that there are far more ways of damaging the workings of an already elaborate and well-constructed organization than there are of improving it even further. This situation is analogous to that of the second law of thermodynamics. In the latter case the energy of particles subject to random motion tends to become dissipated because of the fact that there are more directions and amplitudes of movement by which the energy can be scattered than those by which it can be concentrated. So, in general, there are more types and degrees of change that are disorganizing in relation to the production of a specific result (in the case of living things, their multiplication) than those that are further organizing.

Simplifying the situation by first considering only nonsexually reproducing organisms, and taking the conservative estimate of 99 detrimental to one advantageous change of perceptible degree, it follows that, on the average, the mutant type must multiply at least a hundred fold after each advantageous mutation if evolution is to continue. This multiplication is necessary to make the individuals, or rather, the lines of descent, of the advantageous type numerous enough to allow just one of these hundred lines to give rise to a second advantageous mutation, added to the first one. And so on after that, for each successive advantageous mutation that is accumulated in the same line of descent, there must on the average be a further multiplication of at least a hundred times.

In the meantime, the individuals with the disadvantageous mutations, and in some cases those of the original type also, will have tended to die out, thus making room for the line having the concentration of favorable changes. For the latter, however, the rate of multiplication will have averaged so high that, had this same rate characterized the entire population, their final number would have been at least 100 to a power equal to the number of successive advantageous mutations, that accumulated in the favored line. Thus, for three beneficial mutations this number would have been 100^3 (or 10^6) and for 100 mutations, 100^{100} (or 10^{200}).

These figures are relevant to our inquiry into the degree of our own improbability. For suppose that, instead of having started with just one individual which, in its more favored lines of descent at least, was able to multiply at a rate that would have given the number calculated, we had, instead, *started* with as many individuals, and therefore with as many lines of descent, as that imaginary final number that would have resulted from the equal multiplication of all lines at a rate as high as that of the favored lines. There need in that case have been no multiplication at all, or any ability to multiply, but only a persistence of the individuals, or of their single-file "lines of descent." In fact, even this persistence need have occurred only in the lines in which successive "favorable" changes happened to occur. Yet, given the same rate of "mutation" as before, we should on this system have ended up with just as many individuals having the maximum number of "favorable" changes as on the other system. For in both cases an equal number of individuals would have been provided, in each generation, in which disadvantageous (i.e., self-eliminating) mutations had not yet occurred, and in which "favorable" ones (i.e., those of types analogous to the mutations which would have favored multiplication had it been possible) could therefore have accumulated instead.

4. *Differential multiplication as the extractor of the improbable.* This "thought experiment" (to use the physicists' term) is, like most such experiments, fantastic, but illustrative of a principle. In this case it shows not only the degree of improbability achieved by the succession of mutations in the favored lines but also the role played by the process of biological multiplication in allowing this degree of improbability to be achieved. Thus the scheme on which there was no multiplication shows that the individual that had accumulated 100 favorable mutations represented a combination of chances that could happen only once in 10^{200} trials. There is no possibility that this number of trials could ever, on our earth, have been achieved. Yet the process of multiplication, by being differential, that is, largely confined to the lines that continued, accidentally, to have the favorable mutations in them, succeeded in providing the opportunity for the realization of this degree of improbability.

Within the narrow confines of our world, this multiplication of the favored lines was able to occur only because space was left by the dying out of the other lines. That, then, was the role of selective elimination: to make room. But advantage could be taken of that room only by reason of the gene's faculty of reproducing itself, and thereby multiplying. And even this could not have resulted in evolution if the gene had not been so constituted as to reproduce its mutational changes also in the process of reproducing itself. Evolutionary adaptation is thus the automatic result of the differential multiplication of mutations. And living things are so much more elaborately organized than nonliving ones because the gene's unique property of self-copying constitutes the basis for this differential multiplication of its changes.

Thus, on the primitive earth, after the myriad interactions of diverse substances, occurring in a medium of water and powered by high-potential discharges of photons and electrons, had resulted in the production of nucleotide molecules and then attachments between some of these molecules to form naked genes of the most rudimentary type that fed on those nucleotides that were free, their further evolution to produce their protoplasmic wrappings and finally all the complications of the intricately adapted organisms of today followed from the pressure of their differentially multiplying mutations.

But we have not yet followed far enough in applying this method of estimating the degree of our improbability. This method, it may be recalled, proceeds by first estimating, conservatively, the probability that a given mutational step will be successful, and it then raises this figure to a power equal to the estimated number of such steps.

On reconsideration of the probability of success, which is the reciprocal of the number of mutations necessary, on the average, to include one that is successful, it might at first sight seem that, for a given nucleotide pair, the number of possible substitutional changes that would include one successful one should be no more than three, since there are only four types among which to choose and one of these four types is already present. This inference, however, besides overlooking possible losses, insertions, and inversions, neglects the much more important fact that on the great majority of occasions any change at the given point would be disadvantageous. Usually there would be no possibility of any change at some *given* point in the nucleotide chain being advantageous until some change or combination of changes, of given kinds, had occurred elsewhere, which somehow upset previously attained adaptations. In other words, a group of successful steps accumulated over a period that, in terms of evolutionary time, is very long, would not have been successful if they had arisen in a radically different sequence from the actual one. This restriction explains why the chance of success for a change occurring at any given point, at any given time, can be less than one in 100 or even less than one in 10,000 despite the fact that the number of possible changes at that point is (if we exclude the comparatively rare cases of insertions and inversions) very limited.

Accepting, then, the very conservative figure of one in 100 for the chance of a given mutation being successful, what shall we assume for the exponent of this figure, that is, for the total number of successful mutations in the ancestry of a given higher organism? This total number may obviously be regarded as the product obtained by multiplying the number of successful mutations that have occurred per gene by the total number of genes. As for the number of past mutations per gene it is to be observed that, as was realized long ago (e.g. Muller 1929b), each individual gene must be highly adapted and complicated and have arrived at its present form through numerous steps. Knowing, today, that it contains thousands or tens of thousands of nucleotide pairs, we might estimate the number of steps per gene to have been as great as this or even much greater; that is, we might assume a past history of several or many substitutions of each pair. Nevertheless, we are, to remain on the conservative side, contenting ourselves at this point with the undoubtedly far too low figure of only 100 successful steps per gene.

In taking this figure we are bearing in mind the fact that in the distant past the genes were derived from one another, through rare accidents such as occasionally happen even today, whereby a block of them derived from one chain becomes inserted at some point into another chain. In consequence, many of the earlier mutational steps occurred in genes that were common ancestors of several or many present-day genes, and our assumed number of 100 steps per gene refers to the total number of independently arisen mutations, averaged out per gene. Yet even considering this, the actual number of steps is more likely to have been many thousands than only 100 per gene, because there are grounds for inferring that gene numbers of the order of those at present existing were already attained more than half a billion years ago.

Taking now the number 10,000, derived from flies, as a minimum estimate for the number of different genes in a higher organism (despite the fact that the higher organism contains a far larger total number of nucleotides), we see that there must have been at least $100 \times 10,000$, that is, a million separate successful mutations in the ancestry. Applying this million as an exponent to 100 (our conservative figure for the reciprocal of the probability that a mutation will be advantageous) we then get $100^{1,000,000}$ (or $10^{2,000,000}$) as the total number of trials that would have been necessary, in the absence of multiplication and selection, to obtain one combination as well organized as our own or as that of some other advanced organism.

Although so much smaller than our other estimate of about $10^{2,400,000,000}$ based on the number of nucleotide pairs, the present more conservative number deserves some scrutiny, some comparison with more familiar things. In this connection we may ask, how much room would it have taken to contain this many combinations of genes at one time, in order that among them our own constitution might find a place as one of these random occurrences? A sphere having a diameter of six billion light years goes far beyond the most distant galaxies now detectable. For our present purposes, however, we shall call it, by a stretch of terminology, "the known universe." A little arithmetic will show that in this vast expanse there would be room, if they were all packed closely together, for about 6.25×10^{100} packets or skeins of nucleotide chains, such that each skein contained as many nucleotides as we have taken to exist in a mammalian sperm nucleus, namely, 4,000,000,000, the number that we previously found it necessary to employ 133 volumes to represent. Yet we see that this enormous number of packets, 6.25×10^{100}, is inordinately smaller than the number of $10^{2,000,000}$, that on our more conservative estimate could be expected, as a random event, to include a packet with a composition as select as our own. And even if we had some science-fictionist's method of reducing the size of a genetic packet to that of a proton, we could still get only about 10^{128} of them into the known universe.

Suppose, now, that in order to attain our desired number we allowed each of these packets or genetic combinations to exist for only a millimicrosecond, that is, a billionth of a second, and then caused it to be replaced by a different combination, and so on every millimicrosecond in succession for six billion years, which is probably longer than the earth has existed. This would have allowed some 2×10^{26} changes and we should thereby be able to accommodate in the "known universe" during this period about 2×10^{154} genetic combinations. Let us institute next the radical procedure of allowing each of the evanescent proton-sized spaces thus obtained to be itself expanded to the size of our known universe, and to be granted a time-span of six billion years, within which it in turn became subdivided in both space and time just as we had previously subdivided our own known universe. The total number of genetic combinations that we could get in this way would now be the square of the previous number, and thus come to 4×10^{308}. But we should have to go on in this way, expanding protons into worlds and millimicroseconds into eons and then subdiving them as before, through about fourteen cycles, before we attained the more conservative number, $10^{2,000,000}$, that we are seeking.

This result, then, may give us some glimmer of an image of how improbable we are. How right, then, in a short-sighted way, were those ostensible "savants" who, so they declared, found it "philosophically unsatisfying" to believe that they, or any other living things, had come about by accident. For what an unthinkable multitude of universes would have had to be searched through, before so improbable a combination of accidents as themselves could have been found. And yet, the near-magic faculty of multiplication by self-copying, possessed by the nucleotide chains, does give the opportunity for these most select combinations of accidents to arise. For the multiplication rate in their lines of descent was enough, had it been extended to all lines, to have produced that superlative number, of which our own combination formed just one unit. And after all, the persistence of the defective lines was not necessary for the outcome. In practical fact, on the contrary, their elimination was necessary.

5. *The role of sexual reproduction.* We may next inquire whether the period during which life has existed on the earth has been long enough to allow such a succession of multiplications as here required, that is, a hundred-fold multiplication occurring one million times in succession. Dividing these million steps among the three billion years or so during which fossil evidence indicates life to have existed on the earth, we find 3,000 years allowed, on the average, for each of the hundred-fold multiplications. Now the number of generations occurring in every period of 3,000 years has diminished from, potentially, millions, in stages corresponding to bacteria, to about 3,000 (or one per year) for many of the lowlier many-celled forms, and then down to some 100 (or one in 30 years) in the case of modern man. At the same time, among many-celled forms, the potential amount of increase per generation has also diminished greatly. However, even modern man in America is now doubling his numbers every forty years, a rate which if continued would give a hundred-fold increase in a mere 266 years. Of course, an advantageous mutant could seldom be expected to multiply so rapidly as this, relatively to the rest of the population. If, as seems reasonable, it had only a one percent reproductive advantage over the other individuals, it would require some seventy generations to achieve a doubling, and 465 generations for a hundred-fold increase. This in man would occupy some 14,000 years. But since the human generation is so much longer than that which obtained in our ancestry until relatively recently, there was undoubtedly plenty of time for a million steps altogether.

We do become pinched for time, however, if we attempt, by this method, to squeeze in as many or more successful steps as our number of genetic nucleotide pairs, that is, some 4,000,000,000. For this would give only about a year, on the average, for each hundred-fold multiplication. If, as seems likely, each nucleotide pair has a history of several independent substitutions, and if by reason of the rarity of advantageous steps each period of multiplication requires an increase of 1,000- to 100,000-fold rather than one of only a hundred-fold, then, as can readily be reckoned, each successful mutation would have had to double its numbers, on the average, every few days! This means that it would have undergone something like a one percent relative increase every hour.

Fortunately, the genes have found a way of meeting this evolutionary difficulty. Their answer is sex! Or, more precisely stated, it is sexual reproduction. The function of this arrangement is to expedite evolution by making it possible to obtain an accumulation of advantageous mutational steps without having the respective multiplications of these steps occur in series. They are allowed, instead, to occur in parallel, with concomitant interpenetration and combination of the respective lines of descent (Muller 1932).

Let us first be clear concerning the basic genetic process involved in sexual reproduction. The act of fertilization that produces the child brings together two groups of chromosomes, or chains of genes, of somewhat different ancestry. Although each of the two groups by itself comprises one virtually complete set of genes, there are some mutant genes present in each set. Now the mutant genes of one set are represented in the other set by a gene of the original type, or, more rarely, by a different mutant gene, lying at a corresponding position in a chain of that other set. At some time before the act of fertilization that results in the next generation—we shall call these the grandchildren—the two sets of gene-chains line up parallel with one another, with their corresponding genes in apposition, a process called synapsis. In some viruses, at any rate, even the corresponding nucleotide pairs lie in apposition at this stage. Following this synapsis, the apposed chains again separate, and they become distributed to different germ cells, each cell now receiving just one complete set instead of both of the sets that had come together.

The function of the coming together or synapsis is, for one thing, to accomplish an orderly separation that insures each germ cell's receiving one complete set. But there is an even more important function in the synapsis. For, during their apposition, a considerable interchange of corresponding parts takes place among and between the chains of the two sets. Not only may a given germ cell thereby receive a whole chromosome (call it number one), that had belonged to one set, and simultaneously another whole chromosome (two) of the other set, but many of the individual chromosomes that it receives are themselves mosaic. They are mosaic in the sense that their gene chain up to a certain gene, or nucleotide pair, has been derived from a given chromosome (call it number three) of one of the sets, and from that point on has been derived from the corresponding chromosome (three) of the other set (Morgan et al. 1915).

In higher organisms this interchange of chromosome parts, called crossing-over, occurs by means of an actual breakage of the two corresponding gene chains or chromosomes, one from each set, at the same point along their length, followed by the attachment of the left-hand part of one chain to the right-hand part of the other, and conversely between the other two parts. However, in the virus studied by Levinthal (1956), the interchange is accomplished by the reproduction of the gene chains in such a way that one daughter chain is the daughter of one original chain up to a given point and of the other original chain from that point on. But in either case the outcome is the same. That is, each germ cell comes to contain, and bequeaths to the grandchild, just one complete set of genes, of which however certain ones trace back to the grandfather and the others to the grandmother on that germ cell's side. A grandchild, then, may receive mutant genes from both sources at once, and it is able to transmit them together to its descendants. Remote descendants may thereby come to inherit this combination from both their parents, and to "breed true" for it, as we say.

Let us try to visualize mentally how this process expedites the accumulation of successful mutations. Suppose a horizontal row of dots at the top of a diagram represents a population at a given time, comprising n individuals, say 100,000. On the next line down are their descendants, averaging one apiece and therefore also n. If one *favorable* (i.e., advantageous) mutation occurs among f individuals, say 10,000, the number of favorable mutations in the first generation is n/f or 10. Suppose the reproductive advantage, r, averages one percent, in that 100 favorable mutants of this kind would in this setting tend to produce 101 offspring, as compared with 100 offspring from 100 nonmutants that did not have this competition. With this linear logarithmic increase it will take about 70 generations, on the average, before the number of these favorable mutants that arose in the first generation, 10, had been doubled to make 20. It is true, however, that the number of generations actually taken by the doubling would have a relatively high error. Moreover, many of the mutants would die out accidentally along the way while, as if to make up for these, there would be a much higher than average multiplication of some of the others. Here, however, we need consider only the averages. We may then ask the question: How long would it be before two favorable mutations had been accumulated in the same individual?

We shall take first the simpler case, that of organisms that do not reproduce sexually. In a case of this kind a second favorable mutation may be expected to arise in the same line of descent as that already containing one favorable mutation at such a time, on the average, as f individuals had been produced altogether, in that "line." That is, we do not have to wait until there are f (or 10,000) individuals of that line in one given generation but only until their sum in all generations has become f. The number of generations, g, required to attain this sum, f, is readily obtained, since g in this case represents the number of terms in a geometric series beginning with 1, in which each term is $(1 + r)$ times the preceding term, and in which the sum of the terms is f. (Here $g = [\log(1 + rf)/\log(1 + r)]-1$.) Where, as in our numerical example, $f = 10,000$ and $r = .01$, g, the number of generations required to accumulate one favorable mutation in addition to the first one, turns out to be approximately 464. Moreover, the number of generations, g_m, required for the accumulation of any given number, m, of such additional mutations is simply mg (e.g., in our example 9,280 generations would be required for 20 of them). Or, conversely, $m = g_m/g$.

We may now compare this result with that in a sexually intermixing population having otherwise the same characteristics. In this case, by the time the generation g (or 464) is reached that in the asexual population would on the average have been necessary before a second favorable mutation was superimposed on the first one, there would have been a total population of gn individuals produced, and among all these there would have been gn/f favorable mutations. Now if we are dealing with a long period, of the order of tens of thousands of generations, such as those usually involved in considerations of "macroevolution," we can ignore the length of time needed for any two favorable mutations of independent origin to become recombined so as to be present together in the same individual, or germ cell. For, in a relatively small fraction of such a period, the great majority even of mutations with as low an advantage as $r = .001$ would have had time to spread over practically the whole population. In so doing, these different mutant genes would have undergone the recombinations necessary to bind them together, that is, to incorporate them into the same chromosome sets.

Accordingly, in the sexual populations, virtually all of the gn/f favorable mutations arising during each period g (that in the asexual population allows just one more favorable mutation to accumulate) will have the opportunity of being eventually accumulated within the same descendants. Thus in any extended period represented as a large multiple of g, such as mg, the individuals of the sexual line can accumulate some mgn/f favorable mutations while those of the asexual line accumulate only m of them. That is, over a long period the speed of evolution in the sexual line will be gn/f times that in the asexual lines. Even when a more unfavorable combination of numerical values is assigned to these terms than would often occur in practice (as when g is taken as only 10^2, n as only 10^6 and f as 10^6) this ratio is considerable (in this case 100). It may be inferred then that, ordinarily, sexuality increases the speed of evolution by a factor of many thousands and in some cases even millions. This enormous acceleration explains how it has been possible for several or many billions of mutations to have been accumulated by natural selection in the course of three billion years.

There is one factor that tends to make the situation even worse than this for the asexual as compared with the sexual population. This lies in the fact that in the former the favorable lines usually enter into an increasingly restrictive competition with one another, thus reducing each other's selective advantage, whereas in the latter the formation of combinations of them tends increasingly to substitute cooperation for competition.

When a considerable period is under consideration, comprising tens of thousands of generations, the effective population number, *n*, to be used in the above formula, is that of practically the entire area between the parts of which any intermixing occurs, rather than the average number present within the partly isolated local groups usually dealt with in population-genetic studies. For in the course of the long period in question sufficient migration usually takes place between these groups to allow locally multiplied genes that would have a favorable influence in the group as a whole to become spread throughout the area. Because of the prodigious size attained, for many species, by the population of the all-inclusive area, the speed of their evolution becomes, over a long period, enormously enhanced by sexual reproduction. It should therefore be no matter for surprise that, having once arisen in primitive organisms, this procedure should have been retained by the great majority of species.

The above outlined mode of action whereby sexual reproduction allows evolution to proceed more rapidly has sometimes been misunderstood. According to this misconception, one of the ways in which sexual reproduction aids evolution is by allowing combinations to become formed and tried out, the individual genes of which would not have been advantageous in the general population but which, taken together, constitute a favorable complex. Undoubtedly there are many cases of such genes and they do play a significant role in evolution. It is to be noted, however, that in these cases there would be no greater opportunity for the lucky combination to arise in a sexual than in an asexual population. Only mutant genes that are advantageous in at least a local population, and thereby spread within it, have a greater chance of forming combinations through crossing than through successive mutations that occur in series as in asexual organisms. The fact that sexual reproduction is so widespread therefore attests to the great evolutionary importance of genes whose favorable effect does *not* depend on their presence in combination with other special mutant genes of independent origin. In other words, it attests to the prevalence of so-called additive effects of genes as opposed to complementary ones.

Sexuality got a far earlier start in evolution than was realized until, some thirteen years ago, the recombination process was discovered in bacterial viruses by Delbrück and soon afterwards in bacteria by Lederberg. Moreover, at about the same time, the idea arose (Muller 1947) and was later shown to be correct, that the so-called transformation of one line of bacteria by application of nucleotide chains from another is really a modified instance of the sexual recombination process.

It is true that some groups of organisms, including even higher organisms, in every period of the earth's history, have dispensed with sexual reproduction in fact or in effect, and that this has given them the considerable temporary advantage of being able to multiply without having to wait for the nuisance of finding and pairing with one another first. But these can have only a transitory splurge and are doomed to fall behind in the long evolutionary race and to disappear. They furnish an illustration of the shortsightedness, the opportunism, of natural selection. The stem forms of evolution, from which the organisms of later periods will be derived, are those that pay their tax to sexuality and are repaid in novel developments.

That even forms which have not undergone outwardly appreciable evolution for scores or hundreds of millions of years, such as some mollusks, have for the most part retained sexual reproduction, testifies to the continuing value for them of evolutionary adjustment of less tangible kinds. Among such adjustments are to be classed relatively temporary ecological adaptations, often largely invisible, that bring them into line with shifting conditions of their physical, chemical, and biological environments. Sexual reproduction allows much prompter genetic accommodation of this kind. Another important group of changes in seemingly unchanging species are those, further discussed in section seven, that result in improved regulatory responses, including both more accurate, wider range, and more versatile stabilizing mechanisms, and in the improvement of means of exploiting the environment. Such evolution is to a considerable extent cryptic, i.e., beneath the surface open to our present means of observation, for there are undoubtedly far more reactions of this kind in any organism than those of which we are aware. Progress in such directions must often involve selectional steps that individually confer only a minute advantage. Thus the selective pressure, being of only third or fourth order magnitude, requires, even with the aid of sexual reproduction, a very prolonged period for the achievement of important results. Nevertheless, taken together, these results, which the asexual species would be far slower still in attaining, may eventually be of decisive significance in the competition for survival.

6. *The importance of localized evolutionary experiments.* A factor materially affecting the establishment of advantageous mutations is the degree of subdivision of the species into semiisolated groups. This factor, which has been treated mathematically by Sewall Wright in numerous publications, is of especial importance in the case of genes of the type referred to above, i.e., those that have a net favorable effect only as special combinations and not on the average when acting in connection with the genetic constitution of the population in general. We have seen that in such cases sexual recombination, operating widely throughout a large population, does not facilitate the formation and spread of these combinations. Yet in the long run such combinations are often of great importance and if established may act as turning points that allow evolution to proceed in a new direction. As Wright has clearly shown, populational subdivision can greatly facilitate the establishment of these combinations.

There are two ways in which such subdivision can have this effect. For one thing, the number, n_1, of individuals in the local groups is often so small as to allow some mutant genes that by themselves, even in connection with the genetic constitution of that local group, have no favorable effect, to become relatively numerous, merely as a result of the large random fluctuations to which small numbers are subject, a process termed "drift" by Wright. In some of these cases two or more such mutant genes which would be favorable only, or mainly, when in combination with one another, will thereby accidentally get the opportunity of being present together. This could of course happen just as well in asexual reproduction also. Having now become, as it were, superposed, their favorable joint action will come into play, so as to promote their spread. Under the circumstances of sexual reproduction, they can then spread much more rapidly and surely in the small group than if they were subject to the greater dissipation from one another that a larger group would entail. (A large asexual population, however, is not subject to this limitation.) Finally, by gradually diffusing out from the small group into its neighbors, and sometimes by the gradual advance of the local group as a whole into ever larger territories by competition, groupwise, with its less well equipped neighbors, these combinations can then proceed to "take over" in the general population, n.

The other and probably more important process depends on the many different selectional conditions to which the different local populations are subject. These tend to make some genes favorable from the start in a given local population that would not be favorable by themselves in the population as a whole. Both the peculiarities of the local environment (including the biological environment consisting of other species) and also the peculiarities of the genetic content of the local population itself (that arise as a result both of drift and of this very process of local selection) constitute important factors in the causation of these selectional differences. In consequence of them, some combinations of these locally advantageous genes can become "established" in the sub-population (this time with the aid of sexual reproduction), which as *combinations* though not as separate genes would have a selective advantage even in the larger population or the species as a whole. And again, just as when such combinations had arisen through drift, these locally numerous combinations can then proceed gradually to spread throughout the species.

In both these ways, then, the subdivision of the large population into groups that are locally or temporarily more or less isolated from one another in reproduction allows the carrying out of numerous small-scale evolutionary experiments that would not have been permitted in the freely interbreeding or so-called "panmictic" large population. On the whole not as many evolutionary possibilities, nor as radical ones, are available for the reproductively undivided group. It is this latter type of population that mankind is rapidly approaching today.

The method of local experiments is not, however, the only way by which evolutionary corners can be turned and new directions embarked upon. For even to the large group new pathways may be afforded by alterations in conditions of living. These will oftener result from changes in the biological environment (that provided by other species) than in the inanimate environment, because the biological environment is so much more complex, diversified, and itself subject to change, than is the inanimate environment. The new pathways can also be presented, even to large relatively undivided species, when through the acquisition of given favorable mutations, or combinations of mutations that had been favorable even individually, the species acquires one or more faculties, or passes some threshold in the development of one or more faculties that allows it to exploit a new mode of living.

Following any such turning of a corner there is likely to be a period of much faster evolution than before. For the longer a species has been selected for its old ways of life the harder it is to find new mutations that adapt it to these ways still better. On the other hand, for life carried out in a new way or (what amounts to much the same thing) under new conditions, many mutations that would previously have afforded little or no advantage will now be found helpful.

In such cases it is also much more likely to happen than before that the population, in its different parts, will find different methods of adapting to these new ways and will find the new ways themselves to open up in diverse directions. Thereupon there will be a tendency not merely to faster evolution but also to a splitting of the species into different lines. At first these lines will be isolated from one another in their reproduction mainly by geographic boundaries, but later genetic barriers (including genetically based physiological barriers) will arise between them as well.

The problem of how species split, in genetic terms, is one that is too ramified to permit of treatment here. It should be obvious, however, that the more numerous and the better isolated the local subpopulations are, the more such splitting is facilitated. It should also be observed, that, the more any two subpopulations diverge genetically from one another, even in cases in which they retain great resemblances in their form and manner of functioning, the more likely they are to accumulate sets of genes that can no longer function effectively after having become mixed or recombined with one another (Muller 1938, 1939, 1940, 1942). We must recognize them as separate species after such mixing has become, in a state of nature, virtually impossible in consequence of these genetic incompatibilities.

7. *The development of stability and lability.* But the long course of evolution is by no means concerned only with the dramatic turning of corners and the multiple branching of pathways. Through the prolonged periods of seeming stasis there is, as noted in section five, a gradual genetic whittling away at structures and functions, an increasing refinement of them in adjustment to outer circumstances and to each other. Most of this is beneath the surface that is open to our present relatively crude means of inspection. Even at the turning of corners most of the individual mutations that succeed entail relatively small changes, since larger ones, despite being in some cases favorable in themselves, usually involve maladjustments of the already achieved delicate balances in the complicated interworkings of parts. Thus the other parts must gradually be changed correlatively, before a further change in the primary direction becomes profitable.

In consequence of these relationships the progression in a relatively new evolutionary direction is gradually enabled to go further and further. The appearance is thereby presented of an inner tendency to keep on varying genetically in the given direction rather than in other directions, a fiction denoted "orthogenesis," that has no sound basis in genetic reality.

It does remain true, however, that the organism because of peculiarities of its constitution is able to undergo genetic change much more rapidly in some directions than in others, and in some not at all. Moreover, this pattern of genetic inclinations is itself subject to change through mutation (Altenburg and Muller 1920; Muller 1923). But these limitations are due largely to "canalizations" of its developmental and physiological processes, if I may revert to my original meaning (Muller 1929b) of a term that has since then been used in diverse senses. Such inclinations, be it noted, can never force evolution to proceed in a given direction if the interests of the species are occasioning a selection that works in the opposite direction.

When evolution has not recently taken a radically new direction the visible alterations are, of course, still slower. Yet much is often going on beneath the surface that may profoundly affect the embryological, the physiological, and the ecological reactions of the organism.

One of the most important classes of changes in this category concerns itself with the achievement of ever greater stability of development and of operation for structures and functions that are regularly needed. As pointed out long ago (Muller 1918) and further emphasized since that time (1950), mutant genes must gradually have been selected that gave greater stability and dependability both to the organism itself, in its characteristics, a property that might be denoted as "phenotypic stability," and also those that gave greater stability to the genes themselves, protecting them from the action of agents that might otherwise produce mutations in them.

Too much of a digression would be required for an adequate treatment of this matter in the present article. Suffice it to say that, so far as both kinds of stability are concerned, there is ground for inferring that many different mechanisms have been adopted: in fact, whatever came to hand. Some of these have had the effect of making the reactions in question especially resistant to disturbing influences. Others have worked by counteracting those influences themselves, somewhere along the line. Still others have involved self-regulatory or what are now termed "cybernetic" processes. Moreover, there has been, in phenotypic regulation, the attainment of "factors of safety," or means of doing the same thing through reactions that are somewhat different, involving more or less alternative pathways that are opened up where needed. The term "homeostasis" has often been applied to all this stabilization. It should be borne in mind that this term, like "adaptation" and "physiology" (all of which overlap widely) covers a fantastically great multitude of interwoven biological mechanisms. This complex is so impressive that it has sometimes been confused with the basis of life processes, of which it really forms a superstructure. In its application to matters of genetic variation, the term homeostasis has recently been given a special meaning (Lerner 1954), whereby it denotes an essentially mystical doctrine, representing a revival from pre-Mendelian times. According to this doctrine, an organism's vigor is enhanced per se as a result of the hereditary elements derived from its two parents being unlike one another.

It must not be forgotten that stability is itself only a means of helping to insure survival and reproduction, and that oftentimes these ends are better achieved by lability. In fact, the entire set of physiological reactions of the organism serves as a grand series of examples of what may be called phenotypic lability (Muller 1918). In each normal case, these reactions or changes that the organism undergoes in given situations, instead of representing the passive yielding to environmental pressures that is characteristic of inanimate objects, constitute adaptive responses. By this is meant responses that serve to fend off a danger to survival and multiplication or that serve to take advantage of an opportunity to promote these end-results.

One might beg the question here by declaring that in these cases a deeper or higher stability is served, that of the species or genes themselves. However, this maneuver would stretch the term stability too wide inasmuch as these adaptations are ultimately directed not toward stasis but toward multiplication, of a kind that characteristically takes the form of expansion combined with evolution. It should also be emphasized that these adaptive changes, just like the stabilizing reactions (when, as is only sometimes the case, a distinction can be made!) represent no fundamental property of adaptation on the part of living matter. They are secondary developments, representing (as we have noted in the foregoing discussion) the consequences of the interminably repeated survival and multiplication of the mutant types that happened to be successful.

In addition to the adaptive reactions that have been developed with the function of promoting the welfare of the body proper there are of course those that promote its multiplication. And among the latter are some, of which the prime example is genetic recombination, implemented by sexual reproduction, the function of which is the facilitation of further evolution. Nevertheless, there are no grounds for suspecting that mechanisms have ever become developed that can direct the course of mutation into helpful rather than harmful channels. The process of mutation represents for the organism the taking of an untried step, to the consequences of which it is blind, but which it is ready to profit by if it should make a lucky strike.

It may be reiterated here that the favorable mutation is seldom a large one, and that the smaller its effect is, the more chance there is of its being helpful, and taking part in evolution (Muller 1923). Never do highly organized structures that function helpfully in new ways come into existence at a bound, as they do in "science fiction" stories in which a child is born with telepathic antennae. All organs, tissues, and useful bodily reactions represent the remains of interminable trials, big and little errors that passed away, and little but accumulated successes.

8. *Mutation as destroyer or creator.* Because detrimental mutations are necessarily so much more abundant than favorable ones, it is evident that whenever the rate of elimination of the harmful mutant genes is slackened, as under conditions of easy living or artificial aids, their frequency will tend to rise, and the population will thereby fall off in its natural vigor and in the effectiveness of reactions of types that have been thus protected (Lerner 1950). For it is, in a sense, only selection that holds the body in shape, like the walls of a vessel containing a gas. Thus in the course of evolutionary time, "mutation pressure" will inevitably take advantage of any yielding of the selectional walls and allow the mass to lose its previous nicely adapted form, just as happens with the creatures who after countless generations in caves are found to be no longer capable, genetically, of forming functional eyes.

Sometimes these retrograde developments are all to the good, as when man, having adopted clothing, became relatively hairless, or when, following the practice of cooking and cutting his food, his great jaws receded. However, this process can be carried too far if society not only does all it can to help its genetically unfortunate members, as it certainly should, but if it also gives them every encouragement and assistance in passing along their weaknesses. By an indefinite continuation of this process, society would become overburdened. Moreover, it is evident that an increase in

the pressure of mutations, caused for example by excessive radiation, would exert an influence that worked in the same direction
as a relaxation of selection.

I have no fear that the course of mutational deterioration will
go to serious extremes, because men are in the process of rapid
learning. If they can now avoid self-made disaster they can enter
a period of increasing hope and achievement. The rapid recent
changes in their ways will cause them to reevaluate their ancient
standards. They will then see that, by realistically appraising both
the world without and the world within themselves, by learning
their own basic structure and reactions and the methods of controlling them, they can even challenge and improve upon the
results of that greatest of creative operations, biological evolution
itself. But first let them open their eyes and become aware of this
living world for what it is.

References

Altenburg, E., and Muller, H. J. 1920. The genetic basis of truncate
wing, an inconstant and modifiable character in *Drosophila*.
Genetics 5:1–59.

Benzer, S. 1955. Fine structure of a genetic region in bacteriophage. *Proc. Nat. Acad. Sci.* 41:344–54.

Crick, F. H. C. 1954. The structure of the hereditary material. *Sci.
Amer.* 191:54–61.

Lerner, I. M. 1950. Our load of mutations. *Amer. J. Human Genet.*
2:111–76.

———. 1954. *Genetic homeostasis.* Edinburgh: Oliver and Boyd.

Levinthal, C. 1956. The mechanism of DNA replication and genetic
recombination in phage. *Proc. Nat. Acad. Sci.* 42:394–409.

Morgan, T. H.; Sturtevant, A. H.; Muller, H. J.; Bridges, C.B. 1915.
The mechanism of Mendelian heredity. New York: Holt and Co.
Rev. ed. 1923.

Muller, H. J. 1918. Genetic variability, twin hybrids, and constant hybrids, in a case of balanced lethal factors. *Genetics* 3:422–99.

———. 1922. Variation due to change in the individual gene. *Amer. Natur.* 56:32–50.

———. 1923. Mutation. *Eugenics, Genetics, and the Family* 1:106–12.

———. 1929a. The gene as the basis of life. *Proc. Int. Congr. Plant Sci.* 1:897–921.

———. 1929b. The method of evolution. *Sci. Monthly* 29:481–505.

———. 1932. Some genetic aspects of sex. *Amer. Natur.* 64:118–38.

———. 1938. Bearings of the *Drosophila* work on problems of systematics. *Proc. Zool. Soc., Ser. C.* 108:55–57.

———. 1939. Reversibility in evolution considered from the standpoint of genetics. *Biol. Rev.* 14:261–80.

———. 1940. Bearings of the *Drosophila* work on Systemics. In *The New Systematics,* ed. J. Huxley, pp. 185–268.

———. 1942. Isolating mechanisms, evolution, and temperature. *Biol. Symp.* 6:71–125.

———. 1947. The gene. *Proc. Royal Soc. London* 134: 1–37.

———. 1950. Evidence of the precision of genetic adaptation. *The Harvey Lectures, Ser. 63, 1947–48,* pp. 165–229.

Taylor, J. H.; Woods, P.S.; Hughes, W. L. 1957. The organization and duplication of chromosomes as revealed by autoradiographic studies using tritium-labeled thymidine. *Proc. Nat. Nat. Acad. Sci.* 43:122–28.

Watson, J. D., and Crick, F. H. C. 1953a. Molecular structure of nucleic acids. *Nature* 171:737–38.

———. 1953b. Genetical implications of the structure of deoxyribonucleic acid. *Nature* 177:964–67.

Life

THE path from gene to socially conscious man is not merely explored through calculations of combinational probabilities and the fractions of those numbers sifted through natural selection. Somewhere biological organization, mind, values, and culture emerge in the human story. Muller's essay on life attempts to place man in the universe and to provide a sense of purpose "founded not upon illusions but upon the idealism that is natural to men who engage in a great mutual endeavor."

To many an unsophisticated human being, the universe of stars seems only a fancy backdrop, provided for embellishing his own and his fellow-creatures' performances. On the other hand, from the converse position, that of the universe of stars, not only all human beings but the totality of life is merely a fancy kind of rust, afflicting the surfaces of certain lukewarm minor planets. However, even when we admit our own littleness and the egotistical complexion of our interest in this rust, we remain confronted with the question: What is it that causes the rust to be so very fancy?

In the childhood of our species, the answer to this question seemed obvious: Life is a spirit. This spirit, inhabiting the matter we call *living*, works its will upon it, enduing it with wondrous forms and with purposeful activities. Sometimes the idea of spirit was clothed in more pretentious terms, such as perfecting principle, entelechy, vital force, or mneme, yet all these still implied some sort of conscious or semiconscious entity, striving to dominate matter. The verbal subtlety of the terms veiled a naive animism.

Life as Result of the Mode of Organization of Matter

The animistic view has been increasingly called into question. For instance, with the invention of machinery it was found that entirely lifeless matter can be fashioned into complex forms, capable of engaging in remarkable activities, some of them reminiscent of those of living things. Further, it was found that even in a state of nature some lifeless matter attains considerable complexity, and that in some cases it can give extraordinary reactions, which, although based on the regular principles of operation of lifeless material, simulate one or another supposedly "vital" phenomenon.

These doubts concerning the animistic interpretation were strengthened by the studies on living matter itself. All of its activities were found to conform strictly to the law of conservation of energy. That is, no energy was involved in any of its operations except what had been supplied to it from measurable physiochemical sources, nor was any of this energy done away with by it. Its atoms were found to be the same as atoms elsewhere. They were bound by the same rules into molecules. These molecules could in many cases be constructed artificially, and even the reactions that they underwent within living things could often be repeated in a test tube. Moreover, for some important operations, such as chromosome movements, for which physiochemical formulas were still lacking, regular rules of procedure were nevertheless discovered which elucidated age-old mysteries in terms of orderly material processes.

At the same time, however, such studies have revealed in living things greater and greater complications, which in this respect remove them ever further both from natural nonliving things and from artificial devices. For, as we examine the interior of a living thing and then magnify it more and more, we find at each successive level of magnification a new and different set of complications: first, on naked-eye inspection, that of organs, then that of tissues, then of cells, then of cell parts and of parts within these, until immense molecules are reached, some containing hundreds of thousands of atoms, precisely and intricately arranged into groupings composed of subgroupings of several grades. Such molecules are present in even the simplest microbes known.

Yet this prodigious complication, even in its many still unexplained features, encourages not vitalism but the common-sense interpretation that it is this organization itself on which life's remarkable properties depend. If, on the contrary, an imponderable spirit were the source of life's capabilities, these complications would be superfluous. Daily this inference becomes reenforced as more and more of the operations of living things are traced to the orderly workings of given parts of the complex. Moreover, each living thing as a whole is ever more clearly seen to be one great integrated system, the operations of which are all coordinated in such a way that, collectively, they tend to result in one ultimate outcome: The maximal extension of the given type.

Genesis of the Organization

Granting all this, the question is thereby rendered especially acute: How did these marvelous organizations, constituted in such a way as to achieve so peculiar an effect, come into being? The process of their origination, surely, appears at first thought to require some sort of conscious designing. To begin with, it was believed that all species had been designed and created separately in their present forms; but in the nineteenth century the evidence for their gradual interconnected development out of one or a few primitive forms that were the common ancestors of all became convincing. It was then speculated by certain schools that the ancestral organisms had been endowed with built-in long-range designs that forced them to evolve as they did. Another view, which has been revived by the so-called "Michurinists" of Iron Curtain countries, where it has (until recently at any rate) been obligatory, postulated a generalized adaptive ability in living things. By its means they altered themselves in advantageous ways when they were subjected to changed conditions and, along with this, they somehow implanted into their reproductive cells speculations for these same alterations. Such an ability to select and install just the kind of alteration that is going to work out advantageously, *before it has been tried out,* clearly implies some sort of foresight, despite the disclaiming of this implication by some of the advocates of this view. In this case, then, the designing is merely done in bits, instead of in the grand manner.

Darwin's and Wallace's greatest contribution was to show that, even without planning, complex adaptations necessarily evolve. Since members of any population show manifold variations which their offspring tend to inherit, some of these variations—those that happen to be conducive to survival and multiplication—will find themselves more abundantly represented in the next generation. Thus the population will gradually accumulate more characteristics of an "adaptive" kind, that is, of a kind advantageous for the species' preservation and increase, even though there has been no tendency for helpful rather than harmful variations to arise in the first place.

In confirmation of this principle, modern studies in genetics, the science of heredity and variation, have shown that the great majority of newly arisen variations of an inheritable sort are indeed detrimental, as must be true of unplanned alterations that occur in a complex organization of any kind. Moreover, when outer conditions are changed, the few variations that happen to be useful in coping with these outer changes are found not to arise in greater relative abundance than they did before. Yet of course they do succeed better: that is, they are *naturally selected* afterward, in the actual tests of living.

From Gene to Protoplasm

The major actor in this great drama of evolution by natural selection has proved to be the *gene,* a particle too tiny to be seen under the microscope but immense by inorganic standards. There are thousands of different genes in a cell of a plant or animal, each gene with its distinctive pattern and, in consequence, its special type of chemical influence. For the most part, at any rate, the genes are strung together to make up the threadlike bodies called *chromosomes,* which are visible under the microscope in the inner compartment or nucleus of the cell. Although the genes form only a small part of the cell's bulk, they control through their diverse products, primary, secondary, and more remote, the composition and the arrangement of most or all of the other materials in the cell and, therefore, in the entire body. Their control is a conditional one, however, since the nature of the setting in which the genes' products find themselves has much to do with which of their potentialities are allowed to come to fruition.

Recent evidence indicates that the gene consists of the substance known as *nucleic acid,* in the form of a much coiled chain, or double chain, composed of a great number (thousands) of links. The links, called *nucleotides,* are of only four kinds. Yet there are so many links in each chain that, through their different arrangements in line, they would make possible a practically unlimited number of kinds of genes. How such differing arrangements would result in the very different functional effects that different genes are known to exert is a question now being widely asked, but the attack on it is only beginning.

The most remarkable thing about the gene is that each huge chain-molecule has the faculty of capturing by some specialized sort of affinity peculiar to its links, chemical groups in its vicinity which in some way correspond to these links. The captured groups thereby become matched up alongside the gene's links in an arrangement similar to that in the gene itself, and they are enabled to become bound together, just as the gene's own links are. As a result, they finally constitute another gene essentially like the original one. Thus the gene reproduces itself.

The details of gene reproduction have long eluded investigation. The most direct interpretation was to suppose that each subunit of the gene tended to attract and fasten next to itself a free subunit of the same type that happened to come into its neighborhood (Troland 1917). Although the seeming attraction between like groups of genes (chromosomes) has lent support to this view (Muller 1922, 1937, 1941, 1947), it has met with difficulties on physical grounds. Recently, however, my suggestion that the attraction may derive from electric oscillations has been developed by Jehle (1950a, 1950b). Calculations of his group along these lines are now giving promising results (Bade 1954).

On the other hand, a number of investigators have proposed that gene reproduction, instead of involving the direct capturing or molding of like by like subunits, is a two-step process in which each subunit of the gene captures or molds one of an opposite or "complementary" kind, and that when the complementary structure in turn captures or molds its own complement a formation like the original one becomes reconstructed. An analogy would be the use of a positive print to make a negative one, from which in turn another positive is derived (Friedrich-Freksa 1940). On the most recent and best supported variant of this idea, Watson and Crick, in a series of brilliant papers (1953; Crick 1954), have proposed that each nucleotide has as its complement a nucleotide of a given one of the three other types. By capturing their complements from materials in the medium about the gene, the chained nucleotides in a gene are thought to construct alongside themselves a complementary chain of nucleotides. This at its own next act of reproduction, by constructing a chain complementary to itself, gives rise to a formation identical in types with the original gene. Moreover, since on the view of these investigators the original chain is really a double one, with one member of the doublet the complement of the other to begin with, the construction by each of these two parallel chains of another chain complementary to itself would even at the first step result in a new pair of chains which, considered as a whole, would be identical with the original pair. Further complications have been proposed, involving interchanges of subunits between the original chains and those in process of formation (Delbrück 1954), but as yet these serve to point up difficulties of the hypothesis rather than to answer them.

With the present activity in this field, it may well be that a relatively few years will suffice to establish definitely the solution of the problem of gene reproduction and, thus, to elucidate the most essential phenomenon in the operation of living matter. At this point, however, the important thing to note is the fact that, whatever the means by which it does so, each gene succeeds in constructing a physiochemical duplicate of itself. Later, when the cell containing the genes divides to form two daughter cells, the two identical genes that are present as a result of the duplication of every gene originally existing in the cell become drawn apart into different daughter cells. The fact that the genes are strung together in line to form the chromosomes provides a means for the orderly carrying out of this separation. Thereby the descendant cells come to contain identical genes.

Despite this identity of gene content, however, the groups of cells in different parts of a many-celled body are differentiated from one another. This is because the structure of the cells in each group results from a limited set of reactions, representing only a part of the numerous potentialities of the contained constellation of genes. These limits have been fixed by the special conditions prevailing within the given groups of cells. On the other hand, in a reproductive cell the same outfit of genes is sufficient, when multiplied, to organize the development of the entire body. In this way the genes serve as the basis of heredity.

On rare occasions a gene meets with an ultramicroscopic collision or other accident, which jolts its parts (or those of the duplicate that it has under construction) into a new arrangement that has a different chemical influence from before. We call this event a *mutation*. The mutant gene, in reproducing itself thereafter, tends to copy its new pattern as faithfully as the original gene had copied its old pattern. Thus, if the mutation has occurred in a reproductive cell, it may become evident as a variation inherited by a line of descendants. In this way, the mutations of the genes provide the inherited variations on which the process of evolution by natural selection is based. The reason this role is reserved for the genes alone is that only they have the strange property of making copies of themselves in just such a way as to incorporate within the daughter particles even those features that have been newly introduced into their own structure. In other words, their most important peculiarity is their ability to reproduce, not merely themselves as they originally were, but also their variations (Muller 1922, 1937, 1941, 1947).

The material that forms the bulk of most cells, although often designated by the single word *protoplasm,* is really a most elaborate composite of numerous constituents. The production of many of these constituents, including fundamentally important ones, has been shown to depend upon groups of special genes. Remove one of these genes and a given protoplasmic substance disappears or is replaced by something different; restore the gene and the protoplasmic substance reappears. In contrast to this, the production of any distinctive type of gene is not ordinarily a process initiated by the presence of certain distinctive protoplasmic substances. For, when a new type of gene arises by the mutation of some preexisting gene, this mutant gene proceeds to reproduce itself, along with the growth and division of the cell, even though the protoplasmic substances present were, to start with, no different from those in other cells not containing the given mutant gene. On the basis of this, as well as other considerations (including that of economy of assumptions), it is reasonable to infer that in the origination of life the gene arose first, and that protoplasm came into existence later, very gradually, in the form of a series of products of the chemical action of aggregates of genes that had mutated in such ways as to be able to give rise to these products. Protoplasm would thus consist of substances accessory to and produced by the genes. Its existence would be due to the fact that those mutant genes had been naturally selected whose products happened to afford chemical tools, such as enzymes, that are useful for the survival and multiplication of these genes themselves.

It may be concluded that the essence of life is not protoplasm or its operations, collectively termed metabolism, as has often been asserted, but that these are themselves results of biological evolution. Life's essence lies in the capability of undergoing such evolution, and this capability is inherent in the gene, by virtue of its property of duplicating its variations. At the present time, protoplasm is so highly evolved and complex, even in the most primitive cells known, that we should probably be justified in estimating the amount of advance in complexity between the stage of the simplest gene and that of a single cell, such as a bacterium, to be at least as great as that from the bacterium to the highest many-celled organism.

It is not surprising that, in the remote past, the gene itself should have come into existence. For conditions were such, in the envelopes of the primitive earth, that the accidental encounters of substances, together with the absorption of energetic radiation, continued during many millions of years, must have provided a tremendous accumulation of ever more complicated organic compounds, including many of those occurring today within cells (Muller 1929, 1935). And if, among the myriad types of molecules thereby produced, genes were included (only one successful gene being required!), then the component parts also would already have been formed, out of which these genes could manufacture duplicates of themselves. Moreover, there would also be numerous other ready-made constituents present, which were capable of being utilized as accessory substances after mutations implementing such utilization had occurred in the descendant genes.

Advances in Protoplasmic Organization

The chemical nature of the pathways whereby the genes control the composition and workings of the protoplasm have not yet been made clear. In any case, these pathways today involve so many steps and are so intricately branched and conjoined that much of the control is very indirect. With regard to the primary step in gene functioning, the long-neglected view is now gaining ground that this consists in the construction by the genes in the chromosomes of modified likenesses of themselves which enter the general protoplasm and there act as the genes' working delegates. Now that there is reason to regard the genes as being composed of nucleic acid, it is natural to suppose that the modified kind of nucleic acid, ribonucleic acid, found in high concentration in special protoplasmic granules, represents these gene delegates. Rich and Watson (1954), who advocate this view, present evidence that this kind of nucleic acid, like that of the genes themselves, consists of coiled chains, possibly double, of nucleotides—in this case, however, of the four corresponding "ribonucleotide" types. Since the synthesis of protein and possibly of other substances occurs in association with these granules, it seems likely that it is the ribonucleotide chains in them that conduct this synthesis. Perhaps they also, to a limited extent, carry out some duplication of their own substance. The proteins and other materials, in their turn, engage in the multitudinous other reactions that occur in the cell.

In addition to those ribonucleotide links that are united in long chains to form the ribonucleic acids, there are more or less separated units of them, and these have been found to be indispensable in many protoplasmic reactions. In these reactions they act as conveyors of large amounts of energy (carried on detachable phosphate groups) from one type of molecule to another, under the guidance of proteins and other companion substances. It may be that this special ability to transfer energy is also possessed by chained nucleotides and comes into play when they carry out their synthetic activities, both in gene duplication and in the building of other materials.

Aside from the nucleic acids themselves, the proteins are the most highly organized and diversified of the protoplasmic substances. In connection with most of the chemical steps taken by organic materials in protoplasm, there is some distinctive protein that acts as an enzyme for just that reaction: that is, a substance that induces the given change in other molecules without itself being used up. One or a few molecules of enzyme, because they can continue to do the same job repeatedly, are able to change a relatively large amount of other material. In consequence, an outfit of numerous different enzymes, sufficient for a multitude of different operations, can be obtained within a minute bulk of protoplasm.

The molecules of proteins, like those of nucleic acids, are made up of chains, often coiled, composed of a great number of links. Important in determining the physical and chemical potentialities of any given protein molecule is (for one thing) the exact arrangement in line of its diverse types of links, called *amino-acid groups*. Nucleic-acid molecules, both of those of the genes and those elsewhere (ribonucleic acids), commonly exist in close association with protein molecules. These and other considerations have lent plausibility to the idea that the building of protein molecules involves an activity of the nucleic acids of the genes somewhat resembling that by which they duplicate themselves. Even more likely is the possibility that the ribonucleic acids work in this way.

If, however, the construction of a protein molecule is pictured as a capturing, by the links of a nucleotide chain-molecule, of amino acids corresponding to these nucleotides, with the resultant formation of a parallel amino-acid chain-molecule, the difficulty arises that, whereas there are only four types of nucleotides, there are some two dozen types of amino acids. How then can a given nucleotide specify which amino acid is to be selected at a given point? Gamow (1953, 1954) has suggested what appears to be a likely solution: namely, it takes a group of four neighboring nucleotides to capture one amino acid, and the type of amino acid selected depends upon how these four nucleotides (of their four possible types) are arranged with respect to one another, somewhat as the arrangement of letters determines the meaning of a word. He points out that, at any point in a coiled double chain of nucleotides, the number of effectively different arrangements of four neighboring nucleotides would just about correspond with the number of different types of amino acids in proteins. Whether or not the details of his hypothesis are correct, it would seem that some such relationship must exist if, as seems likely, the nucleic acids synthesize the proteins directly.

Even if the protein molecules are produced in this way in the first place, however, they would still be subject to considerable and diverse alterations afterward, since proteins are among the most modifiable substances known. It would therefore be unwarranted to suppose that any given enzyme or other protein of functional importance is the product of some one special gene alone and that other genes have played no part in the determination of its nature. In fact, there is, in particular cases, direct genetic evidence against this oversimplified view.

Whatever the means by which proteins and other organic substances were synthesized, there must, soon after the earliest stages of their association with genes, have been great advantage in the ability to utilize, as raw materials for them, other materials than those constituent groups out of which they were immediately put together in the process of capture and arrangement by nucleotide chains. These hitherto alien materials would become available for use if they could be subjected to reactions that converted them into such constituents, and these reactions could be brought about by appropriate enzymes and other accessory substances, resulting from given mutations of genes. Moreover, in the construction of some substances methods of their manufacture would be worked out which did not require any direct reshaping of their constituents by the nucleotides themselves. In consequence, as the operations of gene aggregates, gradually aided by more numerous accessory substances, became more complicated through the natural selection of advantageous mutations in the genes, means must have been evolved for transforming into the materials of living things substances that required an ever more extended series of steps for the conversion process. At the same time, increasingly elaborate and effective methods were also developed for obtaining energy, storing it, and transferring it. Thus ultimately some organisms, the typical plants, became able to live entirely on certain inorganic substances and to derive their energy directly from the prime source, sunlight.

Other organisms meanwhile evolved mechanisms for utilizing other substances, some inorganic, some organic, for material, or for energy, or for both, until at last there was one vast interconnected system of living things on earth, diversely specialized chemically. This system kept in circulation the materials for life and also, until it had become dissipated, the captured energy, instead of letting them accumulate in the form of unusable wastes, as many of them must have done before. Life was thereby able to attain far greater abundance, faster turnover, increased diversity, and speedier, richer evolution.

Another circumstance that accelerated evolution, probably even at a prebacterial stage, was the establishment of sexual reproduction, in its more general sense of the coming together of two sets of genes from different sources. Before this process could be biologically effective, the series of maneuvers known as *meiosis* had to be developed. In meiosis some of the genes of each of the two sets that meet become recombined so as to form a single complete set. By the repetition of this process in successive generations, an entire population comes to constitute one great pool of genes, out of the innumerable shifting combinations of which the choicest (from the standpoint of self-perpetuation) tend to prevail. The accumulation of advantageous mutant genes is thereby caused to take place much more rapidly than in organisms that reproduce only asexually, which have their genes confined within mutually isolated lines of descent. Undoubtedly sexual reproduction owes its survival to the other advantages that, secondarily, accrued in its possessors by virtue of their faster evolution. Its function, therefore, is to make more effective the gene's ability to evolve.

Still another innovation the main significance of which lies in its hastening of evolution, or, to be more accurate, in its hindering of the retardation of evolution, is the natural death of the body. Of course this phenomenon arises, in its more typical manifestations, only in the later stages of evolution, in which organisms have become many celled and have had their reproductive cells differentiated from the cells of their body proper. Natural death is not the expression of an inherent principle of protoplasm, but in each species natural selection has tended to develop a length of life that is optimal, in relation to the other characteristics of that species and to its conditions of living. In other words, death is an advantage to life. Its advantage lies chiefly in its giving ampler opportunities for the genes of the newer generation to have their merits tested out. That is, by clearing the way for fresh starts, it prevents the clogging of genetic progress by the older individuals. Secondarily, in higher organisms which as a result of the existence of natural death have allowed defects to develop during senescence, death has become doubly advantageous, in that it now serves also to sweep away these defects for which it is indirectly responsible.

Even before the attainment of the many-celled stage, with its complicated embryonic development, passing into adulthood, senescence, and death, many organisms had evolved regular sequences of transformations, constituting developmental cycles. They had also evolved numerous regulatory mechanisms that adapted them to environmental changes of those types that had been repeatedly encountered. Some of these mechanisms stabilized the organism internally, in reaction to outside disturbances; others set on foot operations that counteracted harmful circumstances or that took advantage of potentially helpful circumstances. Among the mechanisms were those that endowed the organisms with the properties known loosely as *irritability, conductivity,* and *contractility*, all of which were so interadjusted as to result in adaptive (that is, advantageous) movements.

These diverse adaptive reactions all have their bases in specific structures, caused by genes, accidentally arisen by mutation, which had won out in the struggle for survival when the given conditions were met with many times in the past. They are not, however, expressions of any generalized adaptive ability, and they do not control the course of variation in the genes themselves. Thus the pre-Darwinian evolutionists and their Michurinist descendants have put the cart before the horse in assuming that living matter, by virtue of its inherent nature, makes an effort to adapt itself directly to new circumstances, and that evolution has consisted in the accumulation, by inheritance, of the adaptations thereby evoked.

Plant and Animal Ways

In some lines of one-celled organisms, which had probably been typical plants, adjustments of the structures subserving movement enabled the organism to add to its income by capturing and assimilating bits of already formed organic material and finally even other organisms. It then proved profitable for them to concentrate entirely on the predatory mode of life, with resultant loss of most synthetic abilities and ever-increasing development of the motor ones. Thus animals arose.

Although animals and plants thereafter diverged, there were some parallelisms in their evolution. In both groups increased size proved advantageous for some ways of living and was accomplished by the integration of many cells into a larger organism. This in turn allowed the development of far greater specialization of parts. However, in plants the fact that the supplies needed could usually be had best by simply "staying put" and reaching steadily out for them caused this specialization to take the form of relatively motionless branched structures, with (for land plants) roots in the ground for securing minerals and water, leaves above for sunlight and carbon dioxide, and a strong conducting structure between. Movements were still necessary to bring the male reproductive cells to the eggs and to disseminate the products of fertilization, but these were in the main accomplished passively, by mechanisms that utilized motions of water, air, or animals.

On the animal side, the nature of the food put a premium on the development of means of capturing it and of avoiding being captured. It is true that many small bits of food which floated or swam through water could be caught even by sedentary animals, provided that these sifted the food out from the water that was swept by them or sucked into them. Hence such animals are often plantlike in appearance. But more of a challenge was presented by food that was large, well protected, difficult of access, elusive, or possessed of counteractivity. The more the food used had such characteristics, the more advantageous was it for the animal to develop adroitness and strength of movement, including locomotion. The same capabilities also became valuable in protecting it against predators equipped with them. In varied lines of animals, therefore, natural selection favored the accumulation of those mutations that resulted in more effective sensory, coordinating, motor, and supporting systems. At the same time, since the exercise of strength requires a comparatively massive body, in the interior of which materials are not introduced or removed at a fast enough rate by diffusion alone to service a high level of activity, it became important to elaborate systems for ingesting and processing food materials and oxygen, for supplying them effectively to the cells, and for extracting and eliminating the wastes.

The striking divergent forms taken by many of these advances in different groups were, of course, evolved in adaptation to their great differences in circumstances and ways of living. Often these differences were in considerable measure dependent upon one or a few major peculiarities of their construction, such as a gliding membrane or tube-feet, which furnished a key to the mode of construction of many other parts. It is evident that some of the features, including even some of those in the key positions, were originally adopted, at least in the particular form taken by them, as a result of some unusual combination of minor, temporary circumstances, which would be unlikely to recur. Having once arisen, however, they proved their usefulness, which sometimes extended to some very different function, and they thereby became a solid, important part of the pattern of the organism. In this position, they might help to determine the natural selection of a long series of further steps, proceeding in a given direction. Because the method of evolution was thus opportunistic instead of farsighted, it is found that organisms, despite the marvelous interworking of their parts, conceal many imperfections and indirections of structure and functioning. In fact, evolution presents such a curious combination of arbitrariness and consequentialness as to lead us to infer that on another world physically like ours only remotely analogous forms of life would have evolved.

Learning and Consciousness

Among the more regularly occurring of the higher developments in active animals is the elaboration of the coordinating system and the inclusion within it of mechanisms for modifying its operations in adjustment with the individual's experiences. The basic feature in this process, which from the objective standpoint is called *conditioning* and from the subjective standpoint *learning* or *association,* is the formation of connections among different groups of neuronic (nerve cell) reactions that have been aroused at or nearly at the same time, so that subsequently the arousal of either tends to invoke the other as well. These connections form an ever more intricate web, since if reaction-group *A* becomes connected with *B* at one time and *B* becomes connected with *C* at another time, it follows that *A* thereby becomes connected with *C,* in the arrangement *ABC.*

Also essential in learning is the procedure called *analysis,* whereby particular components or relationships existing within a neuronic reaction-complex become dissected out, as it were, so that when they occur in different settings they can serve to cross-connect these other features with one another, somewhat as *B* connected *A* and *C* in the foregoing illustration. Doubtless there are as yet unguessed but far-reaching inherited neural mechanisms that effect the isolation of certain characteristic relationships, such as (on a sensory-motor level) possession of the same color or motion of a given kind across the field of view. However, much of the analysis at deeper levels depends also upon associational procedures in which the neuronic reaction-complex is subjected to various learned operations. These, in modifying it, bring out features implicit in it which it shares with some other complex.

All these processes become useful to the organism only by virtue of their modification of its behavior. This modification is made possible by the fact that the neuronic activities for movements become strengthened or inhibited according to whether these movements have been followed by experiences (neuronic reactions and reaction-complexes) of the types subjectively designated as desirable or undesirable. Which experiences are originally felt to be desirable or undesirable, and which emotional and behavioral ("instinctive") responses are concomitantly aroused by them, are matters determined by inherited neuronic structures. These have been shaped by evolution in such a way that the creature, in working for its own goals, unwittingly furthers the multiplication of its kind. However, through association it learns to achieve its primary desires by more effective means, better adjusted to the circumstances surrounding it, and learns to coordinate and subordinate its different desires to one another so as to attain greater total gratification.

Despite our present ignorance of the nature of the physiochemical bases of all these phenomena, their physiochemical *existence* is attested by numerous facts of observation and experiment.

As, through association and analysis, an increasingly coherent and serviceable formulation or representation of the world outside becomes built up out of the neuronic reaction-complexes, we become justified in speaking of intelligence. Only here, at last, does foresight make its debut in the operations of living things. Moreover, within this same neuronic reaction-system, a representation of the individual himself, including his own association, gradually takes its place. A speaking individual, in referring to this phenomenon, then uses the expression *consciousness* or some equivalent.

Although this term denotes what may be called the inner or subjective view of oneself, it is only a confusion of ideas that it is thought of as implying the existence of two "parallel sides," conscious and material, to neuronic or other processes: that is, two systems of phenomena that coexist and completely correspond but do not interact. If this view were correct the existence of con-

sciousness, being only "parallel," could in no way affect our behavior. Hence we could not speak of it. Nor could we, for that
matter, even think of it (for the conscious could not more than
parallel the material side, and the latter could not be affected by
the former). It follows that the conscious phenomena *are* the
physicochemical phenomena or, at least, are some integrated portion of them. In other words, matter and mind present no real
antithesis. Moreover, in the case of mind, as in the case of life, its
difference from matter and energy in their more ordinary forms
lies in the peculiarities of its mode of organization and resultant
operation.

Pooling of Learning

Turning to a consideration of the native intelligence of our own
species, we find that it is not so very much greater than that of
some other existing animals. However, this relatively moderate
difference, taken in conjunction with man's social disposition and
with his queer proclivities for vocalizing and symbolizing, enables
him far more effectively than other animals to communicate with
others of his kind. This has resulted in his social evolution, by the
accumulation of tradition, a process wherein each individual becomes provided with the distilled experience of a vast, ever-
increasing body of his ancestors and associates. Through this
knowledge and the cooperative activities and resultant material
equipment based upon it, man has become incomparably more
potent than any other form of life on earth, even without any
perceptible improvement having taken place in his genes since
before civilization began.

It is true that ancient tradition is often faulty and tends to over-
elaborate itself by an inner inertia in arbitrary and injurious ways.
Moreover, the strange human propensity for symbolization, although invaluable not only for communication but for thought
itself, has often led men astray, running away with them, causing
them to misinterpret and glorify their own symbols, and to con-
fuse them with the things denoted. But with the increase of useful
knowledge men have come to realize that tradition, even when
ancient, is man-made, and that only the systematic testing, un-

hampered criticism, and rational judgment denoted as *science* can give them a more correct understanding of things. By the conscious, organized use of this method life today, in the form of man, is ever more rapidly reaching out to new spheres and to new modes of existence. At the same time, transcending its role of animal, it is making its position firmer by learning to promote, and in part even to supersede the synthetic functions of the plant kingdom.

It must be recognized that at this point man's social development has lagged far behind his "material" development, and that the resultant insufficiency of cooperation among his own members may bring about the annihilation of his hard-won achievements, if not of man himself. Alternatively, he may begin to advance to hitherto unimagined outer and inner conquests. Such advance, however, will require a wisdom that can be gained only by genuinely free inquiry, based solidly upon our advancing knowledge of the nature of things and backed by the broadest, most unbiased good will.

If our dangerous drifting from one short-range goal to another is to be replaced by really long-range foresight, we shall have to overhaul courageously all our ancient standards of value, for value judgements, far from being immune to scientific investigation as is sometimes asserted, should be a main object of such study. In accordance with the conclusions thereby reached, we shall then have the task of modifying our systems of inner motivation and the relationships of individual with individual and group with group. Recognizing that our conscious objectives, which we subsume under the expression *the pursuit of happiness,* are the complex and modifiable resultants of more primitive urges chosen by natural selection in compliance with the pressure of the gene to preserve itself and to extend its domain, we must seek more *functional* ways of pursuing happiness. These should more successfully harmonize the gene's trend to increase and evolve with the deepest fulfillment of our conscious natures, so that the serving of either of these ends will by that act promote the other. In fact, any other policy is ultimately self-defeating, in this world of interpenetrating competition and cooperation.

Crisis in Gene Increase

It is, however, a mistake to assume that the gene's tendency to increase gives biological victory to the organisms with the highest gross fertility. In general, the "higher" the organism, the greater the security of individual life that it achieves and the lower its production of offspring. Natural selection has decreased the fertility because, with too high a pressure toward population increase, the well-being and efficiency of the organisms are so reduced as actually to lower the potential of the species to undergo biological expansion. In fact, civilized man, through his advanced techniques, has attained such security of life (except for war!) that an even lower fertility now becomes appropriate for him, both biologically and for his individual happiness, than that which was established for him by natural selection in adjustment to primitive conditions.

Civilized man is now going part of the way toward meeting this requirement artificially, by means of birth control, but it will be necessary for him to make much more widespread and adequate use of such technique, in order that he may attain and maintain a world-wide optimum per-capita supply of energy and of food and other materials. Otherwise he would be forced back into a misery and disorganization that would not only rob him of most of the benefits of his previous progress but would find him deprived, perhaps permanently, of the resources needed to raise himself again and at last to expand into new and more commodious realms of living. Thus it is preeminently true of civilized man that his success in pursuing happiness is a necessary basis for the success of his genes in their job of multiplication. Conversely, however, the pursuit of happiness must also be so directed as ultimately to lead to biological expansion, if man is to utilize his opportunities for bringing "the greatest good to the greatest number," and if he is to minimize the risks of disaster and of being left behind in the universal struggle for existence.

But even if we grant that man will achieve adequate control over his numbers and will advance to untold reaches in his social evolution, all this progress must still rest on a crumbling biological basis, unless not merely the quantity but also the quality of that basis is vigilantly taken care of. For the artificial saving of lives under modern civilization will allow the increasing accumulation of detrimental mutant genes, unless this accumulation is deliberately compensated by an enlightened control over the types of genes to be reproduced. This course of action, to be both sound in its direction and effective in its execution, must be entered upon not under compulsion but in the spirit of freely given cooperation, founded not upon illusions but upon the idealism that is natural to men who engage in a great mutual endeavor.

Man a Transitional Phase

The spirit thus aroused would inevitably tend to proceed further, to the realization that the mere prevention of deterioration is an inadequate, uninspiring biological ideal and that instead, by extension and supplementation of the methods followed for maintaining our genetic foundation as it is, it can actually be raised to ever higher levels. Acceptance of this course will be facilitated by the rapid growth of human understanding and technical proficiency that we see under way about us now. This present progress is, as we have seen, not based on any changes in the hereditary endowment but only on the extreme responsiveness of the human organism, even with its present endowment, to educational and other environmental influences. But great as are the advances possible in this way, men cannot remain satisfied with them alone when they become aware of the vastly greater enhancement of life that could result from the combination of this kind of progress with that in their underlying genetic constitution. This would include the genetic remodeling of our primitive urges, the improvement of our intellectual ability, and even of our bodily construction.

There is no limit in sight to the possible extent of such advances, provided that we *will* them to take place. However, the possibility of their coming about automatically, by the type of unconscious natural selection that has operated in past ages, has been done away with, as explained earlier, by the conditions resulting from social evolution. For these conditions rightly lead to the increasing protection, by society at large, of those who are weak and ailing by heredity, as well as those handicapped by misfortunes caused by outer circumstances. Yet at the same time this very social evolution has provided and will provide increasingly effective knowledge and techniques for the voluntary, artificial guidance of biological evolution. These make available, in compensation for the deficiency of natural selection under civilization, novel means of directing many of the processes involved in reproduction and heredity.

Among the methods of this kind that are being, and will be further, developed are those for managing the generation and the storage of the reproductive cells, both within the body and outside of it, those for artificially controlling insemination and fertilization, for instigating parthenogenesis and twinning or polyembryony, and for instituting foster pregnancy. It should be possible eventually to find ways of influencing the behavior and distribution of the chromosomes themselves. Means of substituting, for the original nuclei of eggs, other cell nuclei, of chosen types, are even now being worked out, and such operations may in time be made fine enough to deal with individual chromosomes or their parts. Far more remote and unlikely than these possibilities, however, is that of regulating the direction taken by the mutations of genes.

However that may be, the rate at which biological progress could be made even by the means available today is already incomparably greater than that to which it was limited by the slow unconscious processes of nature. Only fear of the dead hand of ancient superstition today holds most men back from a recognition of these opportunities for greater life. But, with the progress of enlightenment, this fear must wither away. Thus, man as we know him is to be regarded as only a transitional operative in the progression of life, but one who commands a critical turning of the road. For at this point the method of evolution may change from the unconscious to the conscious, from that of trial and error to that of long-range foresight.

Man in the shackles of authoritarianism is incapable of such advances. Should he attempt them, his efforts would be misdirected and corrupting. But, with the amplified opportunity to create that is his when he is free to see things as they are, he will find his greatest inspiration in the realization that he is by no means the final acme and end of existence, but that, through his own efforts, he may become the favored vehicle of life today. That is, he can be the means whereby life is conducted onward and outward, to forms in ever better harmony within themselves, with one another, and with outer nature, endowed with ever keener sentience, deeper wisdom, and further reaching powers.

Who can say how far this seed of self-awareness and self-transfiguration that is within us may in ages to come extend itself down the corridors of the cosmos, challenging in its progression those insensate forces and masses in relation to which it has seemed to be but a trivial infestation or rust? For the law of the gene is ever to increase and to evolve to such forms as will more effectively manipulate and control materials outside itself so as to safeguard and promote its own increase. And if the mindless gene has thereby generated mind and foresight, and then advanced this product from the individual to the social mind, to what reaches may not we and our heirs, the incarnations of that social mind, be able, if we will, to carry consciously the conquests of life?

References

Bade, W. L. 1954. Ph.D. dissertation, University of Nebraska.

Crick, F. H. C. 1954. *Sci. Amer.* 191, no. 4:54:

Delbrück, M. 1954. *Proc. Nat. Acad. Sci.* 40:783:

Friedrich-Freksa, H. 1940. *Naturwiss* 28:376.

Gamow, G. 1953. *Nature* 173:318.

————. 1954. *Danish Biol. Medd.* 22, no. 3.

Jehle, H. 1950a. *J. Chem. Phys.* 18:1150, 1681.

————. 1950b. *Proc. Nat. Acad. Sci.* 36:238.

Muller, H. J. 1922. *Amer. Natur.* 56:32.

————. 1929. Paraphrased from The method of evolution. *Sci. Monthly* 29:481.

————. 1935. *Out of the Night: A Biologist's View of the Future.* New York: Vanguard Press, p. 24.

————. 1937. *Sci. Monthly* 44:210.

————. 1941. *Cold Spring Harbor Symp. Quant. Biol.* 9:290.

————. 1947. *Proc. Roy. Soc. London B 134:*1.

Rich, A., and Watson, J. D. 1954. *Proc. Nat. Acad. Sci.* 40:759.

Troland, L. T. 1917. *Amer. Natur.* 51:321.

Watson, J. D., and Crick, F. H. C. 1953. *Nature* 171:737, 964.

Chronology of
H. J. Muller's Career

1890   Born in New York City, 21 December.

1904/07 Attended Morris High School, Bronx, New York

1907/10 Undergraduate, Columbia University; influenced by
E. B. Wilson for chromosome theory.

1910/11 M.A., Physiology Department, Columbia University.

1911/12 Assistant, Cornell Medical School.

1912/15 Ph.D. research with T. H. Morgan on crossing-over
(coincidence and interference); independent work on
gene and character relations; correlation of chromosome
number and size with cross-over maps and linkage
groups.

1915/18 Recruited by Julian Huxley to Rice Institute; analysis
of inconstant, variable traits.

1918/20 Instructor, Columbia University. Theoretical papers on
mutation and the individual gene; reproduction of
variations as key to definition of gene.

1921   Assistant Professor, University of Texas; analysis of
complex traits with chief genes and modifiers.

1922   Develops CIB method for detecting sex linked lethals.

1923   Marries Jessie Marie Jacobs (divorced 1935).

1924   Son, David Eugene born.

1925   Studies of identical twins raised apart.

1926   Gene as the basis of life throughout evolution.

1927   Artificial induction of mutations with X rays;
          AAAS Research Prize.

1928/32   Laws of radiation genetics; analysis of chromosome
          breakage as basis for chromosome rearrangements.

1932   Attack on American eugenics movement;
          disillusionment with contemporary American society;
          Guggenheim Fellowship to work in Berlin with
          Timoféeff-Ressovsky; analysis of dosage compensation.

1933/37   Senior geneticist, Leningrad and Moscow. Analysis
          of gene boundaries, gene size, viable deficiencies.
          Cytogenetic studies of Bar gene as duplication; gene
          evolution by tandem duplications. Polemic controversy
          with Lysenko.

1935   Publication of *Out of the Night.*

1937   Volunteer in Spanish Civil War, Canadian Blood unit;
          research on transfusion from cadavers.

1938/40   Lecturer, Institute for Animal Genetics, Edinburgh,
          Scotland. Studies of ultraviolet mutation; relation
          of chromosome changes to evolution; discovery of
          mutations induced with low rates of ionizing radiation.

1939   Marries Thea Kantorowicz.

1940/45   Visiting Professor, Amherst College. Studies of
          spontaneous mutation and difference in rates at various
          stages of meiosis; interspecific crosses and gene
          evolution in *Drosophila;* dosage compensation as
          evidence of neo-Darwinian mechanisms of evolution.

1944   Daughter, Helen Juliette (Mrs. Htun) born.

1945   Professor, Indiana University; Pilgrim trust lecture
          on the gene.

1946   Nobel Prize in Medicine and Physiology.

1946/50   Lysenko controversy; concern over radiation hazards; concept of genetic load in man.

1950/57   Critic of medical, industrial, and military indifference to radiation damage; establishment of maximum permissible doses to human population. Banned by AEC as U.S. delegate to first *Atoms for Peace Conference*, Geneva, 1955.

1958/67   Advocate of positive eugenics; proposal for sperm banks; principle of germinal choice (voluntary basis for eugenic use of frozen sperm; donors selected for outstanding cooperativeness, intelligence, and vigor to counteract man's load of mutations).

1967   Died 5 April, Indianapolis, Indiana.

Honors and Awards

Cleveland Research Prize, AAAS, 1927; Hon. D.Sc. University of Edinburgh, 1940; Nobel Prize in Physiology and Medicine, 1946; Hon. D.Sc., Columbia University, 1949; Distinguished Service Professor, Indiana University, 1953; Kimber Genetics Award, National Academy of Sciences, 1955; Rudolph Virchow Society of New York, Medal, 1956; Darwin Medal of Linnean Society, 1958; Hon. D.Sc., University of Chicago, 1959; Hon. M.D., Jefferson Medical College, 1963; Humanist of the Year, 1963; Hon. D.Sc., Swarthmore College, 1964; City of Hope National Research Citation, 1964.

Selected References

A. Books

1. Morgan, Thomas H.; Sturtevant, Alfred H.; Muller, Hermann J.; Bridges, Calvin B. *The Mechanism of Mendelian Heredity*. New York: Holt and Co., 1915.

2. H. J. Muller. *Out of the Night: A Biologist's View of the Future*. New York: Vanguard Press, 1935; London: V. Gallancz, 1936.

3. Muller, H. J.; Little, Clarence C.; Snyder, Lawrence H. *Genetics, Medicine, and Man*. Ithaca, New York: Cornell University Press, 1947.

4. Muller, H. J. *Studies in Genetics: The Selected Papers of H. J. Muller*. Bloomington, Indiana: Indiana University Press, 1962.

B. Obituaries and Evaluations

1. Auerbach, C. "Obituary Note, H. J. Muller." *Mutation Research* 5(1968): 201–7.

2. Carlson, E. A. ed. "H. J. Muller Memorial Issue." *Indiana University Review* 11, no. 1 (Fall 1968): 1–48.

3. Carlson, E. A. "H. J. Muller." *Genetics* 70 (1972): 1–30.

4. Pontecorvo, G. "Hermann Joseph Muller 1890–1967." *Biographical Memoirs of Fellows of the Royal Society* 14 (1968):

349–89. (Contains a complete bibliography of Muller's published works.)

5. Sonneborn, T. M. "H. J. Muller—Crusader for Human Betterment." *Science* 162 (1968): 772–76.

C. Source Materials at the Lilly Library, Indiana University, Bloomington

1. Carlson, E. A. "Indiana University: The Muller Archives." *The Mendel Newsletter*. Library of the American Philosophical Society, no. 4 (November 1969): 1–2.

Acknowledgments

Permission to reprint the essays in this volume is gratefully acknowledged. The following list gives the original facts of publication for all essays here republished.

"Mutation" is from *Eugenics, Genetics and the Family* 1 (1923): 106–12.

"Variation Due to Change in the Individual Gene" is from *The American Naturalist* 56 (1922): 32–50, published by the University of Chicago Press, © 1922.

"Artificial Transmutation of the Gene" is from *Science* 66, no. 1699 (1927): 84–87.

"On the Relation Between Chromosome Changes and Gene Mutation" is from "Mutation," *Brookhaven Symposia in Biology*, no. 8 (1956): 126–47.

"How Radiation Changes the Genetic Constitution" is from *Bulletin of the Atomic Scientists* 11, no. 9 (1955): 329–39. Reprinted by permission of Science and Public Affairs, the Bulletin of the Atomic Scientists. Copyright © by the Educational Foundation for Nuclear Science.

"Physics in the Attack on the Fundamental Problems of Genetics" was first presented to a session on physics of the Academy of Sciences of the USSR, Moscow, March 1936. It is here reprinted from *The Scientific Monthly* 44 (March 1937): 210–14.

"The Gene" is from *Proceedings of the Royal Society*, B 134 (1947): 1–37.

"The Darwinian and Modern Conceptions of Natural Selection" is from *Proceedings of the American Philosophical Society* 93, no. 6 (1949): 459–70.

"Evolution by Mutation" is from *Bulletin of the American Mathematical Society* 64, no. 4 (1958): 137–60. Reprinted with permission of the publisher, The American Mathematical Society, *Bulletin of the American Mathematical Society*. Copyright © 1958, volume 64, no. 4, pp. 137 to 160.

"Life" is from *Science* 121, no. 3132 (1955): 1–9. It was originally prepared for the Columbia University Bicentennial Lecture Series and read in abbreviated form as the third lecture in Ser. B, pt. 1, "The Nature of Things," broadcast on 17 October 1954 by CBS.

Glossary

Adaptive radiation: the rapid evolution of a group of divergent organisms from a common ancestral type; this frequently occurs when a new land area is colonized by a plant or animal not previously known in that area.

Allele: a gene and its variant forms arising by mutation; in older literature the term was allelomorph.

Antigen: a foreign substance, usually protein, in the blood system of an animal resulting in the stimulation of antibody formation.

Aperiodicity: irregular or nonrepeating sequences in a crystal, especially nucleotides in DNA or RNA.

Asexual reproduction: offspring produced by mitosis such as identical twinning.

Autotrophic: cells which synthesize their own biochemical constituents from water, salts, a simple energy source, and a carbon source (such as a sugar).

Bacteriophage: a virus which parasitizes bacteria.

Centrosome: a region near a cell nucleus in which is formed the fibrous apparatus for moving replicated chromosomes to separate cells.

Chromonema: the genetic thread or string of genes which composes a chromatid or chromosome.

Chromosome aberration: a structural change in a chromosome resulting in an inversion, deletion, duplication, or translocation.

Complementarity: the relation of opposites, especially in gene replication, used by Watson and Crick for a pairing mechanism of the nucleotide pairs—adenine with thymine and guanine with cytosine.

Crossing-over: the exchange of segments of paired chromosomes during germ cell formation; a form of recombination.

Deficiency: a loss or deletion of genetic material from a chromosome.

Cybernetic: a regulatory or feedback system which adjusts its activity in response to environmental signals.

Darwinism: the theory of natural selection through the differential survival of minor variations in a population leading to new species formation.

Delayed action: the appearance of a gene mutation in a mosaic condition or several replications after a mutagenic agent was first introduced.

Deoxyribonucleic acid: DNA or the genetic material, composed of nitrogenous bases (purines and pyrimidines), the sugar deoxyribose, and phosphoric acid linked in a double helical pair of complementary molecules.

Diploid: containing two sets of chromosomes; symbolized 2n where n represents the haploid or mature germ cell number.

Dominant: in a diploid organism, the same expression of a gene whether it is present in single (heterozygous) or double (homozygous) dose.

Dosage compensation: the adjustment in expression of a sex linked gene so that both sexes show the same phenotype whether carrying one or two X chromosomes.

Double helix: two complementary molecules, consisting of nucleotide chains, held by a weak bond as a DNA molecule; the model for DNA proposed by Watson and Crick.

Duplication: a segment of genetic material which is repeated either adjacent to the original segment or inserted elsewhere in the cell.

Gene: the unit of heredity composed of nucleic acid, storing the specificity or information for a protein especially an enzyme, a structural component of a cell, or a regulatory molecule.

Gene String: the chromosome in its purified or inferred form, free of associated proteins and linear in organization.

Genetic drift: the tendency of initially small samples of a variable population to differ in gene frequency because of their random distributions.

Germplasm: sex cells, either sperm or eggs and the tissues that produce them.

Gloger's rule: the amount of melanin pigment in a warm-blooded organism decreases with decreased temperature or light.

Gonia: immature germ cells, still in the diploid stage and capable of mitotic cell division.

Haploid: containing a single set of chromosomes, as in mature sex cells; symbolized by n.

Heterochromatin: portions of the chromosome, especially near the tips and fiber attachment point which stain differently during the stages of cell division.

Heterozygous: the diploid state in which a dominant gene and its recessive allele are present in the same cell; the dominant phenotype is expressed.

Homeostasis: a capacity for a cell or organism to maintain its activities despite fluctuations in its environment.

Homozygous: the state of a diploid cell when both of its alleles are identical.

Inversion: a two-break event in a chromosome resulting in a 180° rotation and rejoining of the segment bearing both breaks.

Kappa substance: in the protozoan *Paramecium aurelia,* a bacterial symbiote which releases a toxic substance killing other strains of *P. aurelia* sensitive to it; in the early stages of its analysis, Kappa was thought to be a plasmagene.

Load, mutational: the accumulation of heterozygous mutations which express a slight dominant detrimental effect on the individual, diminishing viability and health.

Lysenkoism: a politically endorsed pseudoscience based on the hypothesis of acquired characteristics and the denial of Mendelism and gene theory; endorsed by Stalin but repudiated after his death. Lysenko called his movement Michurinism.

Marker gene: a gene used to identify a chromosome or some other gene; genetic stocks consist of marker genes and chromosome rearrangements.

Maxwell's laws: laws of thermodynamics, especially the view that all processes produce heat and entropy or tend to a random disorder if left alone.

Meiosis: the process by which mature sex cells are formed by a special cell division which reduces the chromosome number from diploid to haploid.

Michurinism: the name applied by T. D. Lysenko to a modified and politically supported version of inheritance of acquired characteristics.

Mitosis: a cell division in which one cell produces two cells through a precise replication and distribution of genetic material and an approximate distribution of the cytoplasmic components of the cell.

Multiple factors: a character determined by the additive effects of more than one gene; also called polygenic inheritance.

Mutagen: an agent which causes gene mutations or chromosome breaks.

Mutation: a process in which the gene is altered resulting in a change or loss of function.

Mutation, detrimental: a change in the gene having an adverse effect on the individual, slightly increasing its probability of death before maturity.

Mutation, lethal: a change in the gene which, in homozygous condition causes the death of the individual before reaching maturity, usually during the early stages of development.

Mutation, point: a change in the individual gene.

Naked gene: an evolutionary concept of the hypothetical molecule capable of reproducing its errors and hence a progenitor of more complex activity in the origin of life.

Natural selection: the Darwinian theory of evolution involving the differential survival of variations in a population leading to the origin of new species.

Necrosis: the decay and death of tissue.

Nitrogenous base: a purine or pyrimidine found in nucleic acid.

Nucleotide pair: the association of a purine and pyrimidine by hydrogen bonding, such as adenine with thymine or guanine with cytosine.

Orthogenesis: an evolutionary theory, not generally accepted by geneticists, that claims species continue to follow a trend, such as size, by an inner drive or goal rather than through natural selection.

Panmixia: a randomly breeding population.

Permissable dose: the dose beyond which the induced mutation or chromosome breakage would be considered dangerous to an individual or a population.

Plasmagene: originally a theoretical genetic unit in the cytoplasm of nuclear origin; later, a symbiotic organism or a nuclear regulatory system determining cytoplasmic states.

Plastid: an organelle of the cell which carries out photosynthesis.

Pleiotropy: the multiple effects of a single gene.

Polyembryony: twinning or the production of a clone of identical individuals.

Polymer: a chain of molecules forming a larger molecule.

Position effect: the change in function of a gene when it is moved to a new region of a chromosome.

Protogene: in evolution theory, the original molecule capable of replicating its errors; sometimes equated with a naked gene.

Protoplasm: the living cellular substance, including cell membranes, inner organelles, and nucleus.

Pseudoallele: a nest of adjacent genes related in function; sometimes called a complex locus.

Pure lines: highly inbred strains which breed true.

Radiation, alpha: Helium nuclei, consisting of two protons and two neutrons, thus massive, non-penetrating radiation which does its damage to an outer layer of cells.

Radiation, beta: high speed electrons, which, like X rays, may pass through the entire body and result in genetic damage.

Radiation, gamma: energy of very small wavelength which passes through the entire body and which can cause genetic damage; qualitatively identical to X rays.

Radiation, neutron: uncharged particles which usually do most of their genetic damage to the surface cells.

Recessive: a mutation which is expressed when it is homozygous.

Recombination: the shuffling of parental traits in new combinations by crossing-over or by Mendel's laws.

Repeat: a duplication, usually tandem, of a segment of a chromosome.

Salivary gland chromosome: a cable-like structure resulting from the manifold replication (about 2,000 strands) of an unwound chromosome.

Segregation: the separation of two alleles from one another when their homologous chromosomes move apart during meiosis.

Sensitive volume: the inferred target area of a gene based on the number of hits (mutations) induced by radiation within a cell; in target theory, an indirect (possibly erroneous) method of measuring gene size.

Somatic: the tissues of the body other than those making sex cells.

Specificity: the stored information or sequence of coded nucleotides which constitutes the message of a gene; when translated the specificity usually exists as an amino acid sequence in a protein.

Structural change: a two-break event within or between chromosomes resulting in chromosome aberrations.

Symbiosis: a living together of unrelated organisms to their mutual benefit.

Sympatric: species living in a common area.

Synapsis: the association, by pairing, of homologous chromosomes during meiosis.

Target hypothesis: the view that a volume for an object may be inferred indirectly by calculating the number of hits registered by the object when the volume of its container and the number of attempted hits are known.

Transformation: the change in genetic function of a cell caused by insertion and recombination of a fragment of DNA introduced into it.

Van der Waal's Force: a weak attractive force between molecules based on the side groups they contain.

Watson-Crick hypothesis: the double helix model of DNA with pairing of the complementary nucleotides adenine with thymine and guanine with cytosine.

X-ray diffraction: the use of X rays to produce a scattered pattern from crystals; this pattern can be used to infer the structure of the crystal.

Index